BEIRUT AND BACK

Nick Boke

Cover Design by Maha Nasrallah

ISBN-10: 148114281X
EAN-13: 9781481142816
Library of Congress Control Number: 2012922956
CreateSpace Independent Publishing Platform, North Charleston, SC

Canton, MA

To my mother, my wife, and my daughter

{INTRODUCTION}

By Charis Boke

I feel at a distinct disadvantage—a daughter sitting down to write the introduction to her father's memoir. You may say, "You've known him all your life!" It's true. But I have not known him for all of *his* life. I'm not sure that's a criterion for the writing of introductions. It merely makes me reflect, as does the book that follows, on the nature of memory and knowing and on the nature of closeness with the people and places we encounter in these our wild and precious lives.

Nick asks us, through prose paced at a calm walk (interspersed with a brisk trot here and there), to reflect on these memory troubles. This book is a gentle tugging at our notion of time, relationships, and memory. We are prodded to take stock of ourselves, by way of the process of Nick's taking stock of himself—what does it mean to tell the story of a life? What parts do we to leave in, and what do we remove? What should we focus on? How (and this is the question that rings loudest for me, reading this particular tale of my father's life) are we to discern a true story of our lives out of the morass of melting and uncertain images that make up our memories?

There is a resounding sense of loss in this text, compounded with an inexplicable delight in the world. Nick's text feels about in the crowded dark of a room without electricity, not certain what he's there to discover, but needing deeply to find it. Surely this is a sensation we can all recall, whether from our childhoods at night in actual rooms with no light or from the self-searching that many of us engage in, trying to, as Louise Gluck puts it, "go back asking/What am I for?/What am I for?"

I remember other ways that my father told me these stories, and I recognize new stories emerging from the paths of his life, ones I have never heard before. As I read his description of reencountering Beirut for the first time in decades, I recall the glint of tears in his eyes when he described to me, after that trip, how he held his own hand because he was so lonely there. "I put my two middle fingers just like this," he said, holding his hands up in what looked like sign-language for "I love you," "and I walked down the street holding my own hand."

If I have my years right, I was barely seventeen when he told me this story and already full of my own pains, and it was in this moment that I was struck by how vulnerable, how human he was—and how vulnerable we all feel sometimes, going about our lives with not much better than a suspicion of what is coming next.

It is this raw vulnerability that Nick brings to the world that makes his book so moving, especially for any who are familiar with the landscapes of Beirut or of Vermont. He brings himself fully to these places, places that we know other stories of, stories that are told with different words and different goals than Nick's. In telling us his story about these places, he lends us another layer with which to experience them. What does the memory of a stone's texture have to say to the actual sensation of that texture? Nick's wide-eyed curiosity at the workings of human experience as filtered through decades of memory brings us back—not just to Baalbek or to the road or a small prop-plane, but to the ways that we remember things with our senses more generally. How do we do it? Why do we remember the things we do? Why do other things get left out, things that might have been useful or important? When we sink ourselves into the blunt encounter with the world—with happiness as much as confusion, with moments of indecision as much as passion and action—we sink ourselves also into the textures of our memories. We are led, at times, by what it is possible for us to remember. Or what it is necessary for us to forget.

Now, here, I weep when I read his story again. Some of that may be because I can hear his voice as he tells it. I can see why the prose is laid out like it is—I know his voice better than any other, save my mother's, and I hear her voice come alive here too. This book is spoken in the rhythm of Nick's voice, when he is serious or teaching or contemplating. It is also spoken with the groundwork of stubborn determination that guides his life, a determination to find a Purpose, and a way to help other people find a purpose as well.

I have often remarked that the way he spends his days is quite like that of an ethnographer. Ethnography, a longtime tool of the social sciences, consists largely of the ways that Nick runs his life—listening to people, hanging out and figuring out language, pondering the nature of social interaction and asking perhaps inappropriate questions about it in search of a deeper understanding. In the story that emerges in these pages, there is more than an amateur ethnographer at work, though—he weaves together others' stories of joy and struggle, histories of the landscapes he so loves in Lebanon and sometimes even the United States, explorations of the political and social machinations of these places Nick has called home. He weaves these things together with his own aspirations and confusions in a way that reveals the rawness of all of our experiences.

There is no romanticizing of war, civil or otherwise. And I suspect that we would do better, all of us, not to romanticize living through wars. If there is one thing that ethnography teaches us, it is that we cannot truly, fully know or explain the experiences of others. Nick demonstrates here what a challenge it is to know and explain even ourselves. To peel back memory's foil, like phyllo dough before the baklava is baked—except that you don't know, when you peel back memory's layers from a person, whether it will reveal something sweet and delightful, or something bitter, or something deeply moving and impossible to explain.

Let us not romanticize war or joy or pain. Let us, for the time it takes to read this book, be fellow travelers with Nick, as he leads us through the raw experience of parts of his lifetime. As he confronts memory, fear, contentment, gratitude, and confusion, in his relationship to the matter of belonging in one place or another. Let us sit with him, walk with him, look where he looks. Let us allow feeling to wash over ourselves—inexplicable, unguided, and unreasonable. Let us learn from Nick a new way to tell our stories and to hear the stories of each other's lives.

{AUTHOR'S INTRODUCTION}

Writing and the Search for Identity

When I was ten, my mother moved us to Beirut. When I was fifteen, we visited the United States for a few months and then moved to Rio de Janeiro. When I was seventeen, I left Rio and enrolled as a freshman at UC Berkeley.

I've been trying, ever since coming home in 1963, to figure out exactly what it means to be an American.

I wondered this because although I had one of those magic blue passports that will get you through just about any checkpoint anywhere, although the English I speak and write is clearly American (the period goes inside the quotation mark, dammit!), although I've voted in every election since 1968, and although remember the Everly Brothers, Watergate, disco, the Reagan Revolution, and so on, I don't feel very American.

Whatever that means.

I'd begun to wonder who, exactly, I was as I tried to make a place for myself in college and then in the working world and adult relationships. Living overseas for those six years of junior high and high school had done something to me, something that unsettled me, making me feel less at home in America than I'd felt way back before my mother had pulled me out of Lynnbrook Elementary and enrolled me in the American Community School at Beirut.

I've never really figured it out, hard as I've tried. Hoping for insight, I taught high school students a course on United States government and another on Alexis de Tocqueville's *Democracy in America*. I taught a community college course called

"American Identity and Culture." I developed and conducted book-discussion programs for adults called "A Conversation about the Search for American Identity" that were funded by the National Endowment for the Humanities. I've read widely and deeply on the subject.

But I still didn't get it, about American identity, or about myself.

Eventually I decided that the best way to figure out who I was and what it meant to be an American might be by putting myself in positions where my identity would stand in stark contrast to the prevailing identities. So I found work in sub-Saharan Africa, beginning in Tanzania in 2003 and moving on to Kenya, South Sudan, the Democratic Republic of Congo, and Guinée. Then, in 2007, I took a job at my old high school in Beirut.

Maybe that would help.

* * *

Along the way—between Berkeley and Dar es Salaam—I had apparently become something of a graphomaniac. I certainly wasn't a writer way back when my mother uprooted me from my cozy little home in Bethesda, Lynnbrook Elementary, summers at Camp Lakeside and all that.

I was pretty ordinary back then, gradually evolving from deep affection for the Lone Ranger to deep affection for anyone who wore a skirt and all the rest of the transitions boys make as they shift from childhood to early adulthood, from elementary school to high school.

Eventually I began writing: first two-page biweekly letters from college to my mother (still in Rio, then on to Santo Domingo, and finally to Saigon) and my father (in Richmond, Virginia) and then, late in my college career, poetry. Flawed poetry, but increasingly important to me.

Something happened to me, however, the moment I stepped off the Berkeley campus in 1967: I started writing essays.

I saved many of those essays. Leafing through one of the brown folders stacked in the bottom drawer of our filing cabinet, I found a notebook full of musings I wrote on a long-ago trip to Vancouver as I pondered the wisdom of going into exile to avoid being drafted and sent to Vietnam. A little lower in the pile, a few months later I was agonizing over my inability to get sixth-grade boys at Simms Elementary School in Huntington, West Virginia, to pay attention to my unit on astronomy. A few essays later, there was a faded, several-page musing on the flaws of my poetry, and soon after that, something that began, "I remember my ideological rejection of American society."

Month after month, year after year, interspersed among the thousands of poems (still flawed), the essays continued.

But I didn't begin to take essay-writing seriously until the 1980s. It began with occasional newspaper op-ed pieces on being the primary caretaker for our young daughter, on seasonal changes at a nearby pond, on the state of American education. Then came regular commentaries on Vermont Public Radio (on just about anything that came to mind). Finally, there were the eight years' worth of sermons I delivered as minister at the Unitarian Universalist church in Chester, Vermont

Apparently I love to string words together into sentences, sentences into paragraphs, and paragraphs into essays.

And equally apparently I seem to need to write those essays. Given what I've been writing about all these years, the essays help me make sense of the world—of Simms Elementary School, of love, of presidential contests, of illiteracy in Vermont, and of the nature of the divine.

Along the way I learned bits and pieces about how to do this essay-writing thing. Writing for op-ed pages, I learned how to think about an audience. Writing for radio, I learned how to write the way I speak. Writing for the parishioners in Chester, I learned something about consistency, about how to write for a specific audience, week after week.

I took this love of—this need for—writing to Tanzania where I went to develop curriculum for radio-based education programs in 2003. Tanzania was terrifying. Oh, not the maybe-I'll-be-mugged or the I-wonder-how-much-they-hate-Americans kind of terrifying. The terror lay in the depth and extent of the poverty that surrounded me. How does one respond to watching a six-year-old hard at work turning big stones into gravel with a small hammer in the hot sun for hours and days and probably years on end—to earn enough for a bowl of rice?

So I started writing essays about what I found and felt in Tanzania and, almost on a whim, sending them as e-mail attachments to a small group of friends. These essays were, I suppose, like all the essays I had written, efforts to make sense of where I was and what I was doing. But the intensity of the need to make and then communicate such sense had been ramped up tremendously.

So I wrote week after week from Dar es Salam and then a year later from Nairobi and Maridi, South Sudan, and then from Kinshasa and Conakry.

By the time I got to Beirut in January, 2007, to teach English at the American Community School—the school where fifty years before I had before gone from being a staunch Lone Ranger fan to mooning around Anne Marie Dinney, hoping she'd let me carry her books—I had a habit and an audience, so I kept on writing. I wrote week after week, examining topic after topic. My audience grew from a few dozen to a few hundred. Eventually, somebody—maybe my sister Sara's partner Tommy Lee—said something about assuming that someday all this would come out in book form.

* * *

This book grows from two threads that have interwoven themselves throughout my adult life: a very deep and longstanding need to put my experiences into organized language and an equally deep and longstanding desire to figure out who I am and how I got that way.

To satisfy both these needs, I set out to dredge up memories. I began with memories of Beirut in the middle of the twentieth century, and memories of who Nick Boke was in that Beirut. Then I interwove the Beirut I found in the first decade of the twenty-first century, trying to determine who Nick Boke is in this city now.

Hence, *Beirut and Back*.

TABLE OF CONTENTS

PART I

Preparing for Beirut

CHAPTER 1
The Boy in Beirut

I wonder how this little boy staring into the dark night through the airplane window would adjust to his new home so far from his old home.

I wonder what he was thinking as he watched the thin blaze of blue flame stream from the engine exhaust as the propellers whir throatily,.

I remember little things he asked, probably not long after he and his mother boarded the plane from the tarmac, like you used to board airplanes, up the metal staircase that clanked with footsteps.

"Will we live in a pyramid, Mom? Will we ride on camels?"

I think he was trying to be clever. But his mother couldn't have been sure, could she? So she must have said things to comfort him.

"No, no, Nick," she said with a soft mother's laugh, "We'll have a nice apartment. And our furniture will be here soon." Something like that.

The engines throbbed; the cabin was dark. How long did the flight from Rome take? How long did I watch the engine exhaust, wondering and imagining?

Before the cabin lights were dimmed, a girl a few years younger than I had stood beside our seats. She wore a little dress, as I wore a necktie and a sport coat—you dressed for travel back then. More important, she had lived in Beirut, so she knew things. Yes, there were cars and streets. Yes, there were schools. She whispered something to my mother.

"What did she say?" I asked after she returned to her seat.

"She said sometimes people pee on the sidewalk."

The airplane droned on through the night. I must have slept, and I must have slept well—for the rest of my life, the throaty whir of a big window fan has reminded me of the sound of those DC-6 propellers, and the sound has comforted me, lulling me to sleep.

* * *

My mother, Genevieve Vivia Adele Ford Boke, and I lived in Beirut for four years. Something happened to me there. It was nothing tangible; I did not go on to become an Arabic scholar or—as I later thought I was planning to do—enter the foreign service. It took me almost forty years to come back for a visit.

But those years in this city did to me the same sort of thing my wife's summers on Cape Cod did to her and my friend Steve's summers on his uncle Ashton's Colorado ranch did to him.

Beirut got inside me: its cacophonies, its cultural interminglings and antagonisms, its smells, its juxtaposition of the antique with the ultramodern—the way the high-polished marble and brass clash with a willingness to just let things crumble to rot and ruin.

As anyone who has visited will tell you there is no city like Beirut. When I lived here, it was the "Paris of the Middle East," though this did not, of course, mean much to the Palestinians crammed into the "camps" scattered about the city or to the shoeshine boys or street vendors who tried to eke out a living hawking their wares along Rue Hamra or Rue Bliss.

Europeans and wealthy Arabs loved the city, the Europeans because it was exotic but safe, the Arabs because the city seemed to abide by no rules.

I'd never been to Paris, and, at eleven years old, who cares about the things Paris has to offer, anyway?

Today, fifty years and one long civil war, numerous assassinations, occasional bus bombs and kidnappings, off-and-on political stalemates later, the Europeans have dwindled to a trickle. The Arabs, just so long as no one is actually shooting in the streets, have remained fairly steadfast in their loyalty to this city that is so willing to ignore their transgressions.

I have no idea what it was about the city that crept inside me.

CHAPTER 1

All I know is that now, as I approach my sixty-fifth birthday, I'd rather be here than anywhere else on the planet. This city, where I've worked for almost three years, is the only place where I don't feel out of place. When I step out the door of my building on Rue Commodore—or Rue Baalbek, Sharia Commodore, or Baalbek, depending on whom you're talking to—I feel at home.

Stepping out of the building, struck by a burst of car horns, the chatter of construction workers, the rumble of generators, I smile. I turn left or right and, energized, step off into the day.

* * *

My mother and I arrived in Beirut in the summer of 1957, staying until 1961. We went there because she had been appointed Deputy Program Officer of the United States Operations Mission, the foreign aid program which was later renamed USAID. It was her first overseas posting, though she had spent a month or so in Libya a few years earlier when she had served as Washington Desk Officer for that country's aid program.

Though my question about the pyramid was probably asked tongue-in-cheek, I had grounds for the one about riding a camel. My mother had brought black-and-white photos from her Libya trip, and many of them featured her sitting on or standing near a camel, riding in a jeep through the desert, or standing by a well beneath a cluster of palm trees at an oasis.

There she was, again and again, wearing a calf-length dress, her hair in a bun, her bag slung over her arm, standing next to village elders wearing burnooses and *galabiyas* or government officials in dark suits and wide neckties. In one she held a lamb in her arms.

I'd turned the photos into an album called "Adele Boke Conquers Libya" and given a talk about her trip to my fifth-grade class. I was proud of my mother.

This kind of work she was doing was new. Sometime in 1950 or '51, Harry Truman had proposed what he called the Marshall Plan for the underdeveloped world. The proposal was the fourth point in a speech he'd given, so the program, initially called the Technical Cooperation Administration, was often referred to as "Point Four," or *Nu'tta Arba9* in Arabic.

My mother had gotten in on the action early.

She and I had driven across the country in our 1949 Plymouth Suburban station wagon in 1950 or '51, after she'd decided to leave my father. His philandering was just too much for her.

Years later she told me she had confronted him. "You can't go around sleeping with women," she'd told him.

"If you don't like it, leave," he'd said.

So she did.

Ah, that must've been a blow. Dick Boke was a handsome man, and a powerful one for his age. He'd been appointed Regional Director of the Bureau of Reclamation in his early thirties, overseeing the agency that built and oversaw the dams and canals that made life in the American West possible. He and my mother had met in the early 1940s when she was working for the Farm Security Administration, a lynchpin for Roosevelt's New Deal, and he was between jobs—and, though they didn't know it yet, between wives. Eventually he left Sally and their children, Richard and Sara, for Adele. He was appointed Regional Director, he married Adele, and the two moved to California.

My father soon infuriated California's big farmers by enforcing a law that required them to pay for the water they were getting from the federal government. So they took him on, first unsuccessfully accusing him of being a communist, and finally resorting to withholding his salary for a year.

This political and moral drama was all well and good, but my mother decided she couldn't live with the sleeping around. So she packed up, and we left, heading east where she knew she could find work. (Did she chuckle when her five-year-old son asked childlike questions about our adventure, maybe wondering if we'd meet George Washington?) After arriving in Washington, she got touch with her old New Deal buddies who helped her line up work with Point Four.

Meanwhile, my father left the government and found work running Reynolds Metals' agricultural division. He finally married Betty, the secretary he'd been fooling around with when my mother had left.

"You'd like her, Mom," a seven– or eight-year-old me had said after returning from a visit to their home in Louisville. "Maybe we could all live together."

I don't remember if she responded.

My father wrote me letters every month, nice letters about his work and his travels and what life was like at home. I couldn't read his handwriting, so my mother read them to me.

He signed them, "Lots of love, Dick."

I wrote back. My letters began, "Dear Dad."

* * *

My mother read me these letters in the small living room of the two-bedroom house on Windsor Lane in Bethesda, just outside Washington, for five years. It was from that house that she left for Libya, and it was that house that she sold when we left for Beirut in 1957.

We would stay in Beirut for at least the standard two-year tour, or perhaps four years. No more than that. The State Department worried about its employees going native and regularly shipped them hither and yon. After Beirut we went to Rio, and then—after I left for college in 1963—my mother was posted first in the Dominican Republic and finally Vietnam.

I had just turned ten when I left for Beirut, so two years must have seemed a lifetime. I don't recall minding the prospect, though. I don't recall being upset that we were leaving our little suburban neighborhood. I do remember being disappointed that I would not someday join the big kids at Bethesda-Chevy Chase High School.

Maybe I was sorry I'd not see the friends I'd known since kindergarten, Steve and Jessie, for a long time, or my friends from the neighborhood, Johnny-Boy, Ace, and Ace's little brother Tommy.

Maybe. But I don't remember.

All I remember is snatches of that ending and others of the passage toward the new beginning. I remember giving Johnny-Boy the pea shooter I'd just bought and then stomping off furiously because the first thing he'd done was to shoot peas at me. One had lodged in my ear. I remember nothing about our flight to New York, where we spent a day with my half-brother Richard before boarding the ship for Naples, the Saturnia; my mother was very proud that she had finagled passage an Italian steamship line.

All the way across the Atlantic I played with a little Italian boy who spoke no English. Eventually the pain in my ear got so bad that the doctor had to pull the sprouting pea Johnny–Boy had shot at me.

Years later I returned to Naples, and all I remembered was the train station.

We took a carriage ride in Rome before we flew to Beirut.

I vividly recall the flight from Rome to Beirut through the dark night.

* * *

My mother had warned me that things we were accustomed to might be more expensive in Beirut. Did she explain import tariffs? Probably not. That kind of detail is that sort of thing that my generation built into its child-rearing practices.

But I was not ready for the price I found on the label stuck to the jar of Postum at the grocery store. We had gone shopping, probably at Smith's, which was stocked with Western goods, not long after arriving in Beirut. This may have been part of my mother's effort to reassure me that there would be familiar things in this strange city. Or maybe we just went to the grocery store because that's what we had to do.

Postum is a grain-based powder that offers a coffee-like taste when added to hot water. It had been an occasional treat back home, and I was excited to find it on the shelf there.

I found the price four hundred! There were three Lebanese pounds to the dollar, so that would be around $133 for a jar of instant breakfast drink. Embarrassed by a taste that could cost us so much—why is this the kind of thing one remembers?—I quietly set the jar back on the shelf. I kept the price and my greedy desire to buy the product a secret.

Months later, when I described this shocking experience to my mother, she laughed. Not the soft isn't-he-cute mother's laugh. This was an uncontrollable wow-that's-dumb laugh.

"It was four hundred piasters," she said. "Four pounds. A little over a dollar. It's expensive, but not *that* expensive."

I don't recall that we ever bought Postum in my years in Beirut.

* * *

Looking back, I still wonder who this little boy was who whose mother uprooted him from a relatively normal life in a relatively normal American suburb where he walked a quarter mile or so each morning to the relatively normal Lynnbrook Elementary School, where the only unusual event I can remember was the arrival of a shy, tall girl wearing pigtails, and we were told to be nice to her since she and her family were refugees from Latvia.

Her name was pronounced "Leema," but once we saw how she spelled it, she became "Lima Bean."

There was not much out of the ordinary about this blond, skinny little fifth-grader with his crew cut, wearing his house key tied to a shoestring around his neck. He was cute in the way mothers think of cute, not the way girls think of cute. As his fifth-grade teacher Mrs. Wanless repeatedly told his mother and him, he was not much of a student, but his grades could have been so much better if he'd only applied himself.

At recess he drew houses with Johnny Cofer, and they had plans for the Bo-Co Architecture Firm. Catching a fly ball of Donald Orso's in a kickball game made him something of a hero, briefly.

Mrs. Wanless read Thor Heyerdahl's account of his raft trip from Polynesia to Peru, *Kon Tiki*, aloud to the class day after day. He loved the book. Everybody loved the book.

He played cowboys and Indians with toy guns. He loved Superman and Green Lantern comic books. He thought Annette was the prettiest Mouseketeer. Before he left for New York, he apologized to Johnny-Boy for getting so angry about the pea-shooter.

* * *

My four years in Beirut, with a several-month home leave after the first three, somehow turned this normal little boy into…an abnormal one? They changed him—changed me—into someone who never again felt at home amid what would have become normal had I gone on to attend Leland Junior High and then crowned my academic years with a diploma from Bethesda-Chevy Chase High School. Had I stayed in the United States.

Those years in that place changed me from a person I could not have become had I not walked down Rue Bliss to school every morning, or reluctantly toured the ruins at Byblos, or for whom the call to prayer would become such a part of my normal world that I could not, decades later, remember even hearing it as a boy.

This is the part of the narrative when I wish I could recount my Beirut epiphanies, the moments I suddenly understood what living in Lebanon would help me understand, how it was changing me. I'd love to be able to describe the close relationships I developed with Lebanese boys and girls as we explained the nuances of our cultures—or the teenaged versions of such nuances—to each other. I wish I could tell you that the first time I had hummus my taste buds' cravings began to withdraw from hamburgers and hot dogs as I went gastronomically native.

But none of those things happened. I recall only a few experiences that even slightly approached epiphany.

Regarding hummus, for example, I remember being offered some by a friend's mother at a cottage they had rented at Saint Simon, an upscale beach just south of the city.

"What's it taste like?" I asked.

"It tastes sort of like peanut butter," she replied.

"OK."

I tasted it.

"No. No thanks. I don't like it."

Oh, that's not to say that tabbouleh and kebabs never graced our table, but whenever I had the chance I headed up to Uncle Sam's Restaurant just across from the Main Gate at the American University for a hamburger and a Coke.

The only street food I remember is *kaak*, a round sweetish flatbread into the center of which the vendor tossed a few spoonfuls of *zaatar*, an oregano-based mix of herbs. But I also recall occasionally finding it amusing to tip the vendor's carefully balanced tray from his head so the breads spilled on the sidewalk; my friends and I—all of us American—laughed as we ran off, the vendor's fury fading in the distance.

If occasional random cruelty is normal, I was normal, but none of this—not the hummus nor the adventures harassing street vendors nor wandering the ruins at Byblos, hoping my mother would soon have gotten enough culture for the day—taught me anything specific that I can recall. They were all just what happened during this normal boy's days far away from home.

Among the experiences I had that might come close to being classified as an epiphany was one that took place on the narrow stairway we called "the steps" that connected the seaside school with the Hamra district high above on the Ras Beirut plateau. My friend Tim and I came upon a young man playing a shell game on a makeshift table. We watched as he lost his wager. I knew I'd seen which shell the pea had ended up underneath.

So I plopped down my allowance, five pounds—almost two dollars.

The hustler's hands zipped the shells back and forth and then stopped. I knew where the pea was.

"There. That one," I said, pointing to the one under which I was certain the pea had ended up. I knew it was there.

But it wasn't there. I'd been had, but I knew there was nothing I could do about it.

I never gambled again.

But a comparable epiphany could just as easily have taken place on the playground at Leland Junior High, couldn't it? Being in Beirut had nothing to do with my learning that lesson. It lies in wait for every teenage boy everywhere.

* * *

Reflecting on my years in Beirut, I consider how we live our lives as narrative, wandering through the days, weeks, and years, all sequenced, one after the other, unfolding with an organic logic that seems reasonable enough, allowing us to feel secure in the likelihood that one thing will lead to the next, which will lead to the next, and so on, as everything blends and flows, connected.

But we don't recall the narrative. It fades. We remember vignettes.

So the story of my years in Beirut is not the story of what happened in early March, then what followed in late March, then early April, and so on. The story of my years in Beirut is the story of clusters of moments and of my effort—mostly in vain—to coalesce those clusters into something that carries a narrative-like heft.

I have, in short, no story of my years in Beirut. Only stories. If that.

* * *

I have no idea how long it took us to move from a hotel—what hotel? a memory, like most, long disappeared—into our third-floor apartment not far from the seaside Sporting Club. The building still stands. It's next door to the Lamb House restaurant, today a familiar Ras Beirut landmark, but back then it was the site of an abandoned, half-finished apartment building guarded by an aged couple who lived on the second or third floor of the open-air concrete frame.

Entrepreneurs in the city then, as is occasionally the case now, seemed to have no problem raising enough money to get the building started, but then they ran short, leaving a grey, poured concrete hulk, rebar protruding, collecting wind-swept debris, waiting for another investor.

Our building had been finished just before we moved in. I had never seen anything like this, much less lived like this. Three bedrooms, two living rooms, a dining room, two bathrooms, servant's quarters. Balconies everywhere. A view of the Mediterranean.

Years later, I stood on Wassim's Hamra rooftop on a summer evening. I was talking with Michael, an old friend of his who'd just returned for a month. Our conversation jumped from this to that until, oddly, it landed on where we had each lived years before.

"Yes! Yes! The narrow building with the rounded balconies," I said.

"Oh my god. That's where we moved to," Michael responded.

"Where? Which apartment?"

"On the third floor. The apartment facing the sea."

"My apartment. That was my apartment. We moved out just before you moved in."

"Oh my god."

We had a nineteen-year-old maid named Jackie. Jackie from Jacqueline, the French name her Maronite parents had chosen to clarify their allegiances. But she had changed it to Jackie to clarify her own. She spoke almost flawless English and French.

We had a concierge named Habib, which means "lover" or "sweetheart." He was misnamed.

The first Arabic word I remember learning was *khatt*. It means "line," and it's what you asked for—adding what sounded like "amoanmaroof"—"please"—when Habib picked up the phone downstairs after you had picked up the phone upstairs.

"Allo!" Did he take grumpy lessons? Did he ever smile?

"*Khatt*. Amoanmaroof."

And you got a dial tone.

* * *

You might entitle this vignette "Nick begins to grow up." It all began the joyful day when our belongings arrived from the States. It wasn't, of course, the sofa and chairs I'd been waiting for, but my own stuff.

To be specific, my toys. Yes, toys, the things children play with. I was eleven years old, but I was a child.

I'd long been eyeing the empty hillside that faced our apartment. Its rugged limestone and scrub would be perfect for my toys. Perfect as the setting for my toy soldiers, hidden behind a pile of stones, climbing a tiny tree, and as a setting for me, playing soldiers and cowboys with my toy guns, hiding behind a small boulder, ambushing an imaginary German soldier from behind a bush.

So when our belongings arrived, I called Bob Brooke, one of the boys my mother had found to fill the empty summer months before school began. I invited him over, excited to show him my toys and to play with him on my hillside.

Bob—Robert Taliaferro Brooke, he had explained was his real name, but Bob would do—was an embassy kid, not a foreign-aid kid. Somehow early on I began to understand that this mattered, that his was the real foreign service. They had diplomatic passports, while ours were just special passports. These were the ones whose parents got all dressed up to meet with presidents and princes and speak in hushed, nuanced tones about policies and relationships, while those of my mother's ilk met with deputy ministers to talk about building roads and refurbishing schools.

Bob knew this too.

But he too was new to Lebanon, and his parents also knew he needed to fill the time till school began, so he came over.

I took him to my room, rummaged through a box of toys, and handed him a plastic pistol and army helmet. I kept for myself the Mattel submachine gun that had a little lever you cranked so that when you pulled the trigger it went "Ack-ack-ack-ack" till the spring wound down.

"Come on. Let's go outside and play!"

Sure.

He came. He'd be the Germans and I'd be the Americans. OK?

Sure.

I ran off, hid behind a boulder, and raced out, shooting, "Ack-ack-ack-ack."

"Bang. Bang," he replied, half-heartedly loping off toward another boulder.

"Ack-ack-ack-ack."

"Bang. Bang." He paused.

"Um, Nick, you know, I don't really play with guns anymore. I gave that up a few years ago."

"Oh. OK."

I suppose we went inside and found something else to do. I never played with the toy guns again. But I didn't give up on the toy soldiers. There's just so much you can do at one time.

It seems I hadn't destroyed the relationship, though.

Sometime later he called and asked if I wanted to go out with him one night soon.

Sure.

So we met and caught a tram, Beirut's wonderfully rickety turn-of-the-century-style open-air streetcars, painted grey and maroon, with wooden steps. Usually two cars hitched together.

This line ran from the end of Rue Bliss to downtown, Martyrs' Square.

"Where are we going?" I asked.

"To the red light district."

"What's that?"

"That's where the whores are."

Whores? Whores? I was eleven years old. I was going into seventh grade, but only because there was no room in sixth. I'd just given up playing with my Mattel submachine gun that had the special lever to make it go "Ack-ack-ack-ack."

Whores?

We paid our five piasters, and rode on through the night.

We stepped from the tram onto the brightly lit street. I don't remember if women leaned against lampposts, or if there were red lights, or what I said to Bob, but I do know I got on the next tram heading back to Rue Bliss.

* * *

Trams.

Those rickety old street cars that wended their ways around the city were one of the three ways I got around.

Mainly I walked. Rarely I rode the bus. Oh, I don't mean I got on a bus, paid my fare, then took a seat. I mean that every now and then a school bus or a long-distance bus came by, the ones with the double ladders on the back leading to the rooftop luggage rack. You'd circle around behind the bus, keeping low. Then you'd grab onto the ladder, hoist yourself, and ride, either until you reached your destination or you got caught. Then you'd hop off. Joyous!

For twenty-five piasters I could take a service, a taxi-turned-bus that collected passengers along the way. But six cents was a little steep for me.

Trams. Five piasters. One American cent. Pretty reasonable price.

Trams were wonderful relics of a vanishing age. They had wide wooden windows were almost always open; a driver stood at the front, dinging his bell, cranking his accelerator, squeezing the brake levers, as they rattled and clanked through the Beirut's narrow streets. With steps at each end, you could hop on as it came by, stand on the steps, and then hop off as you reached your destination.

Trams, however, were not merely for getting places. They posed a challenge for any teenaged boy worth his salt. How far could you go without paying?

It worked like this. Two tram cars usually ran together, connected. The secret was to see where the fare-collecting conductor was on either car. Noticing that he was, say, at the front of the rear car, you'd get on the rear of that car. As he approached, you'd hop off and run alongside to the front of the car—they never went very fast anyway. When he turned and approached the front, you'd get off, run alongside till you caught up with the forward car, and hop aboard, watching the conductor's progress toward you.

We probably fooled no one. Some conductors probably grumbled about the rich Americans' stinginess. Others probably laughed, recollecting their own boyish efforts to thwart the authorities.

Decades later, I was reminiscing with Ibrahim Bedeir, a man of my age who'd returned to Beirut from Canada in the late '90s to oversee ACS's physical plant. We had already discovered that he'd lived near the school as a boy and that we'd both been chased out of the nearby vacant lot by Abed the caretaker, so we'd figured that our paths must have crossed now and again.

We got to talking about trams: what they had symbolized for the city, how we missed them. How both of us had scooted from car to car to avoid paying the five piasters.

* * *

In Beirut, I grew up.

I never went back to the red light district, though I did soon decide that young ladies—the Nesbitt girl, Anne-Marie, Beth, and the like—were much more interesting than toy guns.

Much of growing up in Beirut involved the same things that it would have involved anywhere, any time: the fascination with girls, with its concomitant interest in how my hair looked and whether my sleeves were rolled up just right, concern about the sprouting of a new pimple, wondering if I smelled bad.

But some of growing up in Beirut had to do with being in Beirut.

Ras Beirut where we lived was then, as it is now, one of the most fashionable areas of the city, with its upscale clothing stores, movie theaters, and restaurants, with the Hamra district at its center.

But Ras Beirut when I was a boy, unlike now, had a visible dark underside. Like most of the city, it was riddled with narrow alleyways and cul-de-sacs. And in many of those out-of-the-way places the poor had built their homes, often of scrap lumber and corrugated metal. The district then, unlike now, had its share of deep and visible poverty.

I passed by this hand-to-mouth poverty on my way to school every day. I saw it in the unwashed, shoeless boys wearing tattered clothes, some of whom occasionally threw rocks at me and cursed at me as I passed, just because I was a clean-scrubbed and well-dressed American. Some sold *kaak* from trays they balanced on their heads..

This was part of my daily living, walking past people who had next to nothing and seemed to have little hope of ever having anything.

It was not just the poverty that I saw. As Beirut had spread to the west, it was engulfing the remnants of a dying world.

Still, from time to time a Bedouin would bring his sheep to forage on the hillside where I had wanted to play soldiers with Bob. I'd awaken in the morning to the tinkle of bells and bleating. Then they would move on.

On the top of that hillside, a bit to the east, stood a farm. The farmer and his family lived in a low concrete-block house, next to which stood a deep concrete cistern for capturing rainwater. The farmer grew dark leafy vegetables on several acres of what would soon become prime real estate. For him, it was just a place to grow vegetables and raise a family. For me, it was a place to notice, a place out of place, fronted by a row of seven– or eight-story apartment buildings set atop the hillside, overlooking the sea.

The rawest, most visible poverty has been pushed out of Ras Beirut now, and the farmer and the Bedouin are long gone. But they were there when I was a boy, and I saw them, unexamined, integral parts of the world I lived in, going about their business as I would shift my gaze from them to the PanAm 707 passing overhead, descending toward the airport just south of the city.

* * *

I remember only bits and pieces about Lebanon the country.

There was Byblos, whose old, old ruins my mother (enthusiastically) and I (reluctantly) and a friend of hers (probably siding with my mother) visited one rainy afternoon. There was Sidon with its castle.

There was Baalbek, the magnificent ruins of the Roman temple to the sun on the eastern edge of the Bekaa. I seem to remember visiting the site a few times, but when I visited a half-century later, I realized that I had created an image of the columns and the temples that had nothing to do with the real thing. Over the years, I had somehow transformed what I had seen. In my Baalbeck there were no steps leading up to the temple. Instead it was a wide, open expanse of stone walkways—in the distance, one could see the columns, far past the rows of eucalyptus trees. There was an amphitheater. It was more a city than a temple.

CHAPTER 1

Recollecting Lebanon, I always recalled loving Baalbek. But had I loved the temple I had visited, or had I come to love the image I had conjured of it over the years?

More than likely the visit had left me with a good feeling, and I had embellished the picture of the place that had made me feel that way so that my picture was more in keeping with things that I love. Adding the row of trees would confirm this, as would opening up the place so it seemed to spread across the valley.

It's a bit frightening to confront such invented memories. You wonder how much one recalls or knows has anything to do with what really was or with real knowledge.

On the way to Baalbek, we stopped at an open-air restaurant in Chtura for lunch. One always stopped for lunch in Chtura after one had crossed the mountains. Someone told me that.

I visited the cedars, high in the northern mountains, once, not long after we arrived in 1957. There was lots of snow; I skied for the first time. Bobby Weiland chose the songs on the jukebox: Buddy Holly and the Crickets sang "Maybe Baby" and "That'll Be the Day," and the Everly Brothers sang "Wake Up, Little Suzy." This was new to me. We played strip poker, three junior high school boys and one junior high school girl. I don't remember how far anyone stripped. It was all new to me.

The cedars? The remnants of those vast mountain forests that had built Solomon's temple and the Phoenicians' ships that set off to create Carthage, and, if the suppositions are correct, voyaged through the Straits of Gibraltar and into the Atlantic?

I vaguely remember wide, dark trees on a snow-covered hillside.

We visited Jackie's family in their village several times. She was Maronite, so they must've lived north of Beirut. It seemed a long drive, so it might have been as far as the Qaddisha Valley, near the cedars, but it could've been as close as the Metn, a few miles above the city. Distances are so confusing when you're young.

Her father had olive groves on terraces on the hill slope. He proudly took my mother and me on a tour, showing us row by row, tree by tree, gesturing, smiling, saying something now and then in the hopes that there might be some relationship between what his Arabic had to say about trees or crops or soil and what we could hear. We heard, of course, nothing but that he loved his trees and the hillside they grew on. Even a young boy who didn't like olives could hear that.

Afterward we sat together in chairs set along the wall of their living room. My mother probably drank coffee; I probably had a Pepsi.

We went to her sister Laura's wedding in the village. I had gotten to know Laura when she had visited Jackie at our house. She too was a maid, but she hated the work, got out as often as she could, and spent all her money on clothes and jewelry. She was flashy and beautiful, aspiring to, but never quite reaching, glamour.

Laura had fulfilled the dream held by so many young Lebanese women in those days—to marry an American. Her American was a Lebanese emigrant, returned home to find a bride. He was older. Jackie thought the marriage was a mistake. Laura didn't care—he would take her away and give her things. Even at my age I could see she was flighty and had no sense.

We drove up to the village in our 1958 Volkswagen, twisting along the winding roads. I did not want to go—what twelve-year-or-so-old boy wants to go to a wedding? It was a hot day, even in the mountains.

The small church was packed. We waited, listening to everyone else's conversations, understanding nothing. As I recall, no one paid us much attention. Looking back, I wonder how it seemed to the villagers that this American woman and her little boy had come so far into the mountains to watch the wedding of a village girl, brought by the girl's sister who worked for the American woman?

What would people have thought? What did I think, being there? I didn't have anything to compare it with—this was the first wedding I had attended.

We waited, first inside the church and then, when it got too hot in the church, outside where everyone milled and chatted. Finally they arrived.

Laura smiled so broadly as she walked into the church in her white gown, carrying flowers. The groom? I don't remember anything about the groom but that he was old, but perhaps this is a Baalbek sort of memory, something long forgotten that I have used Jackie's words to embellish.

We followed them inside, where the swelling crowd stopped milling but continued to chat. We refused the seats we were offered—so many people were standing that we couldn't have seen a thing from the pews. Laura and the groom stepped up to the altar and the ceremony began.

Everyone continued to chat. I watched the priest—did he have a beard and wear a round black Maronite hat, or have I imagined these?—saying whatever he had to say, perhaps praying; I think I remember Laura and the groom kneeling at one point. But the clamor from the congregation never faded.

A woman fainted from the heat.

A gasp. Silence. Chatter and bustle. The ceremony paused long enough for her to be taken outside.

Then the ceremony—and the clamor—resumed.

The church bell rang when the ceremony concluded. I remember no more.

Laura left for America soon after the wedding, and I never saw her again.

* * *

Jackie too eventually married an American. But by that time we'd already lost track of her—she'd gone off to Khartoum to work with another family when we'd left for a three-month home leave.

Of all my regrets, among the greatest is that I lost Jackie. I spoke with her once almost thirty years ago when I found her phone number in my mother's address book. She lived in Lebanon, Pennsylvania. But my mother died soon afterward, and I lost the address book. My efforts to find her over the Internet and through various Lebanese-American organizations failed.

Jackie was like an older sister. Never having lived with an older sister, I'm not exactly sure what that might entail. But I'm pretty sure it would have been like living with Jackie.

With Jacqueline Tannous Khoury.

Jackie was short and pert and pretty: dark hair and dark, bright, often flashing eyes, thick lips she painted with bright-red lipstick, and a ready smile. She wore bright, wide skirts with petticoats. Sometimes she wore a ponytail.

She cooked and cleaned for us. She cared for me. I think she cared about me.

She taught me how to swear in Arabic, pointing to the places and making the motions as she said the words, blushing, but knowing I needed to know these things. I told her how to say them in English, also blushing.

She took us to the vegetable souk downtown, its smells, the vendors' calls and the labyrinthine stallways overwhelming me. But following her we were safe. She knew everyone, and she knew what she was doing. I carried the bags of vegetables she bought.

Beginning in December, a young man began arriving at the apartment, asking for her. I would call her name resentfully, "Jackie, that guy is here again." Then they'd go off into the kitchen and speak in hushed tones in Arabic. I hated him. I must have loved her.

But he was just the dog-arranger, the one who would, on Christmas morning, show up at our door—"Jackie, that darned guy is here again! Tell him it's Christmas!"—with a tan puppy called Crezle that we renamed Skeezix. Sometimes I walked him; sometimes she walked him. My mother came home too late during the week and slept too late on weekends to walk the dog.

I guess Jackie was my best friend in Lebanon. When I was in eighth grade, I told her the heart-breaking news of my girlfriend's decision to break up with me so she'd be available for Pete Gossens. I showed her the new model airplane kit I had bought downtown, at Martyrs' Square at the far end of a tram ride.

She must've cleaned up after me. I was an eleven-year-old, so somebody must've cleaned up after me.

Jackie wanted so badly to go to the States. She seemed truly to believe that with its streets paved with gold, she could find a better life there, a place where she'd not have to clean and cook for others—no matter how nice they may have been or how well they paid her—and where she could be her own person, live her own life.

She listened to my rock and roll records—Little Richard, Elvis, the Everly Brothers—asking what "All Shook Up" and "Ready Teddy" meant as she snapped her fingers and moved her body to the beat.

She took up for a while with Sergeant Shirak. He was an embassy marine. Saturday nights he'd come by to pick her up. He was polite to my mother and manly to me. I must've moved on to a girl my own age by that time since I remember being glad she'd found such a nice boyfriend.

But somehow that didn't pan out. Maybe he got shipped back to the States. Maybe they broke up.

Nothing panned out for her. She cooked and cleaned and listened to my records and my junior high tales of woe and triumph. Sometimes, when she didn't think I was looking, a deep sadness would come over her face, the corners of her broad mouth turned down, her eyes dimmed by tears.

Sometimes she talked to my mother. My mother didn't tell me much, other than that she had a dream of a wonderful life in America but couldn't find a way to fulfill it.

I know that she was sure that learning to say, "Hey, man, that's cool!" with just the right lilt at just the right time was somehow a ticket to that life.

* * *

People we knew had places they went outside the city: Aley, Sofar, Damour, Zahle. I know we visited some of those people in some of those places, but I remember nothing specific.

There are so many places that remain only names—Furn Esshubak and Souk El Gharb just outside the city, Jounieh a bit to the north, Tripoli much farther on.

I vividly recall a trip north to see Helen Hayes performing in Tennessee Williams's play *The Glass Menagerie*. I remember the play, but mostly I recall the great distance we drove along winding roads, deep into the mountains to the newly built Casino du Liban, which overlooked the sea, far, far below.

Returning to Lebanon forty years later, I saw that the Casino wasn't any great distance from the city, standing at the northern end of Jounieh, maybe fifteen miles away, and that the Casino wasn't far above the sea, but maybe seventy-five yards.

* * *

How does memory work? What does it do to us?

For years I held a fond memory of the end of W. Somerset Maugham's novel *Of Human Bondage* that I had read as a senior in high school in Rio, not in Beirut. The final image had never left me: the protagonist, Phillip somebody, riding in a taxi through London, the city swirling around him, its vibrant lights and pulsating sounds drawing him toward his final understanding, his epiphany. I never forgot that ending.

In my fifties I took a copy of the book from the library and began reading. The whole experience was merely a joyful anticipation of those last few pages.

But there was no taxi ride at the end of the book. No swirling lights in a pulsating city. Nothing at all like what I had thought I'd remembered.

That glistening city and Phillip's epiphany were in some other book. Or maybe it was all something I had imagined, some dream I'd had that I'd connected to this book for some reason at some time in the past.

In 2000, not long after re-reading Maugham, I returned to Beirut for the first time since 1961. A few years later, in 2007, I returned to work there for six months. During that stay I wrote essays about being back in Beirut, sending them to a long list of e-mail friends and acquaintances.

Pete Moller had been two years ahead of me at ACS, but we'd stayed in touch off and on over the years. He was on my mailing list.

A few months into my stay in Beirut, he replied to one of my essays.

"Thanks so much for writing these," he responded, "I haven't been back to Beirut, but I've had such fond memories and it had been so special to me. But sometimes I'd thought that I was just making it all up, that it hadn't really been that special a place. Now you've shown me that I didn't invent the memories. It really was that wonderful."

* * *

So my Lebanon was mostly Ras Beirut. Mostly, except for tram rides downtown to buy parts for my model airplanes, to an abandoned airport to fly them, or occasionally to the beach with friends or to the golf course with my mother where I played on the sand fairways as reluctantly as I'd toured Byblos.

Lebanon did, however, provide access.

My daughter made this clear just a few years ago, when she was in high school. She told me her art class was going on a field trip to Boston's Museum of Fine Arts, a few hours away.

"Hey, that's great!" I'd responded.

"Yeah. But you took field trips to Cyprus and Damascus. This isn't really so great."

Well, those weren't exactly our field trips, but the sentiment was correct. For our tenth grade trip, we'd gone to the island of Rhodes, just off the coast of Turkey, staying in a big hilltop hotel and touring the island for a few days. My mother, Jackie, and I had driven through Damascus on our way to Jordan and Jerusalem before Jerusalem had been taken over by Israel. My mother and I had spent a vacation at a beach hotel in Famagusta, Cyprus, when Cyprus was still a British colony, long before Famagusta became part of Turkish Cyprus as a result of that country's civil war. My mother and I had toured Egypt and spent a month or two in Greece during Lebanon's 1958 civil war.

The most memorable of all the trips, however, was indeed a school field trip.

I have no recollection of staying anywhere overnight, so it must have been a day-trip.

We went to Palmyra, deep in the Syrian Desert.

We did not, however, board a bus as my daughter did to get to the Museum of Fine Arts. We got on a DC-3, one of those twin-engine propeller-driven airplanes that sits on the tarmac with its tail down; it held twenty or thirty people, This plane had been developed at the beginning of World War II and had proven so reliable that it lasted through the '60s and even into the '70s. I rode one for the last time in 1976, from Atlanta to Brunswick, Georgia, where my mother had retired. We lumbered our way a few thousand feet above southern Georgia. I looked down through wisps of clouds at twisting rivers snaking their ways toward the Atlantic as I cried, remembering all those long-ago travels, my sobs drowned out by the throbbing engines, thinking of the many things that I had known that had disappeared or were about to do so. Like this old airplane.

The Palmyra trip was on Air Liban, the airline that—before it was subsumed into Middle East Airlines—flew short hops using DC-3s like this one.

An Air Liban pilot lived in our apartment building with his family. They were American. His daughter, Debbie, was my age. We played together during the civil war in 1958, when we weren't allowed to leave the house so I couldn't get out to play with my real friends.

My mother said the father drank, and that's why he was flying for Air Liban. She said she just hoped he didn't drink before he flew.

I have vague memories of the trip itself: singing songs, changing seats to sit first with this friend, then with that one. We began the descent to the desert landing strip.

Here, as so often, the memory gets very vague. And here, as so often, the salient part of the memory may actually be constructed from snippets of other memories or from dreams or books I read.

Nonetheless, here's what might have happened to me in Palmyra, when I had something that did, in hindsight, seem nearly epiphany-like.

We stepped off the airplane into the harsh desert heat. Everything was dust, a tan-colored world extending in all directions. I am sure that my memory of stepping off the airplane and walking across the runway to the ruins is incorrect, the kind of shorthand one uses to simplify recollection. We were probably bussed to the ruins.

At those ruins, I remember— or think I remember—beginning to grasp some understandings that would last a lifetime, understandings that, when added to the daily insights I almost subconsciously gleaned as I wandered Beirut's streets, would remake me, turning this normal little suburban American boy into somebody different.

Here is what I think I saw. In the distance stood a castle the Europeans had built on a hilltop sometime in the twelfth or thirteenth century when they had come crusading. To one side ran a series of columns from the earlier Roman occupation. To another—and this is the vaguest part—stood remnants of something pre-Roman, from one of the civilizations that had settled here, using it as a way station for the trade routes between the cities of the Tigris and Euphrates and those of the Mediterranean coast.

What exactly did I see? What did I know about what I was seeing?

I'm not sure.

Whatever I actually saw, this juxtaposition of historical moments is similar to Byblos, only in that city it's both more extensive and less easily discerned by an almost-young-man not much interested in anything except almost-young-man things.

But here at Palmyra it was blatant enough to capture my attention as I stood there with my friends, probably hoping no new pimples had arisen and that my hair had stayed brushed up into its flattop during the flight.

Here I could see the juxtaposition of culture upon culture upon culture. I could ever-so-slightly grasp the spans of time that one continuously encounters in this part of the world as well as the drastic changes that this world underwent as Assyrians overran Akkadians, then were overrun by Babylonians, who were overrun by people enamored of Greek culture, Romans with their legions, Muslims with their faith, Christians with theirs, and on and on.

On and on until here was an almost-young-man unknowingly representing yet another empire, standing in the desert, thinking about all that past. Considering, as best his untutored mind could manage, what this past meant about the present. About his world. About his life.

Then, as I recall, I went off to climb the steep hill to the castle and then run around inside like a little boy playing knights. The castle smelled of urine and feces, but it mostly reeked of the past, of men defending themselves against the people they had displaced, just as all the rest had displaced and been displaced.

Yes, an epiphany.

And then I got back on the DC-3, flew back to Beirut and probably tried to finish my math homework.

* * *

It was years before I began to understand what living in Lebanon had done to me.

I had gleaned early on that it had somehow made me different. I first gathered this when I returned to the US for home leave in 1960.

My mother—she was indeed a clever woman—had decided that we'd go home what she called "the back way." So we flew from Beirut to Teheran, where we spent a few dusty days, visiting a mosque in Isfahan and watching women clean rugs on the rocks by the riverside. From there to New Delhi: the Taj Mahal and the Red Fort, a snake charmer, people and more people, thronging everywhere. Then came Bangkok, which was then a sleepy city set by the river, no high rises or sex trade, Hong Kong, where my mother insisted I have two suits and a pair of shoes made, and Tokyo, where we went on a night-club tour complete with topless dancers and visited the Buddhist shrine at Kamakura.

Then on to Honolulu.

People asked what I was looking forward to.

"Milk and a lawn," I said.

Milk. There being no reliably pasteurized milk in Lebanon, my mother had bought us Klim. She insisted this was the best-tasting of the powdered milks. She may have been right, but it still tasted horrible. Just when one begins to think how clever one is, one realizes, fifty-five years after the fact, that "Klim" is milk spelled backward.

My mother was a fanatic about food safety. In Beirut, we had no milk or ice cream, no fruit that could not be peeled. I watched as she peeled her grapes, one by one. Was she afraid of the pesticides or of *e. coli* and its ilk? I have no idea.

I, of course, obeyed these strictures in her presence but ate what I damned well pleased when I was out in the world: *kaak* from street vendors, grapes at Tim's or Brian's house, ice cream. Her descriptions of tuberculosis made me hesitant about milk, but I somehow figured that the little germs couldn't make it through the process that turned the milk into ice cream. When we sat down to lunch on the terrace at the Royal Hawaiian Hotel on the beach in Honolulu, I ordered a quart of milk.

It was, of course, good to be home. There were lawns, fruit I didn't have to peel, and plenty of milk. Rock and roll songs played on every radio station, not just the Saturday night BBC-Cyprus broadcast of the top twenty, which included as many British stars (several years before any American cared about any rock and roll singer other than American ones) as American.

And in America there were cars. Kids my age driving cars. Kids my age buying old cars and fixing them, turning them into glittering, low-slung, low-rumbling works of art.

I visited my father and his wife Betty in Richmond, Virginia. From there we drove to Evansville, Indiana, to visit Betty's family.

The most memorable member of Betty's family was Gretchen, her sixteen-year-old sister, a late-in-life surprise for her parents.

Gretchen was beautiful. Frosted hair teased high, pale lipstick, curvaceous in her pastel skirts and matching tops. I could not imagine anyone ever being as attractive as she, or as popular.

She was kind to me. Well, except for doing things like looking at the shoes I had bought in Beirut—then, as now, the toes pointier than the toes of American loafers—and saying something like "Eeeewww! Where did you get those shoes?"

What could I say? "In Beirut. It's what people wear there."

"We'll have to get you a new pair," she said, and, as I recall, she did.

Saturday night she and her girlfriend Carlie took me out—in separate cars, of course. Gretchen drove the shiny new Thunderbird her father had bought for her sixteenth birthday. Carlie drove the car her father had bought for hers, a brand-new Dodge something-or-other, sleek, purple, and glistening with chrome.

* * *

It was almost a decade later before I began to consider that I might, indeed, be real. That the person that Beirut had created did indeed matter; that he had substance, however much he was unlike the Americans he spent his university and post-university years with.

Wonderful as the University of California at Berkeley was in the 1960s, with its free speech movement, anti-war protests, illicit drugs, free love, acid-rock music, and all the rest, I found myself living amid a society that took football rivalries seriously (I'd never seen an American football game; I wasn't quite sure how the sport was played. Not knowing the teams' names, I had no favorite) and in which almost every young male had at some point torn apart and reconstructed at least one automobile engine.

The people I met, as they had done in that Saturday-night Evansville parking lot, were prone to withdraw behind a veil of politeness, asking, "So what's it like in Beirut?" or, by the time I graduated from Rio's Escola Americana, "Which did you like better, Beirut or Rio?"

I was, somehow, Other.

My stories of field trips to Palmyra and necking with my girlfriend on an island in Rio's Guanabara Bay just didn't cut it—it just took so long to explain where it had happened that by the time I got to the what-had-happened part, they'd lost interest.

I had no after-the-Big-Game stories; I had nothing to contribute to their tales of trying to find a used carburetor for a '58 Chevy Impala. I'd never needed a fake ID to buy a beer. I'd never covered the oak tree in a math teacher's front yard with toilet paper. I'd never driven to Tijuana with my older brother to watch a strip tease.

There was, however, one thing I had in common with my university classmates: the Vietnam War that hovered over any future we might consider. I spent much of my time after graduating in 1967 doing the same thing most of my left-leaning peers were doing: not being drafted into the United States Army. Every decision I made about every job I held from 1967 to 1970 was premised on whether or not the work would keep me out of the army, so I taught poor black kids in Huntington, West Virginia, and then worked with a mixed group of emotionally disturbed kids in San Jose, California. Given the ideals I'd picked up at Berkeley, I might have chosen to do such work anyway, but Vietnam forced me to find nothing but jobs like this, jobs that would exempt me from the draft.

In 1970, the Selective Service System responded to accusations that the then-current system of drafting young men was unfair by instituting "the lottery." A group of officials drew dates out of a container, one after the other, noting the order in which they appeared. The order in which one's birthday was drawn determined the likelihood of his being drafted.

May 18, my birthday, was the 278th date to be drawn. I would not be drafted. I could begin to live a life that did not entail primarily looking for draft exemptions.

The obvious thing to do under these circumstances was to spend the winter camped on a beach in northern Mexico. Then I drove to Virginia, where I stayed with my father and found work as a substitute teacher. This eventually led my being hired to teach ancient history to eighth graders at the Norfolk Academy in Norfolk, Virginia, beginning in September of 1970.

Not having studied much ancient history in college, I set out to teach myself what I thought I'd need to know, reading widely in the field. I read about the evolution of Egyptian art from the Old Kingdom to the Middle Kingdom to the New Kingdom. About the brutality of the Assyrians and the ingenuity of the Phoenicians. About Ramses, Hatshepsut, Solomon, Alexander, and Caesar. I borrowed books from my father and from the library and read and read and read, taking copious notes in cramped handwriting to save paper.

My mother, having retired from USAID and moved to a high-rise apartment outside of Washington, sent me a shoebox full of photos from our years in Beirut.

There were the several shots I'd taken of the first commercial jet to fly to Beirut, a BOAC Comet, a tiny speck high above our apartment building. There were photos of our visit to Jackie's house in the mountains; I stood next to Jackie's father, amid his olive trees. There were pictures of Marty, Tim, Joe, and me flying our model airplanes at the abandoned airport just south of Beirut.

And there I was, sitting in a felucca on the Nile. Another of me standing by the Sphinx. There I was at Baalbek. There I was at Byblos. There was a shot of that hilltop crusader castle at Palmyra. There, in photo after photo, was that little boy who'd been uprooted from his Bethesda neighborhood all those years ago, who'd been taken to live by the sea, beneath the mountains, amid the unfamiliar that gradually became familiar.

I began to think about what it had meant for me to have lived in Beirut.

And I became real.

I came to understand that it was all right that I didn't know anything about baseball's infield fly rule or why a fuel-injected engine was superior to a carbureted one. I began to realize that all those radio programs with their haunting minor-key songs and their broadcasts of a fiery Nasser exhorting his Arab neighbors to rise up against the imperialists I'd heard wafting from apartments and mechanics' garages on my way home from school, all those old and stony places I'd visited with their histories more than ten times as old as my country's, all those hovels I'd noticed in the back alleys of Hamra and shanties I'd seen as I drove by the Palestinian camps had added up to create a real person.

A person of value.

A person who understood that there were people out there who loved America, and others who hated it. I had become a person who realized that Americans had what they had not because they deserved it but because they'd built a country on one of the most resource-rich regions of the planet, guarded on both sides by immense oceans; they had been enterprising, but they had also been lucky. I was a person who realized that there were other ways of being than America's and that there was much about many of these ways of being that was, in fact, far superior to the American way of being.

In short, all those years after leaving Beirut in 1961,I had an epiphany: Beirut had made me who I had become, and much of what I had become was good. I had certain wisdoms beyond those of many of my peers. I had perspectives on issues they couldn't even imagine thinking about. I was, indeed, a citizen of the world.

* * *

I'm told it's good to grow up with role models. My father being so far removed from my life, it was hard to use him as a role model. I just didn't know him well enough. There was my friend Steve Hatchett's father; I waited after school for my mother at Steve's house every day for a few years, and his father usually got home long before my mother came by to pick me up, so I knew him pretty well. But he was awfully grumpy and strict, so he wasn't much of a contender.

So there was no one. I never really found a model for how to just be a person.

As a model for the profession I eventually fell into, teaching, in Rio there had been Mr. Rosa, a young Brazilian studying for his country's foreign service exam who came to teach advanced placement English at the Escola Americana. He was funny, helped me understand the power of ideas, and genuinely seemed to enjoy being in the presence of young people. Just the kind of teacher one would want to be.

The only person I remember from Beirut was a rather odd old man who taught me Arabic, James Sutton.

Now the problem with talking about James Sutton (did his friends call him Jim?) is that everything I know about him beyond what I can say about his presence in the classroom is supposition. All I have is snippets ofn memory—and we've already seen what how shoddy my memory is—but mostly on memories about rumors and occasional glimpses of him as he climbed rapidly up the stairs (taking two at a time, or did I invent that?),or stood talking energetically with a colleague in the hallway.

Since being back in Beirut, I've tried to ask around about him, as I have about a number of my teachers. I've been able to get a bit of an update on my Egyptian math and French teacher, Mr. Shoucair. He would be impossible to forget, a tiny man lost amid his dark suits, nicotine-stained fingers, and persistent frown. But most of all his love of Christmas and his singing, year after year, "Minuit Crétien," the French version of "O Holy Night," in French class as the season approached. I don't recall that he taught it to us or wanted us to sing along with him—merely that he loved to dip deep into his baritone and begin, "*Minuit cretien, c'est l'heure solonelle/quand notre dieu est descendu jusqu'a nous...*" There was Mr. Thomas, my Lebanese biology teacher. Of him I remember only my dissatisfaction with the inadequacy of his response to my question, "But why couldn't there be life forms on some planet that were not carbon-based, that didn't rely on oxygen?" He said something to the effect that this was simply not the way life has been constructed, just the kind of thing to disappoint an inquisitive adolescent. Madame taught advanced French. There were, of course, the ex-pats, who cycled through, year after year: Miss Lawrence, Mrs. Parker, Mr. Troyer, and all the rest.

But there were also the stalwarts, Elsa and Will Turmelle, whom I had lunch with in New Hampshire in the 1990s. They came to the school in the early '50s and left in the early '80s and became institutions, he as an English teacher, she as a gym teacher and eventually, during the civil war, the head of the school. Ah, they had loved Beirut. He died in 2007, but she still returns every year, accompanied by a niece. She stays with Wajiha and Fatimah, the two Palestinian women who had cooked and cleaned for her, and to whom she turned over her apartment, thereby keeping it under rent control and cheap. Wajiha and Fatimah cook and clean for me and my wife now.

I could get bits and pieces of news about most of the teachers I'd remembered, about Fawzi, the custodian, and about Camille, who'd owned the snack shop just around the corner from the school. But nobody knew anything about Mr. James Sutton. Nobody even remembered him.

He wasn't really on staff at ACS. He taught only one class of conversational Arabic to a group of about twelve of us during my last year at ACS.

This was the first year ACS had offered Arabic, but why did the school ask an American to teach Arabic in a land full of well-educated native speakers?

Looking back, I can imagine that perhaps no self-respecting Lebanese Arabic teacher would consider teaching the language of the streets. Indignant at the thought, they may have insisted that only *Fus-ha*, Classical Arabic, deserved to be taught.

But that's just a guess. Most of what I have to say about this teacher and this class is guesswork.

All I can say for sure is that I showed up every day, took out my copy of *Eastern Arabic: An Introduction to the Spoken Arabic of Palestine, Syria and Lebanon* by Frank Rice and Majed Sa'id, which had been published by Khayat's on Rue Bliss the year before, and got to work.

I still have my copy of the book, which had been prepared, the flyleaf tells us, under the auspices of Georgetown University's School of Foreign Service. This being the case, the textbook is rather unorthodox. Instead of learning to say "I want to go to the store to buy new socks," one learns dialogues like this one about the newsroom:

> How many news bulletins do you broadcast per day?
> *Kam nashra ixbaariyye bidzii9u filyoom?*
> We have a morning bulletin at seven o'clock.
> *Fii 9inna nashra sabaahiyye, ssaa9a sab9a.*

And so on, all in transliterated Arabic, with the "9" serving for the letter "aign," the "x" serving for "khah," and other examples of using English symbols to represent letters and sounds that don't exist in English. To ensure our correct pronunciation, there were the tapes that came with the textbook. Mr. Sutton would set the tape on the reel-to-reel Wollensak tape recorder, fast forward to the correct lesson, and push the "play" button.

Beyond that, I remember little about the class except that we met in a corner classroom on the second floor, and when I did not want to pay attention to what Mr. Sutton had to say about feminine T-nouns I could watch the waves roll in from the northwest along the Corniche fifty meters away.

So many questions remain about this man and this class, questions I cannot even imagine a procedure for answering. Why conversational Arabic, not Fus-ha? Why had it not been taught before? Did it continue after I left? Why was it taught by an ex-pat armed with a tape-recorder, not a native speaker? Why a textbook that included lessons about the proper way to address the minister of defense, not how to ask directions to the movie theatre?

Why James Sutton?

Who was James Sutton?

We had occasionally seen him around the school before he began to teach the class. A balding man with thick tortoiseshell glasses, widely and consistently smiling, he was usually dressed in a tan Boy Scout uniform decked out with colorful badges, probably come for a Scout meeting. He bristled with energy, but it seemed to be an energy rich with kindness.

He was, I think, a missionary, or at least affiliated with some Christian group. Did someone tell me this, or am I guessing?

He had, one could assume, been in Lebanon for some time, since his Arabic was good enough to lead the class.

He didn't much care about his appearance, usually showing up for class in the same wrinkled khaki pants and long-sleeved white shirt, the armpits sweat-stained yellow.

He never stood still, sometimes seeming to dance in the classroom.

His hearing wasn't as good as it might have been. He would ask you to repeat the question, please, leaning forward.

I enjoyed learning Arabic, as I had been enjoying learning French and as I would enjoy learning Portuguese under the tutelage of Miss Colares in Rio after leaving Beirut. Language came easily to me.

During my years in Beirut in the late '50s, one could practice one's French in the streets. Today Beirut's billboards and shop signs are in English and Arabic—sometimes only in English, rarely only in Arabic—but in those days they were in French and Arabic. Today you have to go to Ashrefieh to practice your French, but back then you could use it anywhere, although you could expect your English to be understood in only a few places.

I didn't think much about James Sutton when I was his student. He was just a nice, rather pleasantly odd old man teaching a class I enjoyed.

As the years have passed, however, I have noticed that he was among the only teachers I remembered from the fifteen or twenty I'd studied with in my four years in Beirut.

Why? Why do I remember this man, even going so far as to think of him as some sort of role model?

What was there about this grinning, zippy, middle-aged man, probably come to Lebanon decades before to spread the gospel, wearing almost tattered clothes when he wasn't wearing his Scout uniform with its short pants and little neckerchief that stuck with me?

I returned to teach at ACS in 2007. This was not long after Israel had decided to see if it could commit as ill-conceived a foreign policy venture in Lebanon as the United States had begun not long before in Iraq, as Israel's thirty-three-day attack on Lebanon essentially turned the country over to Hizbollah.

But I'd come back to a very different ACS from the one I had attended, the student body and faculty having become mostly Lebanese since the Civil War had driven out all the ex-pats. No matter. I loved being there.

A few months into my stint, I looked at myself in the restroom mirror one day after classes were over. There I stood, my hair thinning, my wire-rimmed glasses hopelessly out of date, the armpits of my white shirt stained with sweat.

I was James Sutton.

But who had James Sutton been to me that I could see myself in him, or him in me?

If he had been a protestant missionary, he would have been connected with a long train of Americans who'd been coming to Lebanon since the 1840s, bringing their truths, but often melding themselves into the local culture. As a protestant, he'd have brought a hierarchy-free, ritual-free, democratized vision of the way people could connect with the holy. His smile being so permanent, he must have believed in a loving, nondenominational god, offering nearly universal salvation.

Or so I'm assuming fifty years later.

I didn't know those things about him back then, of course. I didn't know anything about him then. I'm not sure teenagers know anything about anyone; they're so busy trying to figure out the self that they're living within .

But I'm going to guess that I felt some things about this man—from this man—and that those things had to do with openness and affection for others, with respect for unfamiliar cultures, and with an interest in finding one's way out of one's own skin and into the skin of others.

I'm going to guess that I saw such things in him, though I didn't know I saw them.

I'm going to take an even wilder leap and guess that his way of being in Lebanon is how I see myself being here—feeling great fondness for the people and the culture but using my understanding of this people and this culture to help me clarify what I value about my own culture.

And, by extension, becoming a missionary for my own faith.

Like the faith I'm imagining James Sutton to have held, my faith is hierarchy-free and ritual-free and is premised on the assumption that truly, all people are created equal. And that if I'm correctly inventing who James Sutton was, Americans have a lot to learn from other people.

I think that this is what I've brought to Beirut. And I think I owe some of what I've brought to that funny old man I think I may have become. To my role model, James Sutton.

* * *

I couldn't miss the politics in Lebanon, even distracted as I was most of the time by momentous events like the arrival of that pretty new girl, Kathy Croft, to the ranks of the eighth grade and the screening at the Hamra Theatre of "Blue Denim," a movie about the plight of a teenaged couple after the girl found herself pregnant. The Hamra Theatre is long gone, though the marquee still stands, and teenaged pregnancy barely raises an eyebrow any more. I don't know what happened to Kathy—seems to me she didn't stay long.

Distracted as I was, it would have been difficult to miss the ubiquitous Jamal Abdul Nasser, Egypt's charismatic president. Nasser was America's regional bad guy, but he was the hero of many in the Middle East, with his ability to stand up to the imperialists, his leadership in the Non-Aligned Movement, and his call for Arab solidarity against the West and its Zionist ally. When he convinced Syria to join Egypt in the creation of the United Arab Republic early in 1958, the talk at the dinner table turned ominous.

Politics took an in-your-face turn at the beginning of the school year in 1958. The father of one of my classmates had been working in Iraq when General Qasim had overthrown the West-leaning King Faysal in a bloody coup in July of that year. One of my teachers gave us time to look at the grainy black-and-white photos of political opponents hanging from lampposts on a bridge across the river. Those grisly pictures remain etched in my memory. This, I could understand even through my adolescent hormonic fog, was how bad things could get.

And of course there was Lebanon's own 1958 civil war. I vaguely understood that the country's Christians had been staunchly resisting the Muslims' call for a census ever since independence. They understood that their own birthrate was much lower than that of the Muslims and that if the ratio had shifted significantly in the Muslims' favor, there'd be no real argument for the Christians' hold on the positions of power they had been granted in the 1942 National Pact. My mother didn't like the idea of the Christians losing control, but she also didn't approve of their unwillingness to face facts.

It was summer. The swimming at St. Simon and the Sporting Club were great. I was getting old enough to be invited to dance parties. I was courting Babs Nesbitt's younger sister, whose name I've forgotten.

But then it all ground to a halt, as the fighting in Tripoli and Sidon made its way into parts of Beirut. We weren't allowed to leave the building. Confined to the building, my upstairs neighbor Debbie and I would pause our play from time to time to listen to the not-so-distant machine gun fire. It would stop, and we'd go back to our business.

Then the United States Marines landed. They were surprised, the news reports explained—and *Life Magazine* dramatized with a photo essay—to be greeted by vendors selling Pepsis and snacks as they deployed through the surf south of the city, submachine guns at the ready. One group bivouacked on the hillside just across the road from our house above the Sporting Club. My mother says I took a pitcher of lemonade to them, announcing, "Courtesy of the American Embassy." My mother fell in love with a United States naval officer, and I was given a tour of the Sixth Fleet's command ship.

But the situation remained difficult, so my mother and I were finally evacuated to Greece, staying in a hotel in the hills outside Athens for a few months.

When we returned, her officer had gone. She found us another apartment, just up the hill, above the farmer's hut and cistern. We were on the seventh floor, looking far out over the sea, just above the field where the farmer worked his land, growing leafy green vegetables.

The political scene in the Middle East grew quieter. In Lebanon, General Fuad Shehab was named president, his military leadership having won him the respect of all factions. In Iraq, the blood-letting ended, and the new military leadership kept a tight lid on things. Nasser's voice still resonated over the airwaves, but squabbling within the UAR eventually led to its dissolution, leaving a bad taste in Pan-Arabists' mouths but bringing relief to America's leaders.

* * *

One question nags at me about my teenage years in Beirut. It's a fairly simple one, not having to do with sectarian violence or role models or even with what my years in that city did to transform me into the person I became.

I'd just like to know who Fuad and Fadool were. Oh, I know that they were young Lebanese men who worked in the USAID program with my mother, she enjoyed their company, and they, apparently, enjoyed hers. And I know that they were friends of Dalles Ostergaard, a prematurely balding, hunched-over, dour young American who also worked with my mother. And that they all got together from time to time, maybe for cocktails, maybe to play bridge.

Fuad and Fadool were handsome young men, their white shirts neatly pressed, their sleeves stylishly rolled up. Fadool wore his long hair slicked back almost in a pompadour, while Fuad had shorter, bristlier hair. They were nice to me.

But who were they?

What did they want in life, from life?

Were they, like Mr. Rosa in Rio, laying foundations for positions in the Lebanese government?

Or were they hoping to rise through the ranks in the USAID office or even to switch over to the embassy? Were they hoping that the connection with American institutions would get them out of Lebanon? Maybe they were just saving money for graduate school?

Or was there something else?

Dead-end questions, every one.

Sometimes I wonder what became of them. Did they, like Jackie, find their ways to Lebanon, Pennsylvania, or even Washington, DC? Perhaps they lived out their working lives writing reports and attending meetings in some labyrinthine ministry building in downtown Beirut. Perhaps they assumed important positions in one faction or another during the 1975 Civil War or even in one militia or another.

Maybe they're dead.

More likely, as I write this, they are sipping coffee as they read Alnahar at the house they retired to in Aley or Nabatiyeh or Zgharta.

But I don't know, and I can't find out. I didn't even know their last names. I was too young to understand that knowing something about these two young friends of my mother's would matter to me years later.

When we're young, all we know is the moment. It almost never occurs to us that there really is anything beyond our desire to buy that shirt or listen to that song or sit next to that girl.

Life mostly passes us by—or we pass it by. Whichever.

CHAPTER 1

As it mostly seems to have passed by the teenaged me who lived in Lebanon while that country's complexities swirled around me and engulfed me. We all live in the thick of our worlds, but we barely notice, until one day we lift up our heads and begin to wonder: who am I? And how did I get this way? How could I unearth the things that made me, me?

If we can, we go home, hoping for hints.

CHAPTER 2

Coming Back, the Visits

In Arabic, my name is Nqoola. I'm not quite sure why—no one I've asked is quite sure why—but being named Nqoola automatically earns you the honorific "Hajj" in Lebanon. A Hajj is someone who has gone on pilgrimage.

It's all rather complicated: I'm automatically Hajj Nqoola—or "N'oola," since you never pronounce the letter "qaff" in Beirut—without ever having set foot in Saudi Arabia, much less visited Mecca. I've visited Jerusalem, though I doubt that visiting as a twelve-year-old really counts as a pilgrimage. People named Nqoola are almost invariably Greek Orthodox.

Nonetheless, I like the honorific.

And I like the implication that I'm a pilgrim, someone on a spiritual journey. Maybe it's even better that the destination can't be determined. I think that's how I've seen my life, as a pilgrimage, for as long as I can remember thinking about things like this.

The summer after graduating from Berkeley I read Nietzsche's epic parable *Thus Spake Zarathustra*. It opens as the prophet Zarathustra comes down from the mountain to share what he has learned in his thirty years in the wilderness.

"What is great in man is that he is a bridge and not a goal," he tells the people, "What can be loved in man is that he is a going-across and a down-going." I never really understood the "down-going" part, but I loved the "bridge" and the "going-across." I loved the idea that life was a journey, a pilgrimage to somewhere, toward something, without knowing what.

I still have the dog-eared copy of *Zarathustra* I kept in my back pocket for a year or so, several layers of tape barely holding the spine to the cover, pages yellowed and loose.

Years later came a family synchronicity: our daughter, Charis, studies Buddhist and Hindu pilgrimages in Nepal and India. They're the focus of the doctoral dissertation she'll begin in a year or so when she's finished her coursework at Cornell. I think she too is a goalless wanderer, hoping the journey will suffice.

* * *

It took me a long time to make my way back to Beirut, almost forty years.

Forty years in the wilderness? Certainly they were forty years of never quite feeling at home, of never quite feeling like I belonged. Forty years of standing in the dark in that Evansville parking lot, knowing my shoes didn't quite make it, marveling at the handiwork of young men who could rebuild automobiles from the ground up, making conversation the best I could, but never quite believing. Never quite at ease.

I returned to Beirut in December of 2000.

I'd begun to consider the possibility of returning several years earlier, after my wife, daughter, and I had taken a summer trip to Greece. It was the sun that did it. When we stepped out of the airport terminal in Athens, I felt the its rays strike my skin like no sunshine I'd felt since leaving Beirut. It beat down on me with a familiar ferocity, prompting me to begin to consider what I'd been missing.

Weeks later, as we wrapped up a tour of Greek islands with a stopover at Rhodes—one of the school field trip sites my daughter had envied—I gazed toward the southeast, realizing how close I was to my old home, that Lebanon was just over the horizon, just past Cyprus, a hop, skip, and jump away.

If I could come to Greece, I thought, I could go to Beirut.

Lebanon seemed possible in a way it had never seemed before, even though my years in Beirut had never been far from my thoughts. I thought about it every time I heard a bit of Arabic in a movie or over the years as I heard newscasters talking about the Six-Day War, the oil embargo, Iranian zealots taking American embassy personnel hostage, the Iran-Iraq War, the Intifada, and the First Gulf War.

Or about the devastation Lebanon wrought upon itself during its fifteen-year Civil War.

I tried not to think much about that. Sometimes I wondered what had happened to Fuad and Fadool. Sometimes I wondered if any of my teachers were still in the city. What might have happened to the apartment buildings I had lived in? Or to the trams?

But I had my life, so such thoughts remained in the background. My little pilgrimage was unfolding: failed relationships finally being replaced by a successful one when I married Buffy in 1980, followed by the birth of our daughter and the move from teaching in Virginia and Maryland to Cape Cod, where I took care of Charis while my wife wrapped up her preparation for the Unitarian ministry with some courses at Harvard and an internship at a nearby church, finally followed by the move to Vermont, where we lived for twenty years.

Vermont was wonderful. With its brief, lush green summers, its glorious autumns, and its long and serious winters, it was a place filled with fine people who believed that what mattered was one's character, not one's lineage, wealth, or social status. A crusty old newspaper editor who lived in a hilltop farmhouse in rural Weathersfield Center, Armstrong Hunter, told me the rules: "Do what you say you'll do, and do it as well as you can, and you'll have no trouble here."

He lived his life that way, as did so many of the people we met on this part of my life journey. So I followed the rules as best I could and found that doing so opened doors to a variety of fields I helped a failing Unitarian church bring itself back to life; helped create an organization that became nationally known for its work with family literacy*;* wrote commentary for Vermont Public Radio about education, the arts, politics and—increasingly—America's role in the Middle East. All the while I wrote for a variety of newspapers and magazines and, finally, creating a statewide program to help middle- and high-school teachers help their students understand the materials they were asking them to read.

Along the way, I found out that Will and Elsa Turmelle—teachers from ACS—had retired to New Hampshire, not far from us. I decided to write a piece about Beirut from their perspective for the *Valley News* (based in West Lebanon, New Hampshire), which I had begun writing for. I called. We met for lunch.

Their memories of Beirut were as fond as mine, only they had stayed on, remaining from the early '50s until the early '80s, when Elsa was finally replaced as headmistress at ACS. They had stories of the good old days—the "Paris of the Middle East" days—and of the civil war: once, during the period when foreigners were being kidnapped, Will was stopped on Rue Bliss by young men who seemed likely to do him harm until he was saved by guards who rushed over from the AUB gate. But the couple never lost their affection for the place. And their affection helped rekindle my own.

My wife had always wanted to tour the Holy Land. In the late '90s we'd begun to make tentative plans for a trip that would begin in Beirut and end up in Jerusalem. But then came the Second Intifada. So much for our plans.

But dammit, I wanted to go back to Beirut. So we agreed that we'd postpone our big trip and I'd take this simpler trip alone.

I was scared. Lebanon had been quiet for almost a decade, but who knew? The country had been removed from the State Department's don't-go-there list on the inside of my passport only a few years before. So every week for the month before my December, 2000, trip I called a nice young man at the State Department's Lebanon desk. Every week he told me the same thing: "It's still quiet. Just don't go south."

Friends told me I shouldn't go at all. But one of those friends had recently told another friend she shouldn't go to Rome—it was just too dangerous there, he insisted. So I didn't pay these friends much mind.

But you never knew, did you? After all, the fighting never made much sense, and it lasted for fifteen years. You never knew.

I made my arrangements. I booked an Air France flight to Paris and then, after a several-hour layover, the Middle East Airlines flight to Beirut. The Mace Hotel on Rue Jeanne d'Arc in Hamra, the *Lonely Planet* guide told me, would cost me twenty-five dollars a night. I called and booked a reservation, checking the twenty-five-dollar figure several times just to be sure.

CHAPTER 2

I prepared. I found my rather tattered high school Arabic textbook, *Eastern Arabic*, sat myself in the striped chair near the piano every morning, and practiced: "*Sabah al kheer, ya Mr.West. Keef haalek?"* My words would bring my wife scurrying into the room to see if something was wrong—the strong "h" and "kh", to say nothing of the guttural "aign" and "ghaign", sounded to her like I was at least choking, if not worse.

Then my wife remembered that Munir Saada, the former minister of the Woodstock Unitarian Universalist church, was Lebanese. Hey, I could call him.

I did, explaining that I wanted to practice my Arabic before traveling to Lebanon in December. Would he mind my stopping by on Saturday mornings?

Of course not. *Ahlan wa sahlan*. Welcome.

And so every Saturday for a couple of months I visited Munir. He was well into his eighties, stooped over, nearly blind, staying in an upscale assisted living facility. He tired easily, but he clearly loved the visits.

I'm not sure how much Arabic I learned, but I learned a lot about Munir. Raised a protestant in Damascus, he had studied at AUB and then gone on to for post-graduate work at the Near East School of Theology a couple of blocks away. He had known one of the founders of the Syrian Baath Party. While teaching history at a prep school near the Woodstock church, he had created a scholarship fund for poor but qualified students from Syria and Jordan to attend AUB. He had returned to Beirut in the early '80s, hoping to lend his voice to those calling for an end to the civil war, but a blast of machine gun fire hitting the balcony he was standing on not long after his arrival in Beirut showed him the futility of his mission, and he flew back to the US. He ended his working life filling the pulpit of the Woodstock UU church.

In hindsight, I think he considered Lebanon a part of Greater Syria, but he was never explicit about the issue, and I didn't know enough about the historical and cultural complexities to press the point.

Before I left, Munir asked two favors of me. First, would I please take a picture of the Near East School of Theology, to prove to his satisfaction that it had survived the war unscathed? Second, would I see if his master's thesis had made it through the civil war. He'd lost his copy, and wanted to be sure it was still on the shelves there.

Sure. Be happy to.

"*Allah maak*," god be with you, he said as I shook his hand a few days before leaving.

I'd made it to lesson twenty-one or twenty-two of *Eastern Arabic* by the time I caught the shuttle to Boston's Logan Airport one snowy morning. It was an uneventful bus ride. The Air France ticket agent expressed a bit of curiosity about my travel to Beirut, but my story passed muster. Into the boarding area—this was before 9/11, so security was pretty perfunctory—and to the gate to wait. Boarding time came and went. Finally, "Ladies and gentlemen, we regret to inform you that there's a minor technical problem with the aircraft. We're trying to get the part and will let you know when we're ready to depart."

Time passed. I don't believe in signs, but I did wonder if somebody was telling me something.

Several announcements and two hours later, we were told that they hadn't been able to find the part they needed—a bulb for a cockpit instrument—so they were going to put us up in a hotel, and we'd fly out the next morning. Any connecting flights would be taken care of.

Was somebody trying to tell me something?

We were given meal tickets, bused to a nearby hotel, and brought back to the airport the next morning. It was an uneventful flight.

OK, I thought, as I settled in to wait in Charles de Gaulle's Terminal C for the MEA flight to Beirut. Here we go. It's gonna happen. I'm going back to Beirut.

Not long after settling in with my book I noticed two policemen escorting a dark-haired young man toward the departure gate. He began shouting. The policemen grabbed his arms, trying to force him through the boarding gate onto the gangway to the airplane while he struggled to free himself, still shouting.

"What's going on?" I asked a young woman sitting next to me. "Do you speak Arabic?"

"Yeah. Wait." She listened. "It seems he's a Palestinian who's being deported back to Beirut, and he's shouting that he won't go."

Is somebody trying to tell me something?

The policemen finally decided that Plan A was not a good idea and escorted the young man out of the terminal.

CHAPTER 2

It was an uneventful flight.

The plane dropped through the clouds and into the rain as we flew just above Beirut, toward the airport south of the city.

I'd bought my visa in the States, so there was no problem getting through passport control. The customs inspectors weren't interested in my backpack, waving me through, into the airport. Into Beirut.

I was swarmed by taxi drivers. "Taxi! Taxi, sir? Taxi to Beirut?" This was long before European or American tourists had begun thinking about visiting Lebanon, so my light skin and northern European features marked me as a rare and lucrative target.

The *Lonely Planet* guide had told me that I could catch a bus to the city by walking just a few meters onto the main road outside the airport. I was too tired and too discombobulated to try to figure this out, and besides, I told myself, it's raining out there.

"OK. Hotel Mace bi Rue Jeanne d'Arc bi Hamra." I'd been practicing that for hours. "*Adeesh?*" How much?

"Hamra. OK."

"*Adeesh?*"

"Hamra? Twenty dollar."

"OK." That's what *Lonely Planet* had told me it would cost. A good start, even with the grey skies and rain.

The first thing that struck me as we drove to town was that, well, we didn't have to drive to town. We were already in town—apartment buildings and shops lining the highway—the moment we left the airport. No longer was the airport out in the middle of nowhere. No longer—I noticed as I looked east, to the mountainsides on my right—was there a middle of nowhere. Buildings and buildings and buildings everywhere.

Beirut had spread.

The driver turned left off the sleek airport highway, driving toward the sea, then turning right when he reached the coast.

"*Raouche*," he said, pointing to the familiar coastal landmark, Pigeon Rocks, before he turned into the city, heading for Hamra.

"*Rue Jeanne d'Arc. Sharia Jeanne d'Arc*," I said. "*Ta9rifha?*" Do you know it?

"*La.*" No.

We entered the Hamra district, and things became familiar—not the specifics, but the generalities—but then I saw an old landmark on the corner ahead, the ABC—Ah, Beh, Ceh—store.

"Stop here. *Wa'if hone*," I said. I wasn't sure exactly where Jeanne d'Arc was, but this was close enough. I was tired of being in a vehicle. It was time to take things into my own hands.

The driver pulled over. I took my backpack from the trunk, paid him, and made my way back to the ABC store through the gentle drizzle.

Here. The hotel is right near here. I'm sure.

And there it was, on the left-hand side of the street, half a block from Rue Hamra, the modest neon "Mace Hotel" sign shining above the entryway.

I had arrived.

I was back.

* * *

I sat on the bed in my stark hotel room, wondering what to do next.

Beirut in the rain. It must've rained in Beirut when I was young, but I didn't remember it. I had no memory of these grey skies, of this raw, damp breeze. But I'd come all this way, so…

I set out to see what there was to see.

And for the next several days, that was what I did: wander, seeing what there was to see.

Michel, the Egyptian night clerk at the hotel, told me there was nothing to worry about, so I could wander where I would. Beirut was safe. Nevertheless, I was wary. I began close to home—close to the hotel—and then gradually expanded my circle until it encompassed a several-mile radius.

Walking, looking, smelling, listening.

What had changed? What was the same? The apartment buildings where I had lived were still standing, though the farmer's field had turned into a parking lot and the rocky hillside across from our first apartment was taken up by a glistening new high-rise, still under construction.

AUB remained beautiful, with its lush greenery, winding pathways, beige-stone and red-tile-roofed buildings. I snapped a photo of the nearby Near East School of Theology for Munir and photocopied the first several pages of his master's thesis, which was safely catalogued and shelved in the library stacks.

But the AUB field where I'd played left field for the Uncle Sam's Rangers softball team was being replaced by a state-of-the-art gymnasium.

More ominously, there were all those bronzed plaques on the walls of College Hall, the ones that read, "AUB thanks its faculty, students and staff for their help toward the reconstruction of College Hall," "AUB is grateful to the American people for their contribution to..." "AUB thanks Shafik Hariri," and so on.

At one corner of the building, "College Hall Rebuilt 1999." The year before my visit. It took that long to undo that particular part of the damage wrought during the war, the truck bomb that had destroyed much of this landmark and the adjacent library (where Munir's master's thesis was still stored) in 1991, about the time everyone thought the worst was over. I learned later that the rebuilding was completed just about the time that the painstaking reconstruction of the equally devastated National Museum was wrapping up.

Down on the Corniche, the American embassy, blown up by a car bomb in 1983 (had Fuad and Fadool still been working there?), had been moved to a more isolated location high above the city in Antelias. In its place a twenty-story apartment building with high-priced views of the sea and the mountains was going up. The curve of the Corniche where it bent around in front of the embassy, then turned left along the coast, was gone—now the seaside road ran straight from AUB Beach to Ain el Mreisse, the little harbor for fishing boats having been accommodated by access under the bridge carrying the four-lane, palm-tree-lined boulevard toward the familiar electric guitar icon announcing the Hard Rock Café, just across the road from the Nasser Monument and from a Sunna mosque. And a McDonald's.

Ah, Beirut. Still such a blend. Still so perplexing.

Back on Rue Bliss, Uncle Sam's restaurant had become Baguette. Student waiters still served hamburgers and fries, but now I could order pasta dishes too. Khayyat's bookstore, just down the street from the AUB main gate, was on its last legs, its shelves half-stocked, its customers rare, its skimpy collection of postcards yellowing, the pictures long out of date. I spent several pleasant afternoons with the owner, sipping coffee, talking about the good old days.

Was it Smith's grocery store where I had considered buying that hundred-dollar jar of Postum? I had remembered wooden floors and a location a bit farther east. But who knew? The sign said it'd been operating since 1952, so it might have been here. Sifri's grocery store, not far from our seaside apartment, was gone—that's where I had bargained with Mr. Sifri, insisting that fifteen pounds was just too much for such a scrawny Christmas tree. OK, ten. OK.

The Manara? Where was the Manara, the lighthouse? Where was that stubby black-and-white symbol of Ras Beirut? Oh, there it was, hidden among the tall apartment buildings that had sprouted around it, dwarfing it. And there was its replacement, a sleek, silver minaret-like—or was it rocket-like?—spire set on the rocks at the far tip of the peninsula.

The trams were gone, the tracks on Bliss paved over. The long stairway I'd walked to and from school every morning—the place I'd learned my lesson about gambling—had been closed off, both ends bricked up, razor wire spun across the top of the tall wall.

Downtown was gone. Place des Martyrs was a wide, flat expanse at the center of which stood the heroic statue commemorating the 1916 rebels against Ottoman oppression. But I didn't remember the statue; it had been set here just before I left. Workmen were refurbishing and renovating the mandate-style buildings just west of the Square. The el Amine mosque that Hariri had endowed was just a hole in the ground behind a fence covered with artists' renditions of what was to come.

Much of Beirut was still visibly scarred by the Civil War. Bullet holes riddled the Martyrs Square statue, even though it had eventually been removed to safety from its position on the Green Line and then brought back after the war. Buildings pocked with bullet scars and wide holes blasted by rocket-propelled grenades and artillery stood everywhere. Entire blocks lay abandoned, the buildings uninhabitable, balconies dangling by their bent steel rebar above the street, bushes growing in rubble-filled, roofless houses.

The Holiday Inn stood empty, overlooking the sea. It was battered and war-riddled, a tall, ragged remnant of the worst of the fighting. But the St. Georges Hotel, at whose beach I had occasionally swum with my friends, was still standing, still symbolizing Beirut's entry into modernity in the 1930s, when the hotel had served as the first host for European and American travelers looking for the familiar.

I paid a brief visit to ACS. Two new floors had been added to the old classroom building where I had studied. The library was on the top floor, and a French class was going on in a far corner. The school was still using the old four-story boarding department for faculty housing, so classroom space was limited. The students—all Lebanese—spoke French as poorly as any American student would. This was no longer a Francophone world.

Well and good, all these sights. But what did I feel?

I certainly did not have anything approaching an epiphany—there was no, "Aha! This is who I am and where I belong!" And I was mildly frightened a fair amount of the time, wondering just how much I could trust the seemingly peaceful world I'd stepped into. I was very lonely. The only people I spoke with on a regular basis were Michel at the hotel, the owner of Khayyat's, and the waiter at Marrouche restaurant.

I was pretty much the only European or American I encountered.

Back at the Mace, I asked Michel the best way to go to Baalbek. He knew a reliable company and would book a tour for me. But no luck. They needed at least four passengers, and I was the only one interested. Day after day I checked. Day after day, no luck. Finally a Canadian couple came to visit the ambassador, so I traveled with his wife and friends. Baalbek was not as I remembered it, smaller and more self-contained. But the Bekaa was beautiful. And we stopped for a snack at Chtaura.

Though I'd not much enjoyed my Byblos tour with my mother fifty years before, I knew I was ready for it now. *Lonely Planet* told me the best way to get there was to go to the Charles Helou bus station, get on the bus to Tripoli, and ask to get off at Jbeil.

Fair enough. I looked at the city map and started walking, keeping my eyes peeled for the bus station.

The only thing the guide book forgot to explain was that the bus station stands under the highway overpass. The highway overpass that I traversed. On and on I went, past Electricité du Liban, past the phone company, over the Beirut River, till finally—at what I later found out was the Dora roundabout, three miles past the bus station—I saw some buses, asked for one to Tripoli, got on, and half an hour later was deposited at the Jbeil off-ramp.

I picked up a guidebook in the souk just outside the entrance and made my way across the narrow bridge to the castle keep, up the stone stairway to the ramparts to get the full panorama, and then, slowly, alternately reading the guidebook and the placards set at various sites, though the ruins, civilization by civilization, epoch by epoch.

This, I realized as I wandered the path among the obelisks, ramparts, and columns, was the Lebanon that had gotten under my skin all those years ago—this and its modern counterpart, the arm-in-arm promenade of young women along the Corniche, one modestly covered head-to-wrist-to-toe, the other in skin-tight sequined jeans and a halter top. It was this little seaside plot that had gotten to me, where everyone who was anyone in history had passed through to conquer and convert, only to be conquered and converted in turn, century after century, millennium after millennium.

All the way back to the Late Stone Age. All the way through the Amorites and Canaanites and Egyptians and Romans and Crusaders up to the Ottomans. All the way up to the restaurant just around the corner from the ruins where I could get a hamburger, fries, and a Pepsi or hummus, tahini, and tabbouleh. Or, just around the corner from that, where I could buy a bit of stone into which was etched the fossil of a long-extinct fish, dug from the side of the mountains that tower above this busy little coast.

I was the only visitor that day, as I was the only customer in the souk, jam-packed with Byblos scarves and Byblos t-shirts, water-pipes, headdresses, postcards, and pashminas. The shopkeepers were pleased to see me.

* * *

I wandered Beirut's streets, looking for the familiar. Andy Harada's building had been torn down, but where was Tim Rasmussen's? Was that it, just up the street from Dream Suites? Not sure. Didn't Art Pfau live in one of these buildings on a side street near the hospital? What had happened to the small prison just up the hill from our apartment in the Bissat-Kassem building? What were the names of the other buildings we lived in? What were the names of the streets we lived on?

Bobby Wieland, who had made the jukebox selections in the hotel at the Cedars fifty-three years before, had lived in that building, the one just across from Pigeon Rocks, the one whose 1950s architectural hipness was proclaimed by a huge modernistic concrete curlicue gracing the entry way. But the building was collapsing, waiting, like so many others, to be torn down to make room for the new Beirut. "The Syrians took over that building," someone told me," and they destroyed it."

Where had the Eagle's Nest restaurant been—second fiddle to Uncle Sam's but where we had gone when there were no free tables at Uncle Sam's—on Rue Jeanne d'Arc? Was that it, where there was now a photography store on the corner? Yes, I thought so. Yes, the owner confirmed it used to be a restaurant, though he didn't remember the name.

Where was the spot on the Corniche where I'd had the only fight of my life, a tussle and tumble with a Lebanese boy, down the hillside toward the sea near the Bain Militaire? What had come of that fight? What had caused it? Who had been with me that day? What had I told my mother?

What had the Corniche looked like before they widened the sidewalk and straightened the Ain al Mreisee end? When had the rather scruffy Military Beach been turned into this slick resort-like expanse, taking up most of the western edge of the Corniche? A little farther south, next to Pigeon Rocks, the sea access and swimming pools at Sporting Club and Long Beach seemed about the same, resembling, as an acquaintance later described them, "construction sites masquerading as public beaches."

The beaches just south of the city—Saint Simon where I had first tried hummus, and Saint Michel, with its palm-lined entryway—were gone, the wide sands turned into two– and three-story structures built during the war by people looking to get away from the center of the city where the fighting never seemed to let up.

The once forested and farmed mountainsides, similarly, were covered with buildings as people had sought safety from the relentless violence of the cities.

Christians had built on the hills and mountains to the north of the city, the Druze just to the east and south, the Sunni farther north, the Shia farther south.

The Lebanon that had once been made up of tiny antique villages surrounded by terraced hillsides tended with loving hands by farming families was gone. In its place were vast agglomerations of small retail shops and apartment buildings, stretching along the roadsides connecting the villages, a mountainous megalopolis running almost seamlessly along the coast from north to south. The terraces, like so many of the buildings in Beirut, were collapsing, overrun by weeds and scrub. The farms and the farmers were long gone.

The abandoned airport was gone. That wide expanse of cracked tarmac where my friends and I had flown our model airplanes, like the beaches, was covered over by houses and stores and apartment buildings. It was long gone, like the shepherds who occasionally herded their flocks along the edge of the airport, stopping to watch the band of American teenagers playing with their little airplanes so far from the city.

It was at the old airport that I'd driven for the first time, Harold Snell's 1958 Peugeot, nervously steering and missing my shifts on the wide, empty pavement one dark night. Was Harold Snell still alive? He was the man who taught me how to tie my necktie in a Windsor knot. What would my mother's life have been like if she had married him, that widowed, kind, cultured black man who, I'm sure, she loved at a time when American society still did not allow love between a black man and a white woman?

* * *

Still, I wondered. What had living in Beirut done to make me the me I had become?

Walking along Rue Sadat one afternoon, I got an inkling. But it was an inkling, not of the answer to this specific question. It was more general, an inkling of the profundity of the impact the city had had on me.

As I walked past Smith's grocery store, the sounds of a radio playing Arabic music came from a window across the street. In the distance, the call to prayer began. The smell of grilling kebabs wafted toward me in the gentle breeze. A passing taxi driver beeped his horn, letting me know he was available if I needed a ride somewhere. These sounds, sights, and smells all came together, an overwhelming wave of sound and sight and scent.

Bathed in memory, I began to cry.

I stood stopped on the sidewalk, tears wetting my cheeks, my vision blurred.

"Thank you, Mom," I found myself saying aloud, through my soft sobbing. "Thank you for bringing me here."

* * *

Once I'd felt included. I'd been wandering around downtown, watching the workman bring the old buildings back to life as they replaced pocked slabs of beige stone facing with new ones. I noticed the steeple up the hill, and walked toward it.

A church. A capuchin church, to be precise. The steeple was new, but the stones of the church were old, some still showing the scars of war.

Huge vases of flowers were being delivered to the church. There was bustle everywhere. A wedding maybe?

"What's going on?" I asked an official-looking young man.

"Tomorrow we dedicate the church," he said, beaming with pride. "We have finished the renovations."

"What time?"

"Ten. In the morning."

"I'll be here."

Of course, I wasn't sure if I would be there. What right, I often found myself wondering, did I have to be any of the places I took myself to? I often felt like an intruder. The afternoon I had stepped into a small mosque just off Rue Hamra, untied my shoes, walked into the sanctuary, and sat among a few men kneeled at prayer, I had felt this way. I felt this way during my brief visit to ACS. I had even felt this way at Marrouche and Stambouli, restaurants noted for their regional cuisine.

Why would I feel this way?

I'd guess it's left over from the fact that I almost always feel a bit like I don't belong. Others in the motel coffee shop in Ascutney, Vermont, or on a ski lift just around the corner on the mountainside belong. This is their coffee shop; they are true skiers, not just paying a brief visit to the sport.

But I think such feelings were intensified in Beirut.

Wherever I walked I felt a mild awe. After all, most of the people I passed in the streets had, only a few short years before, lived through a hell I could not imagine. Not the hell of a full-blown, formal, declared war with explicit enemies whose airplanes dropped bombs and lobbed artillery shells, one set of foreign uniformed soldiers overrunning another set of uniformed soldiers No. The people I saw walking the streets had lived through something different, where no one ever quite knew who was who and what was what. Christian against Muslim, then Muslim against Muslim; the Druze first there, then there while Israelis invaded, and Syrians invaded, and Americans invaded, then, one after the other, they left, and the fighting returned to what the fighting had been.

I tried to imagine what it would have been like to own a curio shop during those years or run a vegetable stand. I tried to imagine what it would have been like to try to study algebra. Who could have considered having children?

There. Those two men, passing each other on the Corniche, I'd think. Was one of them, a decade before, hidden around the corner from the other, his automatic weapon aimed to shoot him if his head appeared? Did one of them kill the other's cousin? Mother? Wife?

Everyone I passed, I felt, had stories I could not imagine having, lives I could not imagine having lived.

Or perhaps what I mean to say is that I could not imagine having lived them and then gone on to walk along the Corniche, passing people I knew might have, only a decade beforehand, wanted with all their hearts to kill me and my cousins, mother, and wife.

I was in awe of whatever it is in human beings that allows us to get on with things. I think that's what I felt. Feeling that, I felt like an intruder, a person who had not earned the right to live amid such brave and resilient people.

But once I'd felt included. I decided, the next day, to attend the ceremony at the church. Bathed and dressed, I left early enough to get in before the church filled up. I took a seat in the back—I did not have the right to be front and center; I could watch, but not pretend to belong.

The service was in French. After a few hymns and readings, the sermon. Was it a priest who spoke? I don't think so, but I'm not really sure.

What did he talk about? He praised the commitment of this small community to its church and its faith. Without elaborating on the horrors of what had happened to the church and the city and its people, he commended their bravery.

Then he spoke about the future. About the fact that this rebuilt church and renewed faith were what mattered. Beirut was being rebuilt and reborn.

And there I was, sitting in a tangible, rock-solid symbol of that rebirth, welcomed as a guest to the re-inauguration of the life of that symbol. For the second time during this visit, I wept.

* * *

It wasn't long after attending this church service that I went home. I actually left a few days earlier than I had planned. I had, apparently, seen enough, felt enough, heard enough. I think attending the capuchin service brought me closure. I had felt enough and knew enough. For the moment.

So I had marveled at the alternating neon lights festooning Rue Hamra, the first reading "Merry Christmas" and the second "Ramadan Kareem," blessed Ramadan. I had walked the familiar streets and some unfamiliar ones. I'd realized how little Arabic I actually knew and wondered how much I had known when I'd studied it all those years ago. I had, briefly, felt like a part of things.

It was time to go.

To change my ticket I had to go to the Air France office, which was near Sassine Square in Ashrefieh. I'd not traveled that far within the city, so the bus ride seemed interminable. Every time we approached a widening in the road, I asked the driver if this was Sassine.

"No, don't worry. I will say," he said in friendly, faltering English. Again and again.

At Sassine, I asked directions to the Air France office.

At the Air France office, I changed my ticket.

And then I went back to the hotel, packed, and flew home the next day.

"It was good to go back," I told Buffy when I got back to Vermont. "But I don't think I'll want to go again. I sure wouldn't want to live there."

* * *

But I was wrong. On both counts.

I came back. And I—we—ended up living in Beirut.

First, the coming back part.

Something happened to me between that "I sure wouldn't want to live there" and, oh, maybe 2003. I found myself suggesting to Buffy that she might like to see Beirut.

"You know, I've been talking about this place for all this time. You really oughta come see it. It's really a pretty neat place."

The civil war seemed safely a thing of the past—all the news reports were of peace and security—and the Hariri assassination, which set in motion years of off-and-on violence and political instability, was a year and a half in the future. A visit to Beirut seemed a good idea.

Then we were given a job to do, making it an even better idea.

Our Weathersfield neighbors Cookie and Ernie Shand got wind of our plans to visit Lebanon. It seems that the couple, whose adopted son had just graduated from the local high school, had, a decade prior to that adoption, adopted a little Lebanese girl, Wafiqa. Wafiqa was coming to the US for surgery to correct deformities caused by rickets, but her visa wouldn't allow her to stay in the US long enough to get the necessary follow-up therapy. Kind-hearted souls that they were, the Shands adopted her.

Wafiqa had spent much of her childhood in an orphanage before coming to the US. Her mother had been killed in a crossfire during the civil war while hanging laundry on the roof of her house. Traumatized by this event, and by the war in general, Wafiqa had become shy and withdrawn, able to recall only fragments of her past as she tried to pull herself together.

She'd lost touch with her relatives in Lebanon. She had vague but fond memories of the people who cared for her at the orphanage, she told us over coffee and cakes in the Shands' living room.

Would we, she asked shyly, be willing to see if we could find the orphanage, talk with the staff, and take some pictures?

Sure.

Her face brightened. The orphanage was somewhere in Jounieh. She wrote down its name, her full name, and the phone number of an aunt she hadn't been able to reach for years. She gave us a couple of pictures of herself and Ernie and Cookie.

We booked Air France from Logan to Paris and Paris to Beirut. Since I was bringing my wife, I'd decided to upscale the visit, paying fifty dollars a night for our room at the Berkeley Hotel just up the street from the Mace. I wouldn't even consider the bus from the airport, rain or no rain.

"Just don't go south," the nice young man at the state department told me. I got out *Eastern Arabic* again, pretty much starting back at the beginning.

And then we left.

* * *

The flights were uneventful, as was the taxi ride to Beirut, as was locating the hotel. Other than getting stuck in the snow on a trip over the mountains to Baalbek, the visit was uneventful. Other than spending a few minutes chatting informally with the new headmaster at ACS, that is.

The trip, however, was important in a much larger sense. It contributed to a mental evolution I'd been undergoing ever since a summer trip to Portugal a few years previous.

Portugal had been wonderful. Our family had been joined by my nineteen-year-old niece Heather and my old friend Lee. We'd spent a few days wandering about Lisbon and then taken the train north. We stopped for a night or two at Coimbra, then at Vigo, Spain, renting a car there and driving to Santiago de Campostella, a pilgrimage site packed with believers, the exquisite church overflowing with people and humming with energy. We spent the last few days before turning back toward Lisbon in Finisterra, a picturesque fishing village jutting far out into the Atlantic.

As much as I loved the trip, something was missing.

The something, I finally realized, was purpose.

Every morning we got up, got dressed, got breakfast, and figured out what we would do with ourselves. Then we went and did it: visited a castle or a museum or a church, walked along the river or up a hill or around a park, had lunch, did more of what we had decided to do—or maybe something else that had occurred to us along the way. We had dinner, walked some more, read, and slept. Then we got up again, got dressed, and all the rest.

But I never felt the sense of purpose that I feel when I live somewhere. I get up because I have obligations, relationships, things to look forward to other than seeing a painting, and things to worry about other than whether the train will leave on time.

This realization prompted me to start looking for work overseas when I returned. I wanted to live somewhere outside the United States, not merely to visit other countries.

Then Wafiqa gave us our little task. One sunny morning not long after arriving in Beirut, the hotel concierge got us a driver who knew Jounieh. We shared with the driver as much as we knew about where we were going and why, and set off.

In Jounieh, we turned east and into the mountains, the roadside crowded with houses and buildings. Not far up the road, the driver stopped and went into a pharmacy. He came out with the owner, to whom we explained what we were looking for and why.

He gave us directions. Another mile, another stop. Another consultation, and soon we turned left off the main road. Another consultation, and we pulled up in front of a *garderie*, a nursery school.

We rang the bell. A woman came to the door. She didn't speak English, so we explained what we were looking for in French.

"Oh, yes, this used to be an orphanage. Now it's a boarding school, but all the children are gone. Please come in. Please, sit."

We sat. Not long afterward, a middle-aged woman came out.

Now director of the garderie, she used to work at the orphanage. We showed her a picture of Wafiqa and her American family. She remembered her fondly, with her misshapen legs and her kind heart.

We sat together talking in the office for some time as she tried to recall specifics of Wafiqa's years there. I took notes. Then she took us on a tour of the building: the classrooms, the dining hall, the dormitories. We took pictures, including several of her.

Then we hugged and drove back to Beirut to see if we could find Wafiqa's aunt somewhere in Ashrefieh. No luck there. So we returned to the hotel and took a nap.

But that little job, when we were doing something that mattered for someone else, not just inventing our days, strengthened my resolve to quit visiting places and start living in them.

In less than a year, I found work on a project in South Sudan.

No, not in Beirut. Not yet.

CHAPTER 3

Leaving Home

I'd been looking for work outside of the US in a somewhat haphazard manner for several years. Charis had made it successfully through a rocky last few years of high school and seemed to be well on her way toward a solid life, one way or another. I began to search more seriously. My second visit to Beirut inspired me to ramp up my efforts.

How hard could it be to get a job overseas? I'd spent my teenaged years in Lebanon and Brazil, had traveled widely since then, spoke more-than-passable French and Portuguese, and had a CV rich with a variety of experiences that demonstrated how creative and energetic I was.

I found the websites, talked with friends, sent the letters and e-mails, made the phone calls, and did everything I could think of to get my foot in some international door.

Nobody bit.

So what was I doing wrong? How come, even when I could spice up the intro to my phone message or letter or e-mail with "your colleague Julie (or Tereza, or Peter, or whoever) suggested I get in touch with you," they wouldn't even respond with, "Sorry, but…"?

I persisted, but it was pretty frustrating.

An NGO in Washington had posted an opening for a curriculum specialist on USAID's website. All they'd wanted was a quick blurb. I sent one. They responded: send your CV and give us a call.

I sent it.

I waited. Then I called. And called. And called. I left voicemail message after voicemail message. I wasn't about to give up—they had actually responded to something I had sent them!

One afternoon I was working at Newfane Elementary School in southern Vermont, talking with teachers about their students' difficulties reading the texts they were assigning them. Finding myself with a bit of free time, I went into the library office, got an outside line, punched in my phone card code, and dialed the NGO number.

A real person answered.

"Mike Laflin here."

I introduced myself, saying I was wondering if he'd had a chance to look at my CV.

"Yeah, I got it. But we can't use you. You haven't worked overseas."

Ah! So the reason I wasn't having any luck getting a job overseas was because I hadn't held a job overseas. OK. I could understand that.

Sort of.

But at least I had the guy on the line, so maybe I had a chance at something.

It was at this point that I realized I'd really made a mistake here. Oh, not about trying to get this guy interested in me. Not about sending the CV or about following up.

The mistake was to make the call from the Newfane Elementary School library on a day when the fifth graders were putting on a play in the library just outside the door and were going to use the office as a green room, where they would change into their costumes and wait to go on stage, giggling, chattering, scurrying, and, basically, being fifth graders.

As I tried to gather my thoughts to keep the NGO official—Mike Laflin, Vice President of the Education Development Center, or EDC—interested, noisy, excited kids zipped in and out of the crowded little office, then milled about in the tiny space, about to burst with adrenalin and kid-energy.

"Well," I began again, at which point a hectic fifth-grader tripped on the phone line, knocking the phone on the floor and yanking the receiver from my hand.

I picked up the phone and the receiver.

"Are you still there?"

"Yes."

"I'm sorry. I'm in a pretty noisy place. But...but...I think I have some skills that would serve me well overseas, even though I've never worked there," I went on, blurting out whatever came to mind, hoping he wouldn't give up on me as I dodged kids and held the phone close to my chest.

"Listen, give me a try. Send me somewhere, house me and feed me, and let me show you what I can do. I'll work pro bono. You don't have to pay me anything."

I was about to say, "Never mind the 'house me and feed me,'" when he said "So tell me, why do you want to do development work?"

Development work? OK. Good to know what it's called.

But I knew that I had him. He had engaged. I was going to pull this one off.

The kids continued to scurry in and out of the room, laughing and whispering and poking and tripping, but the phone never fell again and, more importantly, Mike and I tentatively arranged a trip to Washington for a face-to-face interview.

Two months later I was on my way to Dar es Salaam, Tanzania, for a month's stint transforming the Ministry of Education's math, English, and Kiswahili curricula into the scope-and-sequence for the Interactive Radio Instruction program that EDC was about to develop for that country's rural schools.

The project director told me that she had been reluctant to take me on but that when Mike called her after I'd been there for a week or so and asked her if EDC should consider hiring me, she had replied, "You can send Nick anywhere to do anything."

So it turned out that breaking down, almost in tears, in her office, hadn't done me in.

Here's what had happened. After a brief here's-what-we-do-here orientation—international NGOs seem to allow up to thirty-five minutes before plunging new employees deep into the fray for this sort of activity—I was handed the Ministry's English curriculum, shown sample scope-and-sequences from other projects, and assigned the task of breaking the curriculum down into a series of units and then subunits. From this, the scriptwriters would be able to decide what they'd teach in each radio lesson.

Fine. A little grammar, syntax, vocabulary. No problem. I wrapped that up in a few days.

Then the boss, an energetic, outgoing Canadian named Suzanne, handed me another Ministry curriculum booklet. This one was for teaching math. Great. I went back to my office, opened the booklet, and almost cried.

It was in Kiswahili. Not English or even French or Portuguese. Kiswahili, that strange mix of Bantu and Arabic that tradesmen from the north had developed a few centuries before.

I recognized a few Arabic words. But knowing that *arabaaine* means forty in both languages wasn't going to help me much when almost none of the other numbers matched up. Ten is *kumi* in Kiswahili, *aashra* in Arabic, and so forth.

After a while I made my way back to Suzanne's office.

"I can't do this. I just can't figure out how to do this. I can't even figure out where to begin," I said, hanging my head. Not crying.

"Hey," she replied. "We'll find something else for you to do. Don't worry about it."

I went back to my office, picked up the curriculum guide, and began leafing through it. Then I picked up the Kiswahili-English dictionary my wife had bought me. I started looking up words and then translating sentences. Every now and then I'd jump up and run into the scriptwriters' room, asking one of them how close my translation of a sentence was to what the sentence actually meant.

Usually pretty close.

OK. OK. I can do this.

"Suzanne," I said, bursting into her office, "I can do it. I can do this."

She smiled. "Great."

And I did it. And then I did the same thing with the Ministry's curriculum guide for Kiswahili.

And then I went home.

But not before I'd seen a bit of Africa. Not the Africa I'd noticed wandering around Dar es Salaam in the hour of daylight that remained after work or the Africa I'd seen when I took a bus inland to spend the weekend at Morogoro, which Lonely Planet had billed as a provincial college town. OK, maybe I did pass a couple of high-fenced freshly painted institutions as we approached the town.

This was another Africa.

Suzanne invited me to visit the site where we were going to put the radio programs they were producing to a test. They'd record the actors reading the scripts, teaching the first grade curriculum to a cluster of kids sitting on rocks and logs in the shade, just outside the community center.

The kids, most of whom appeared to be eight to fourteen or so, seemed to like repeating the lines the radio characters were saying, and the "teacher," a local volunteer with three or four years of schooling under his belt, seemed to understand what he was supposed to ask them to do during the musical interludes.

When the lesson was finished, we drove a little further. We stopped at the abandoned quarry where most of the students worked.

Here's what they were doing.

They would take a small hammer and hit a big stone, making smaller stones, then smaller stones, then gravel.

They would pile the gravel into cones, which contractors would buy from them.

They did this in the direct sun. All day long. Every day.

My first taste of Africa.

I flew home and picked up where I'd left off my life.

Six months later, Mike called to ask if I'd like to go to South Sudan to oversee work like that I'd been doing in Tanzania.

"Hold on a second."

"Sure."

"Hey, Buff," I called to my wife, who was writing a sermon in her study just down the hall from mine. "Do you mind if I go work in Sudan?"

She didn't miss a beat. "No. Sounds great."

So, undaunted either by the challenges of the work or the realities I'd be confronting, six months after the phone call I was on my way to Nairobi, Kenya, where I was to train and supervise South Sudanese scriptwriters and actors who would create and produce radio programs to be beamed to primary-grades schoolchildren in rural South Sudan.

I did it! I got a job overseas!

* * *

A year and a half in Nairobi—and in and out of Maridi, South Sudan—were followed by a month in Kinshasa, Democratic Republic of Congo, and another in Conakry, Guinea, between which I worked in EDC's Washington offices.

I don't think I have ever learned so much in such a short period of time, except maybe for those first couple of years when I was learning how to talk, that gravity existed, and the basics like that.

Before working in Africa, I had thought that I knew something about the world. I had thought that my early years overseas had taught me things about how the world worked and how it differed from America.

Indeed they had. But I was not at all prepared for what I learned as I walked the streets of Nairobi, approached by little boys in filthy, tattered t-shirts, pleading "Baba, I'm hungry," or when I walked through Kawangware, the slum where Sud Academy, the school where we tested our radio broadcasts on Sudanese refugee children, was located—most of the students could not afford the $3.50 semester's tuition, or when I was awakened in the middle of the night in my thatch-roofed hut in Maridi by drumming and chanting that signaled a funeral and that might last until well into the morning.

Or by Mading's question, "Tell me, Nick, what exactly does 'the rule of law' mean?"

Mading was an interesting young man. He was the only Dinka on our scriptwriting team. He was tall and as close to black as human beings get; his forehead was grooved with a few ritual scars.

We had tried our best to balance the ethnic makeup of the team, given the complexity of the ethnic makeup of the South Sudan and the hostilities among some of the groups. By mixing the groups, we could write scripts that would honor as many of the seventy tribes as possible, while modeling ethnic collaboration. The Dinka, the largest group, were a proud and often aggressive people. The rebel leader John Garang was Dinka, and many southerners felt that he and his people held disproportionate amounts of power in the movement.

But southern South Sudanese tribes like the Moru and the Azande had more university-educated members than the northern groups, so it had been hard to find qualified Dinka or Nuer, their virtual cousins, with whom they competed fiercely.

With the six-member scriptwriting team and four actors selected and trained, we set to work writing, producing, testing, revising, and recording the scripts. It was interesting work.

I ate lunch with the scriptwriters and actors in the small kitchen at our offices in Lavington, an affluent Nairobi suburb. The conversations were always provocative.

One day Mading opened the lunchtime conversation by asking, "Tell me, Nick, what exactly does 'rule of law' mean?"

I had two responses.

The first was amazement. Mading, like everyone else who worked for us, had a university degree, spoke fluent English—though we had to explain to him, again and again, that even though there were no words for "please" and "thank you" in Dinka, he still had to use these terms in English at what were considered appropriate times—and was very knowledgeable about national and international events. But he didn't know what "rule of law" meant.

My second response to his question was excitement. Hey, I've uncovered a real need; I've encountered a truly teachable moment.

So I proceeded. I quoted profusely, things like "the rule of law, not of men," "all men are created equal," and "equal justice before the law." I elaborated on the ideas undergirding the concept, explaining that under "rule of law," one would be treated according to what one was accused of having done in relation to what one was allowed to do, not in relation to who one's uncle was, that the poorest beggar would be given the same opportunity to defend himself as the richest bigwig. And so forth.

I was so pleased with myself—an opportunity had come to me, I had taken it, and now a young man destined to make a place for himself in this new country understood something of fundamental importance to the way his country was to be shaped.

"Hm. I see," Mading said when I was finished. He paused, thinking.

"I don't like it. I like it our way."

And he went back to his bowl of beans and rice.

* * *

However much—or little—I was able to teach, I certainly learned a lot, experiencing, myself, many teachable moments. There was Taban's resignation from the scriptwriters' team because his relatives ridiculed him for not earning enough money to provide for all of them, as he was supposed to do according to tradition. Or Amelia's willingness to spend three days on buses from Yambio, South Sudan, for an interview, even though she knew I could not guarantee her a job. Or the fact that every time we provided food at a workshop in South Sudan, all the attendees took second and third and sometimes even fourth helpings since this might be their only meal that week.

Once I asked Francis, who had worked for a number of years at Nairobi's *The Nation* newspaper, why Kenyan President Mwai Kibaki hadn't held a press conference to explain his reasons for responding as he had to the plebiscite on the constitution.

Francis looked shocked. "The president doesn't give press conferences! The president only makes speeches. Journalists aren't allowed to question him."

But there was more to it than my learning how the world worked.

In fact, I had wanted to work overseas in large part because I thought this might help me understand the question that had been nagging at me ever since I'd first come back to America from Beirut in 1960.

What, I'd been wondering all those years, is America?

What does it mean to be an American? I mean, if I'm an American, and those guys in the Evansville parking lot were Americans, and the black rock and roll fans who had been required by law to sit up in the hot balcony at the Little Richard concert in Greenville, South Carolina, were Americans, and the football fans and Free Speech Movement folks at Berkeley were Americans, and hip-hop artists and Newt Gingrich were Americans, what did we have in common? What makes us American?

To say nothing of the Laotian refugees in Burlington, the Hispanic day-laborers in Oakland, the dairy farmer just up the road from my wife's church in Weathersfield, and the Unabomber.

We're all Americans.

So who are we?

The question, which had been plaguing me for decades, really hit home sometime in the early '90s, when I was teaching at the Community College of Vermont.

My favorite class was one called American Character and Culture. This gave me a chance to get young—and sometimes old—Vermonters to systematically explore the questions about identity that I'd been informally messing with for so long. Selfishly, I used the students' insights to enhance my own understandings.

So we read widely, from Alexis de Tocqueville to John Kenneth Galbraith, from Walt Whitman to Ayn Rand to Allen Ginsberg. The conversations were wide-ranging and provocative. The point, of course, was not to answer the question "What is American character and culture?" but to ask it and to clarify what the question might mean.

One day, out of the blue, I got an e-mail—or was it a letter?—from the dean of something or other at CCV. American Character and Culture was being dropped from the CCV syllabus.

"What? How can you do this? This course," I said on the phone as respectfully as I could manage though I know my voice was quivering with frustrated rage, "is the most meaningful course in your syllabus! How can you drop it?"

"We've decided that there's no such thing as American character and culture anymore." Did he go on to say the concept was too controversial or too complicated or too…what?

I pushed back. A letter to him, another to the president of the college. Thoughts of a commentary on Vermont Public Radio.

I finally let it go. Well, I let go of trying to get the college to keep the course on the syllabus. But I didn't let go of the question. My question.

The fact that the college had decided to drop the course only added to my curiosity. What the hell is America? Who—I was still wondering—am I?

You can imagine how working overseas and immersing myself in another culture seemed likely to give me more glimmers of insight into a possible answer—or at least into clarifying the question. So as I wandered through Kawangware on my way toward some of the deepest poverty on the planet, watching kids playing soccer on a sewage-strewn beach at Conakry, the question recurred. Again and again.

* * *

One morning in Nairobi, Mike Kuenzli changed the way I looked at everything.

Mike worked for Sudan Radio Service as the CoP—that's "Chief of Party." How in the world do people think up stuff like this? It just meant that he ran an EDC project based in Nairobi like Suzanne had run the one in Dar. Mike was Swiss. As I recall, he had worked in radio in Europe for a while before heading for Africa, where he ran some sort of development-oriented radio programming deep in the Democratic Republic of Congo. He was an old-style, self-made man, no university degree, a life built solely on his accomplishments, not on his credentials. He was proud of this, but as the degree-clad youngsters made their ways up the hierarchies around him, he was also nervous about it.

What were he and I talking about?

Maybe something about how American NGOs differed from European ones, or about how people of different nationalities adapted to life in Africa. I don't remember.

All I remember is his unexpected interjection into the conversation.

I had said something like, "Well, you know, as an American, I—"

"You're not an American, Nick," he said, matter-of-factly interrupting whatever it was I was saying.

"What?"

"I said you're not an American." Just as matter-of-factly.

I was nonplussed. "What do you mean?"

"You don't act like an American. You don't think like an American. You pay attention to people. You listen. You engage. Americans don't do that."

What could I say? What did I say? Not much. Maybe nothing.

I was taken aback. Not an American? Then what was I?

Walking home from the office later that day, I recalled my 1960 home-leave visit, as our PanAm 707 from Tokyo touched down in Honolulu and I stepped off the plane onto the tarmac, looked around, and said to myself something like, "Yeah. This is your country. You are an American."

Mainly what I wanted, of course, was that quart of milk, but that quart of milk—and the grassy lawn I wanted to lie on—symbolized my America. My country.

I recalled having explicitly agreed with myself that this—even this mid-Pacific outpost that had only recently become a state—was my home. I was of it. It was who I was.

Through all the years that followed I had never wavered in this assumption. Not when I felt so out of place drinking beer with Gretchen's friends in the Saturday night parking lot, not when my fraternity brothers referred to me as "Beep-Beep," making the noise they assumed a Martian might make, not when I argued with the Collegiate School headmaster that Iranians taking Americans hostage was only a logical response to what we had been supporting in that country for decades.

Not when I found myself on the edges of things. Faking it. Pretending I knew what was going on and how to maneuver the life I was making for myself.

Trying to figure out what to do when Jim Clardy tried to show me how to fix my broken motorcycle and I found I just didn't care or when the conversation turned to whatever sport was in season.

But these—Americans' affection for machines and for watching one group of people try to move a spheroid from one end of a playing field to the other end, then to put the spheroid through a hoop, or into a net, or just get it across a line, past another group of people who acted like they hated the group with the spheroid—were only the metaphoric tips of the iceberg.

I never felt at home. Through all those years, I never felt especially real.

Now Mike Kuenzli had said it.

"Nick, you're not an American."

Now what?

Well, for starters, I decided to see if he was right. I began watching the Americans around me. How did they encounter each other? How did they deal with the Kenyans and the Sudanese we worked with? What did they do with themselves during their free time? What did they talk about?

The last one was easy—among the many things they talked about was sports.

OK. I knew that. Lots of people talk about sports. Rio went absolutely crazy when the World Cup soccer matches were held at Maracanã Stadium back in 1962 or 1963.

But I did begin to notice other little things. For example, I was the only one to eat lunch with the Sudanese scriptwriters and radio actors. I was the only one not to avail myself of Joseph the driver and to walk home or take the bus, sometimes riding with Nicholas the gardener and exchanging anecdotes about our families and our lives. I was almost the only American who seemed to actually like the fact that my African colleagues touched each other freely and regularly—I was the only one who seemed eager to join in.

Mike was right: I did approach things differently.

My favorite restaurant was…oh, what was it called? The Greenhouse, maybe? It was an outdoor palm-frond roofed courtyard where for not much money I could get excellent grilled chicken and potatoes. It always took a long time to get the chicken and potatoes, though, because the waiters, after setting my Tusker beer on my table, seemed to forget I was there. No matter. I always brought a book. And if it took too long, I'd get up and go find the waiter, who would apologize and go see what was happening in the kitchen. Eventually, my food would come.

But the best part of the restaurant was the music. A *kenga-kenga* band usually played: there was a one-stringed instrument called an *uruto*, lots of drums, and a couple of singers, as I recall. It was a driving, rhythmic music that brought everyone to the dance floor. The dancing was nothing "tribal" or ritualistic, nothing stylized or fancy-footed— mainly moving, bouncing, turning. Dancing. Smiling. Clapping your hands.

I never got up to dance. I did not try to sing along with the band. I didn't make friends with singers or dancers. I just read, ate, sipped my beer, and watched. Then I went home and slept very well.

I didn't spent much out-of-the-office time with my ex-pat colleagues. The one time I remember doing so, we went to a Chinese restaurant.

It was a half-dozen nice young men and women, NGO workers mainly, but as I recall, maybe an embassy employee or two.

We talked. Then the food came, much more promptly than at the Greenhouse. Nobody had to chase anybody down to remind them of our order.

But how vividly I recall the conversation. The interminable subject was why there were no good Chinese restaurants in Nairobi, and why this one, which wasn't a very good one, was the best. On and on and on the conversation went.

Surely we talked about something else, but I don't remember anything.

My fellow diners were American. We'd come eight thousand miles, leaving the malls and freeways and sports arenas far behind, and we'd come all this way to help people learn to read and write and think. We'd come to represent what was best about our culture and to enable people to live lives that offered choice, security, equality and liberty.

And this was all Americans had to talk about when we weren't doing the work?

Was this what Kuenzli had been talking about?

Was this what I wasn't?

Fine with me.

* * *

On the other hand, I did not, in any way, shape or form, go native or even consider going native.

Time and again, I heard British and American development workers remark that "once you've got the dust of Africa on your shoes, you never want to leave" or something like that.

The dust of Africa. But those development workers were chauffeured in air-conditioned cars by nice men you called by their first names while they called you "sir" and "mister," driven from their tall-stone-wall-topped-by-razor-wire-and-an-electric-fence compounds to their tall-stone-wall-topped-by-razor-wire-and-an-electric-fence office, from where their nice driver might take them to a tall-stone-wall-topped-by-razor-wire-and-an-electric-fence restaurant or shopping mall. How many really got much dust on their shoes?

No doubt some did. The Americans and Europeans who stayed for two or three months at a time in the CARE compound in Maridi got plenty dusty. There, they slept in brick, thatched-roof, concrete-floored huts called *tukuls*. Every morning they blended the buckets of hot and cold water that had been left outside their *tukul* door, stood in the little roomlet that had a drain—always hoping curious snakes didn't slither through the drain and into the roomlet—and tossed water onto themselves. Better known as taking a shower.

Only a few years before, the Sudanese Air Force would occasionally drop bombs on places like Maridi from the Antonov bombers the USSR had provided back in the days of the Cold War. So next to each *tukul* was a six-foot deep foxhole you jump into to escape the blast. The latrines were at the far end of the camp; some had seats, and some were made for squatting—take your pick.

After eating breakfast in the communal dining hall every morning the dozen or so NGO workers who lived at the compound went out through the bamboo gate in the bamboo fence to meet with local officials from the Ministry of Education in concrete-block offices that had neither electricity nor running water. They talked about the latest revisions they'd made in the national curriculum and then went back to their own concrete-block offices, without electricity or running water, to continue the work.

Every couple of months, the workers returned to Nairobi to work in the CARE or EDC or Save the Children offices and sleep and bathe and generally catch their breath at the Jacaranda Hotel or in an apartment they kept for such visits.

Everyone flew in and out of the Maridi airport. Well, to call it an "airport" is a bit of an overstatement. It was a clay landing strip cut in the forest. Enough gravel had been spread so airplanes could continue to land until the rainy season really got going in earnest. The development workers came in either on the big UN Lifeline Southern Sudan planes or in the five-seater or eleven-seater Cessnas owned by Mission Aviation Fellowship that flew anybody doing humanitarian work from Entebbe, Uganda, into South Sudan for $700 round-trip.

Once the rains really began, nobody got in or out except by road from Juba, where there was a tarmac landing strip. It took many hours to make the two hundred-mile trip, including spending two hours on the last eighteen miles of rutted road that tossed the four-wheel-drive vehicle from side to side as everyone hoped that the driver would be able to avoid the worst of the mire and they could make it all the way.

People who worked in places like Maridi indeed had the dust of Africa on their shoes. And the mud.

Those people worked right in the thick of things, where families tended half-acre plots of beans or manioc, drew water from wells drilled by a Norwegian NGO, carried five-gallon jerry cans on their heads back to their *tukuls*, and walked however many miles it was they needed to walk when they had to go somewhere. Those people had better things to talk about than the quality of the food at the best Chinese restaurant in Nairobi, although they certainly frequented that restaurant, and every other restaurant they could find, when they came back to the city for a break.

The longest I stayed in Maridi was two weeks.

I got Africa's dust and mud on my shoes, but it didn't stick in the sense Africa-lovers meant.

After I'd been in Nairobi for six months, Buffy and Charis came to visit. We went on a safari, and—making one of the stupidest vacation-decisions I've ever made—went to Addis Ababa for a few days. Nairobi's poor seemed positively affluent compared to the begging mothers nursing emaciated babies that lined the streets of Addis. We saw Lucy, our however-many-million-year-old ancestor, in the basement of the local museum, and took a taxi to a hilltop church to watch a dedication ceremony. But mostly we were perplexed there, troubled by almost everything we saw.

Buffy and Charis tutored for a while at Sud Academy, and had dinner with me at the Greenhouse Restaurant. Then they flew to Nepal, where Charis was about to begin a semester abroad. Even that turned out to be fraught. Buffy had a very difficult time getting on a flight back to Nairobi, but she didn't know that this was because after her flight left the airport—and the entire country—would be closed off from the outside world as the king tried to get everybody back in line. Buffy and I sat watching the CNN crawl, always pleased when it read something like "no new events in Kathmandu." Finally, after three weeks, we heard from Charis. All was well.

Buffy flew back to the States.

Then I flew to Kathmandu at the end of Charis's stay there, allowing her to be the guide and the guru about what was cool to do in this unusual city.

Then Charis flew home. Not long afterward, so did I, leaving Nairobi after nearly a year.

Africa tore me up. As hard as I tried to lift my spirits with thoughts such as "Isn't it amazing how everyone continues to smile, even though they have so little?" it was the depth of Africa's problems that stuck with me.

The depth of the problems and the hopelessness I felt as I considered them.

Maybe I just started working in Africa too late in life. Maybe I'm just too emotional, too much of a softy. Maybe I think too much. Maybe it's my propensity to consider worst-case scenarios. Whatever. I just couldn't see a way out for Africa. Its dilemmas, its problems, its burdens just seemed insurmountable.

Africa tore me up.

So I went home. Which was, at that point, a nice little house in a pleasant neighborhood in Newport News, Virginia.

* * *

Before I left, Fiona Edwards, a British early-math expert who had visited Nairobi periodically to support our scriptwriting efforts, gave me a bit of advice. Fiona had begun her working life by spending a couple of years in Bangladesh, working in the British version of the Peace Corps. Most recently, she and her family had lived in Lusaka, Zambia, where she had worked for the British foreign aid program.

"When you get back to the States, Nick, everybody will ask you lots of questions about what it was like living here," she began.

"Yeah. Of course. I'm looking forward to that."

"Well, don't believe them. They don't really want to know. You'll start talking, and they'll listen for a couple of sentences, and then their eyes will glaze over."

Indeed, I'd already had inklings of that possibility. A well-traveled and well-read old friend, responding to one of the narratives I had sent about Sudan, had expressed a consternation.

"I read your e-mails, and I love reading them," she had concluded. "But, in all honesty, I just don't have to context to begin to understand any of it. This is why I hardly ever respond. I just don't know where to begin—it's all so alien to what I know and how I live. But keep writing, and I'll keep reading."

On returning to the US, I found that by and large, Fiona was right. The only ones who had much inkling of what to ask and how to respond were those who had lived outside the country.

But I found something at least as unsettling as others' lack of interest in the world I'd lived in.

I found that I had been changed in profound ways. Before I wasn't sure how I fit in my mother culture. Now I wasn't so sure I wanted to fit.

Oh, I don't mean the run-of-the-mill post-sixties stuff like vestigial anti-materialism and scorn for truly committed capitalists or disdain for the hypocrisy of politicians who spout democratic rhetoric while supporting Noriegas, Mubaraks, and Shahs.

No, this was deeper and more basic. It was mostly little things.

To wit, the impatient grumpiness that is quickly transformed into boisterous public irritation at, for example, having to wait a few extra minutes in a grocery store line. Or the gastronomic finickiness that results in restaurant customers asking if white pepper could be substituted for black in such-and-such a dish, or requesting that a piece of fish be grilled, not fried.

Americans' self-absorption revealed itself to me in ways I'd never imagined, and on a level I'd never conceived. The standard critiques of our culture—from Herbert Marcuse to Christopher Hitchens—seemed to have missed how deeply we were flawed, how petty our focus had become, how paltry our daily concerns.

The concerns expressed by those American Chinese-food-eaters in Nairobi, I began to understand, were not the exception. They were, in many more cases than I had noticed before immersing myself in Africa, the rule.

No wonder the people I met didn't want to hear my stories. Too many seemed to have long ago given up thinking about social justice and meaning-of-life issues, to have traded curiosity about the world for curiosity about when a Trader Joe's might move into their neighborhood. For too many, the insights about the world beyond their immediate reach provided by Nova and the National Geographic channel seemed enough. For some, maybe more than enough.

Oh, not everyone, of course. But a lot more people than I had imagined seemed locked in little boxes of acquisition, honing their preferences and their insights into their preferences with an uncanny precision. So many people seemed exquisitely clear on what they wanted, when they wanted it, how much of it, and of what quality. And so many of these lacked any interest in concealing, or perhaps lacked an ability to conceal, those preferences from the rest of us. We've all heard about them: restaurant wait-staff, supermarket cashiers, and innocent bystanders, subjected to these puffed-up people's insistences, grumblings, and minor tantrums. All over the slightest infringement on their time, their space, their sanctified preferences for crookneck squash over summer squash.

Maybe, I thought, the Community College was right to insist that we no longer teach American Character and Culture. But maybe for the wrong reasons. Maybe the culture had just become too embarrassing to be shared with the general public.

* * *

But Abdechafi Boubkir had another take on America. A Moroccan who'd been educated in the US, he and I traveled together to Kinshasa, Democratic Republic of Congo, to train a group of scriptwriters. His French being a lot better than mine, I relied heavily on him to unscramble what I told the group of intern scriptwriters, like his continually having to correct my *on peut observer* to *on peut constater.*

So over the course of my three weeks in the DRC I learned a bit more French, and the scriptwriters learned something about how to create a radio lesson—the hardest part is to figure out how to explain something with no visual props, no facial gestures, no gesticulations and, most importantly, no opportunity for your listener to say, "Wait a minute. Can you go over that again? I missed a few points."

So we taught them to write the script. Then it would be recorded, tested, broadcast, revised, and rerecorded. The program has to be clear enough that a seven-year-old living in a hut far off in the bush can figure out what the radio characters are trying to say the first time around.

It's a tricky business.

But it's fun.

Abdechafi also taught me, however, what is probably the most important lesson I learned about my country, my culture, in all my time in Africa.

Although he was generally an admirer of Euro-American culture, Abdechafi was not a total convert. When, for example, that Danish cartoonist portrayed Mohammed wearing a turban and sporting a nuclear arsenal, he went ballistic.

"They can't do this!" he exclaimed. "It is not right! It's blasphemy!"

"But it's the way it works, Abdechafi. Free press, freedom of speech, and all that. If somebody wants to draw a picture of Jesus carrying bombs, or even raping his sister, they've got the right. Mohammed's no different."

"Mohammed *is* different. It is against our religion to do something like this."

The discussion went a few more rounds, but eventually we both realized we were getting nowhere, and dropped the subject.

So the first Abdechafi-inspired mini-lesson was similar to the lesson Mading had taught me after my explanation of the meaning of the rule of law: even people who admire Western culture have lines beyond which they won't cross; the culture that nurtures us as children keeps a tight grip on much of what we believe and who we are.

The second Abdechafi-inspired lesson, though, was much more meaningful.

He and I were about halfway through the morning's lesson. The coffee-break was approaching. Everyone was tired. We'd been conducting these trainings for almost two weeks and still had another week to go.

Machimango had asked—for maybe the fifth time that morning—Abdechafi to re-explain something he'd tried to explain several times about giving instructions for using manipulatives in math lessons over the radio.

At the end of his tether, Abdechafi had erupted angrily.

Everyone had fallen silent.

Abdechafi had hung his head.

Looking up, he had then approached the whiteboard. He wrote something and covered it with his hand.

"I want to say something," he began, speaking softly in French. "It's about the most important thing working with Americans can teach you. In your culture here, as in my culture in Morocco, we are very proud. We don't like to admit mistakes. We feel like we lose face if we admit to doing something wrong.

"But if you're going to work with Americans, you need to learn a few very important words. Americans are, I believe, perhaps the only people on the earth who can say these words easily and sincerely."

He removed his hand from the board.

He had written the words, "I'm sorry."

He translated them. He explained that they meant that the speaker was admitting to having made a mistake and expressing regret for whatever he or she had said, whatever insult had been conveyed, whatever harm might have been done.

"Americans can say these words, and they are very important. They allow us to move on. To get our work done, instead of holding grudges and hoping for revenge. They are the most important words I have ever learned.

"Learn these words. Say them whenever you need to. Accept them from people who say them. It will change your life."

No one spoke.

Coffee was ready.

* * *

A week later I left for Conakry, Guinée, and Abdechafi went back to the US.

The scriptwriters occasionally sent me e-mails, asking questions about how to convey an idea or how to organize a lesson.

As their work was drawing to a close, Abed asked a question about the reason for an instruction to the teacher to draw rectangles and circles on the board next to the letter "A." Abed wanted to know the purpose of the rectangles and circles.

I explained, in barely passable French, that the shapes were to give the students something to compare the letter with—we wanted them to distinguish the "A" from random shapes.

He replied, "*Merci pour le renseignements. C'est plus clair maintenant.*" Thanks for the information. It's clearer now.

Then he went on, "*Je suis toujours frappé par votre bel état d'esprit et votre humilité malgré votre haute fonction. Tu es un bel exemple à imiter.*"

I am struck by your wonderful spirit and your humility, given your high status. You are a great example to imitate.

He concluded, in English, "I hug you."

Right. That's the "...that all men are created equal" part. One of the parts of American culture we should be proud of. One of the parts that's not embarrassing.

CHAPTER 4

Living in Beirut, 1

Just how many times can you watch a country be destroyed?

How many times was Beirut, was Lebanon, destroyed, then redestroyed, during the Civil War?

How much would be destroyed this time, Buffy and I thought as we watched the TV news clips of Israeli jets bombing southern Beirut in the summer of 2006, bombing bridges and roads and electric plants.

Hey, how about a cease-fire here? But Secretary of State Condoleezza Rice mumbled some non sequitur about how you only declared a cease-fire when the objectives of the mission had been accomplished (huh?), so we waited while Israeli aircraft continued to drop bombs and Israeli troops forayed gingerly into southern Lebanon. Then, finally, after thirty-three days, Israel called a halt to the foolishness.

This halt, of course, had nothing to do with accomplishing the mission. Quite the contrary. Israel decided to stop destroying Lebanon when it realized that the mission itself was flawed—that trying to take out Hizbollah was about as effective as invading Iraq to get rid of the weapons of mass destruction had been for the US.

And maybe it began to occur to America's leadership that destroying Lebanon would boost the status of Hizbollah, the enemy it had been hoping to destroy, or that it had hoped to intimidate the Lebanese army into trying to destroy.

Bad calls, all around.

Bad call, Hizbollah, for taking the two Israeli soldiers hostage. Bad call, Israel, for dropping all those bombs all over this little country. Bad call, America, for encouraging Israel to drop the bombs and then for letting it continue dropping those pointless bombs for more than a month.

Oh well. Silver lining for me.

I didn't tell Buffy that I'd sent ACS Headmaster George Damon a brief e-mail: "Hi, George. You may remember me from our visit in 2004? I'm assuming you're having trouble finding faculty, given the circumstances. I can teach English and history. CV's attached."

He replied almost immediately. This time I had to tell her what I'd set in motion.

He wrote, "Can you come next week?"

She and I talked.

I was teaching a couple of courses at William and Mary at the time but had few other responsibilities. What had seemed like promising meetings with the chairman of Virginia's State Board of Education, the programming manager at the Norfolk Public Radio station, and the director of a literacy program at Old Dominion University had all come to naught.

These meetings had helped me slowly realize how little who I am fit with what Virginia is.

I began to understand that I didn't get it here. All those years in Vermont had made me think that people meant what they said, but I didn't understand how people communicated here, I didn't understand the code.

To me, "The first thing we have to do is get you a contract to do some short-term work; the second is to bring you on board full time," means just what it says. But apparently this statement, and others of its ilk, meant something else to the nice people I had such pleasant, promising interviews with.

So not only did I not have work in Virginia, I didn't have any prospects of work here. Even worse, I realized that if I got work, I wouldn't be able to understand what was going on around me, not understanding the rules by which people communicated. To say nothing of the fact that I wouldn't be able to tell if I was actually getting prospects of work or not in the first place.

On the other hand, Lebanon was shaky. But, we both agreed, Lebanon was always sort of shaky. Hariri's assassination the year before had unsettled things, and that murder had been followed by others. But the country seemed to be holding together. Or close enough.

OK, she said. Go ahead. But come back in the summer. Right?

Right.

"Dear George, I can't come next week, but I'd love to come in January when I've wrapped up my responsibilities here."

"Fine. See you then. I'll put together a contract."

I got out my *Eastern Arabic* book again. Got up to Unit 18:

> And when the elections took place, they elected him mayor.
> *wlamma saarat lintikhabaat, ntakhabuu ra'iis baladiyye.*

* * *

We followed the news, watching Hizbollah set up its tent city downtown in protest of the current state of things political. We found the websites and followed the news.

Oh well. Lebanon's always shaky. After all, there isn't shooting in the streets.

Yeah. OK. We decided and then redecided, again and again.

Finally, on January 7, I headed for Beirut again. Norfolk to Washington, Washington to Frankfurt, Frankfurt to Beirut.

Wahib met me at the airport.

"I bring the 'ACS' sign in case I don't see you, but I can always tell who are the new ACS teachers."

He took me to my apartment at La Cité just up the hill from the school, just off Rue Bliss. There, he and Ismail showed me how to work the stove and the heater, explained where the Sukleen dumpster was, and made sure I had coffee, bread, milk, and a few other basics.

"*Maa salame.*" Bye.

"*Allah maak.*" Bye.

Whew. Here I was. And it was only two thirty on Saturday afternoon. And it wasn't raining.

. I went out for a walk. I got to the corner of Sidani and Sadat, turned right, and then…ooops. I slowed down. I didn't't even know where my building was.

Take your time, Nick, I thought. You'll be here for a while. No rushBut you've done it. You've come back to Beirut, and you've come back with a task, a job, a reason for being here.

Congratulations. But slow down. Don't get lost on your first day living here. Here, where you're not in Newport News or Weathersfield. Where you're not in Nairobi or Dar. Where you're in Beirut.

I started taking notes about where I was. Then I started off again.

* * *

School wasn't going to start till Tuesday, so over the next few days, I wandered. Sunday, as I headed toward the hill that leads from the Hamra district to the seaside Corniche, I heard loud, young voices chanting and shouting. Perhaps the downtown demonstrators have left their tents and made their way to this part of town, I thought. Should I go on?

Sure.

I crossed Rue Bliss and headed down the winding street where the voices were coming from. And there they were, on a broad cement playground at International College: several dozen blue-uniformed kids. Boy-Scout-like youngsters running around a schoolyard on some sort of Saturday Camp-o-ree-like occasion. They ran around, chanting and singing, as though only a couple of miles away no crowd was bivouacked outside government buildings insisting that the government resign, promising to escalate the protests until they did so.

Boy Scouts. OK.

I walked on, down to the Corniche. There I took note of the things every newcomer takes note of. Young women dressed in mini-things and patterned stockings passing couples walking arm in arm, the man in jeans and a leather jacket, the woman wearing an abaya and a head scarf. A covered mother in an ankle-length dress walking with her fashionably-attired daughter, her hair blowing freely in the sea breeze, her jeans tight. An old man in a burnoose smoking his *nargelieh* outside a café, watching us all go by. An old woman selling coffee from a thermos, rhythmically clapping two cups together to get our attention.

Everywhere soldiers wearing camouflaged uniforms. But there have always been soldiers everywhere in Beirut. They're posted in little red, white, and green kiosks every few blocks, automatic weapons slung lackadaisically over their shoulders, the way they might carry their fishing rods or tennis gear. Here and there an armored personnel carrier, though the vehicle's guns were often sheathed in canvas.

Back in Hamra, metal barriers were set on alternate sides of Rue Bliss, leaving just enough space so drivers would have to slow down, weaving from side to side to wherever they were going on a sleepy Sunday morning as they passed in front of Prime Minister Siniora's apartment building, where more camouflaged soldiers stood, more or less at the ready.

As I walked back to my apartment lugging two chock-full grocery bags from Bou Khalil Hyper-marché, the sight of two soldiers running my way set my heart racing. Now what—drop the groceries and run too? Step aside, hoping they're not interested in me? Follow?

Then I saw they were laughing. They were only trying to get wherever they were supposed to get to before the gentle drizzle turned into a full-blown rainstorm. Just trying to stay dry.

OK.

It was going to take a while to get used to this Beirut this time.

* * *

Things had changed.

Not just the obvious changes like the opposition's tent city, scattered around a dozen city blocks downtown, this on-going "sit-in" the grand symbol of Hizbollah's new-found power and the West-leaning government's frailty. Not just the periodic general strikes with the scent of burning tires gradually wafting its way to Ras Beirut, or the occasional car bomb, or the devastations wrought by two bus bombs that killed dozens of people who were simply on their way to work one morning.

Closer to my daily life, the school was so different.

I already knew that two new stories been added to the high school building, taking the library out of the near-basement and giving it the top two floors. It had all been so reconfigured that I couldn't find my old classrooms. In which room had Mr. Shoucair sung "Minuit Crétien"? Where had I, day after day, slept through coach Troyer's "Our Economic World" lessons?

Next door to the old high-school building, the four-story boarding department had turned over to classrooms. The snack bar in the bottom of the old BD where I'd eaten my lunch as I'd watched the lithe Lynn McMurray and every girl in the senior class jitterbugging to the Everly Brothers and Elvis songs on the jukebox now housed classrooms teeming with nursery school kids. The dusty playing field where we'd occasionally flown our model airplanes had been AstroTurfed.

The real changes were deeper. No longer did my class roster read—as it would have for Mrs. Turmelle or Mr. Sutton—Nick, Tim, Marty, Cathy, Kathy, and Beth. Now it was Maya, Hala, Ghida, Raya, Karim, Kareem, Mohammed, Mohamed, Mohammad, and Firaz. Occasionally, there'd be a Tom or a Carla. But not often. People didn't bring their children from the US, the UK, or Denmark to Beirut any more. All the ex-pats had left by the early '80s, and the news was not good enough yet for many to return.

There's a story here, mostly untold.

Somehow, this school held on through the worst of the civil war. In broad outline, Else Turmelle held it together until 1982 or so, followed by headmistress Catherine Bashour, who kept it going through the war and on into the early 2000s. Since the student body was only Lebanese, a Lebanese baccalaureate track was added to the curriculum—students with only one passport, or those who had not lived outside the country for more than three years had to study this curriculum if they wanted access to the various syndicates that govern many professions in Lebanon: law, medicine, engineering, and the like.

During that time, any teachers who could left. Americans essentially had to leave—Lebanon joined Cuba and North Korea as places the State Department would not "allow" its citizens to visit. The faculty became entirely Lebanese.

There is indeed a story here. A story of bravery in the face of fear, a story of commitment. Why hold on? Why not, since the civil war seemed unending, give up, close down, and figure somebody could reopen an American Community

School sometime in the future, if the future ever seemed conducive to such a decision?

But Catherine Bashour and the others held on, through the violence and the devastation. The school remained open. More importantly, the school remained.

By the time I arrived in 2007, Catherine Bashour had handed the school's reins to George Damon. The faculty was almost one-third ex-pat. An international baccalaureate program had been added, so now students could choose from either the traditional American College Prep program, the LB program, or the IB program. The strivers chose IB. The slackers chose the American program. Those who had no choice went LB.

So the Gregs and Annes were gone. Even the Bjorns and Katarinas were gone.

In their place was a student body that responded glibly in English to questions about Newton's Third Law and the causes of World War I in the classroom, but at break, for the most part, turned to Arabic. A student body who, for the most part, knew almost nothing about the Lebanese civil war, their parents perhaps hoping that not talking about it might prevent its recurrence. A student body brought into the world only when their parents figured things might be safe in Lebanon—fingers crossed. And a student body, who, in large part, were affluent far beyond anything I could imagine. "I'll call my driver, sir, and he'll bring my homework." "Ali has a new house in the mountains, sir. It's more like a hotel than a house." "We had a great vacation, sir. We went to our house in Switzerland and skied every day."

Of course, not everyone was so wealthy. But many were, overshadowing the simpler lives of the scholarship students or even of those whose mother and father both worked to keep them here, in the most expensive and reputedly the best school in Lebanon.

But just as when you peel away the foolishness that most cultures impose on most of us, most people are just people, most kids are just kids.

Sixteen-year-old boys anywhere on the planet, for example, appreciate slapstick humor—fall on the floor in the middle of class a couple of times, and you've got them for life. For another example, the simple words, "Hey, your hair looks nice today," will set a sixteen-year-old girl anywhere to blushing and primping.

All these changes, however, didn't affect some aspects of what went on in the classroom. Ninth graders reading *Romeo and Juliet* in Weathersfield or Newport News, for example, had no more idea where or even what Verona was than my Lebanese students, and "e'en," "wherefore," and "Marry!" were equally perplexing to both groups. So teaching *Romeo and Juliet* posed many of the same challenges it would have posed back in the US.

Actually, given the play's premise—that two people couldn't marry because their families hated each other—certain aspects of the play may have been easier to communicate. After all, it was in Beirut, not Weathersfield, where the National Honor Society had decided to attack head-on the problems arising in the lunchroom and on the playground from the recently heightened sectarianism by conducting a "Safe Sects" campaign, insisting that students not wear their party's colors to school or taunt each other for their religious and political affiliations.

And in another of those people-are-just-people lessons, my Lebanese students loved the play at least as much as my American students.

Other ramifications of the changes at the school were not so simple—or, for that matter, so easy to discern. Take *To Kill a Mockingbird*, Harper Lee's best-of-the-best-selling novels about racism and decency in the American south in the 1930s. Oh, everyone loved the book, once they began to understand what was going on.

But it took me a while to realize something pretty obvious: most of these students had no idea where the novel was set.

I could easily explain enough about the Great Depression so they'd generally understand the economic circumstances the community faced. They'd heard enough about Martin Luther King and so forth that America's racism was no surprise to them—I enriched these understandings with stories of visiting my cousin Chuck in South Carolina in the 1950s, my Uncle Harris doing his best to say "nigrah" instead of "nigger" out of deference to my liberal mother, "colored only" water fountains and restrooms, and attending rock and roll concerts where Chuck and I sat downstairs in the good seats, while black attendees sat up in the sweltering balcony seats, all of us ironically assembled to hear black singers like The Coasters and Little Richard.

But the neighborhood where Scout and Jem lived, now that was something else. The students didn't get the neighborhood at all. The Finchs' house, the Radleys', the idea of a yard, a wrap-around porch, a farm field you might cut through to get from school to home. I gradually came to realize that for most of these apartment dwellers—even the ones who had other apartments in London and Montreal—a small-town American neighborhood was a totally alien concept.

So I drew a map of Maycomb on the board, as best I could understand it, showing the relationships between the Finch house and other houses, the school, and the downtown. I even went so far as to draw the house itself, with trees in the yard, a picket fence, the space between this house and the next, the sidewalk. I went online and found pictures of some traditional suburban houses, and of the trees described in the novel—willows, oaks and other such tall, wide deciduous trees. I showed pictures of the trees at different seasons.

What they could never really understand, though, these kids raised in Beirut apartments, was neighborhood. Walking to school, meeting up with friends along the way. Friendly neighborhood dogs who might just walk with you to school, having nothing better to do.

Stepping out your front door on a summer morning to watch Miss Maudie in her garden and the milkman going from house to house. Then seeing your best friend step out of his front door a few houses down the street, calling out to your mother, "Goin' over to Johnny Boy's house," and running off, the screen door slapping behind you.

Playing baseball back in Bethesda at the intersection of Windsor Lane and Ryan Street, stepping aside when the very occasional car made its way down the street. Playing hide-and-seek till long after dark, sometimes all the way up the hill to Mark Maine's yard, five houses away. Trick-or-treating in a skeleton costume, groups of kids wandering the neighborhood, flashlights swaying their beams along the street, occasional screams as some little-boy ghost decided it was time for some little-girl princess to shriek.

Some of the ACS students had their own stories of how they spent their free time like this in the villages—but these were mostly during visits to the grandparents, not where they lived all the time, not how they lived their lives in their city neighborhoods.

Then there were the obvious cultural gaps that showed up as our lessons unfolded. Like the young Saudi boy who, during the discussion of *Romeo and Juliet*, quietly and matter-of-factly explained that he would probably have an arranged marriage. Or the young Sunni who, asked to write about his most frightening moment, described standing on his street corner with friends during a recent flare-up between the sects, AK-47 slung over his shoulder, ready to defend this section of the city.

One day I spoke to a bright young woman who always seemed so tired. "What time do you get to sleep?"

"Oh, around two."

"Why do you go to bed so late?"

"Because my family stays up late."

"Why don't you just go to bed, since you have to get up early for school?"

"Oh, no, sir. We can't go to bed until we all go to bed, not in my family."

Little things and big things, major life patterns and subtle cultural quirks. I gradually began to understand that I knew almost nothing about Lebanon and Lebanese culture. All I had gotten from my years here as a boy were vague glimpses, mere hints of the fact that my life and the lives of those around me—those I passed in the streets, but also those I "knew," like Jackie and Fuad—were immensely different. Different in ways I could not possibly have understood all those years ago, or perhaps even noticed.

Living here, day after day after day, fifty years later, I began to understand something of the breadth and depth of the differences. Not, of course, that the lives I was encountering were like Jackie's and Fuad's, but that these new lives were as distinct from mine as theirs had been all those years ago.

No matter how good their English. No matter that their clothes and mine both might have been made in the same Malaysian sweatshops and been sold through the same international clothing chains.

Now, in my late fifties, I felt almost wise enough to be able to understand something of the character of the differences, of the impact these differences had on the way each of us was shaped, and of the kind of human beings we had become and were becoming: Jackie and Fuad; Mohammed, Mohamad, and

Maya; Nick in both his iterations, as Hajj Nqoola and as Nick the American, the guy still pondering his Saturday evening in that Evansville parking lot.

I set out to understand.

* * *

First, there were the little things, like lunch.

I have to begin by saying that there's no such thing as a "little thing." But we'll save that for later.

Lunch. Meals. Time with friends and family.

It's different here, I figured out. And the way it's different tells you something about lots of other differences.

Not long after I arrived, Huda invited me to come to lunch in the mountains with her and some friends, mostly Lebanese, with one other ex-pat.

"Well, maybe," I replied hesitantly.

But what I meant, what I felt, was, "Are you sure? Are you sure you want me to come along. Are you sure it'll work?"

You see, I felt a bit in awe of almost everyone I met. Even among the Lebanese I knew who'd spent time in the US—who understood my codes and cues and spoke to me in codes I could understand—I did not feel quite up to snuff.

Oh, not in the Evansville parking-lot way; I'd given up trying to get it right about clothing styles and the like. But there was something deeper. There is a directness about the Lebanese way of being that I wasn't quite sure how to respond to. People look you directly in the eye. They come close. They touch you, not just an initial hug, but ongoing throughout the conversation, tapping your hand, taking hold of your arm, resting a hand on your shoulder.

People speak strongly, even forcefully, with a certainty that is rare in the US. I don't mean the disdainful certainty of the pompous and the arrogant. The Lebanese certainty is a human-scale certainty, a way of being that says, "I am here and you are here, so we might as well engage. We might as well engage the whole of each of us. We will modulate our voices, we will gesticulate, we will use our eyebrows, frowns and smiles to enhance what we have to tell each other."

Although I found this dramatic approach to simple conversations a bit intimidating, I recognized it. This certainty, this in-your-face engagement seems to have been one of those things I had picked up in my early years here. In fact, on many occasions in the US I had to intentionally disengage, to pull myself back.

Time and again, I had found myself in what seemed a perfectly normal conversation, only to be told, "Whoa! Sorry! I didn't mean to get you so upset."

Upset? I'm not upset. I'm just talking. To you. With you.

But in Beirut, everyone was this way. No shrinking violets. Nobody just politely listening and nodding. Everybody everywhere jumped into the fray, so conversation was a busy, noisy place to be.

At first I didn't quite know what to do, how to respond to so much energy, familiar as it seemed.

So when Huda invited me to lunch in the mountains with friends, I was afraid I wouldn't measure up, that I couldn't be a way that would work.

Oh well. Might as well give it a try.

I learned several things that afternoon. Relearned them? Whichever.

First, lunch in Lebanon does not begin at twelve or twelve thirty. Lunch begins at one thirty or two. Or later.

OK. That's an easy one.

Second, the time thing in general. Nothing new here, except I'd never seen it unfold in quite this way. We'd agreed we'd meet Huda's friends at one thirty, but at one thirty we were still diddling around a dozen miles west of the restaurant, paying a quick visit to the snow banks. At two, we were sipping coffee at a ski lodge.

"They probably won't be there for a while," Huda explained.

OK.

At two thirty, we arrived at the restaurant, arranged a table for ten, and ordered another coffee.

At three, the friends began to arrive.

OK. That's the time lesson: it's all pretty flexible. Got it.

Then another quick lesson. While the other ex-pat ordered a beer, nobody else did. It's not that nobody else drank alcohol. It's just that nobody else felt that need.

Nobody else, as I was soon to find out, needed any lubricating. Everybody was perfectly happy being who they were, talking about what they wanted to talk about, listening to whomever they wanted to listen to.

And eating. The *mezza*, then the grilled meats with some more *mezza*, then some more grilled meats. Roasted potatoes. Eventually dessert, pastries drenched with honey and sugar syrup. Finally, just before we left, a bit of alcohol—a few sips of arak.

What did we talk about? Our children. Our religious heritages and upbringings. The current political situation in Lebanon, in the US, in the world. Education. The lack of snow. And so on.

We talked about just about everything. But I don't remember a single moment during the conversation in which anyone held forth. Nobody took over, pontificated, insisted on hoarding the attention.

Which is not to say there was no passion or disagreement. There were plenty of both. That was the point—the passion, the engagement, the willingness to lean forward and shake a spoon in your face to make a point, but then to listen fully as you responded, shaking your own spoon, pounding, if the point deserved it, on the table, rattling the silver.

And so lunch went on and on. The food came, the topics shifted. Everyone had something to say about everything.

And then, around five o'clock, we drove home, back to Beirut.

So that was lunch.

That was how friends were together.

* * *

Then there were the bigger lessons. And the most interesting thing about these bigger lessons is that each time I thought I had learned one, I came to realized that I had learned only part of one and had to learn yet another.

Layer on layer of understanding piled up and continue to pile up.

Take, for example, the day I spent in Marakeh, a village a bit inland from Tyre, about fifteen miles north of the Israeli border. I traveled with Wassim,

Rada and ten ACS students so they could team up with students from the village school and then go out into the community to interview some of the oldest residents. They were to ask them questions about life *min zamaan*, in the good old days—which weren't always so good.

As we drove the winding back roads from Tyre, banners in each village announcing whether its allegiance was to Amal or Hizbollah, I was reminded of a conversation Charis told me she had recently had with a cousin. The cousin had asked Charis why our family spent so much time in countries where Americans were reviled—or at least the American government was, though the cousin did not make such a distinction.

The Hizbollah flag is certainly disconcerting, that green fist holding aloft that AK-47 against a yellow background. Given this imagery and much of the organization's history, it's easy to imagine why Hizbollah is anathema to the United States government.

But there Charis and her cousin had been, having a lunch at a pleasant restaurant in Berkeley where all could so easily seem so right with the world—with that world, as opposed to those other, dangerous worlds.

I thought about the question as I recalled Marakeh's village administrator leading me to the platters of food the women had set out on a concrete picnic table at the municipal picnic area after the students had finished the interviews. It was more than enough for forty-some of us, the students, the senior citizens, and the teachers who'd spent the day together talking about Israeli invasions, raising children, harvesting fruit, and life's vicissitudes.

He took my arm in his and escorted me to the table where the *mjdara*, *mshtaha* and *fatouche* were laid out, and, of course, the thick *laban* yoghurt topped with olive oil.

"Are you Swiss?" he asked me.

The day before I'd been asked by the young women who'd needed directions to Rue Hamra, "Are you British?" I'm often asked, "Are you French?" or "Are you Canadian?"

No one ever asks, "Are you American?" They didn't ask it here or in Southern Sudan, Congo, Tanzania, Guinea, or even in Istanbul.

Why not? I wondered, driving north to Beirut along the smooth highway where the themes on the billboards alternated: Persil laundry detergent, Pepsi

Cola, Dove beauty soap, photos of young men who'd been killed during the Israeli attacks. We periodically had to exit this highway because of the work being done to repair the bridges Israel had destroyed with bombs dropped from jets made in America and then sold or even given to the Israeli government by my government.

One doesn't expect to see Americans in places like this because many Americans, understanding the world as Charis's dear cousin understands it, just don't come to places where they think they'd be likely to be loathed.

But the only time I've felt loathed, or even mildly disliked, in all my time abroad, was in the streets of Kinshasa, the capital of the Democratic Republic of Congo. But it wasn't me, or even Americans, who were loathed there. By all accounts, the DRC is among the most dysfunctional and distraught of the world's nations. Nobody in the DRC much likes or trusts anybody in the DRC. It seems to be a society in which loathing is pretty universal and mutual.

Everywhere else I've felt welcomed. Sometimes I suppose it's mainly my wallet and credit cards that are welcomed. Sometimes it's been because I worked for an NGO, which meant three things: I'd be trying to do something good, I might have jobs to offer, and I'd be connected with people who distribute funds.

Most of the time in most of the places, though, the welcome has felt genuine and unencumbered. Just as Charis, during her week-long visit to Beirut, had been welcomed in this same part of southern Lebanon a few weeks earlier when a friend of a friend had brought her to see some projects she was involved in, and they'd spent the end of the afternoon talking politics and sipping coffee with municipal officials.

And as welcomed as I felt by the passenger sitting next to Charis and me on the bus to Tripoli who showed us where to get off for Jbeil, and wished us a good trip as we hopped off the bus, making our way toward the overpass. Just as the people my sister—who had visited a month before Charis—met in the streets of Damascus helped her get wherever she was going. Just as people nodded greetings to me wife and me as we strolled arm in arm along the Corniche in the evening when my wife had come to visit between Sara's and Charis's visits.

My wife, daughter, sister, and I find it so hard to see the world as so polarized, as the us-against-them world that has been so vividly portrayed since the attacks of September 11, 2001. There is no question that there are profound difficulties in the world, and Charis's cousin's worries are not totally unfounded.

I remain puzzled, though. If the world is so polarized, if there are so many demons out there just waiting to get us, why, when I come to parts of the world to which my government has obviously and even intentionally and systematically caused harm, am I welcomed? Why am I not "them" in southern Lebanon, since I am supposed to think of those who run this region—and those who let them run it, Hizbollah ranking high on the State Department's list of terrorist organizations—as "them"? Why am I not demonized?

Take the head-scarfed teacher who led me from house to house in Marakeh. Some of the houses she showed me had been rebuilt, the new mortar and stucco unblemished by weather and time, while others still stood battered and crumbling. From time to time we entered a house, stopping to listen to groups of students asking senior citizens questions about the past and then listening to their often long-winded reminiscences.

Why—either in Arabic, or in the schoolgirl French she resorted to when the Arabic did not work—did she never turn to me, fire in her eyes, and say, "It was your Secretary of State who allowed this destruction! It was she who didn't support a cease-fire for more than a month. It was because of her that so many these houses were destroyed by Israel, and we've had to rebuild so much of our village! It was your airplanes and your bombs that did this"?

Instead, she made sure I had a comfortable seat each place we visited and leaned to whisper to me, making sure I understood the jokes.

What about the heavyset, barefoot woman who laughed as she sat next to me on the bed in the room that served as her family's bedroom and living room, telling how she stood up to the Israeli soldiers who'd kicked in the door and rousted her family in the dead of night.

"Out! Get out! Everyone is asleep, and there's no one here who's done you any harm. Leave us alone!"

Or the tiny, squat woman, sitting in her garden, explaining that she and her family had stayed in the village while planes zoomed overhead and bombs exploded nearby for twelve days before finally leaving for Beirut.

Finished with the village tour, I sat in the third-floor office of the village administrator, sipping thick coffee with Wassim, Rada and a few local teachers when the poet came in. He began to recite, telling the tale of the births of his children. The administrator translated the hard parts: "I studied English in high school, forty years ago," while the poet declaimed.

At no point did I discern any hint of animosity toward me. Nor was there any hint that this was an orchestrated scheme to show me how bad things had been. The questions the students asked were questions they had prepared in their classes—ours, back in Beirut, the others, in nearby schools. The answers the old folks gave were simply tales of their lives.

No one knew I was coming. Many barely noticed that I was there.

No one mentioned anything about what my government had done, or at least had allowed. No one looked askance when they learned I was an American. No one saw me as anything other than an old guy who spoke a little Arabic and seemed interested in watching children learn and listening to people talk about their lives.

At the picnic ground everyone milled about—one thing one learns to do well in much of the world beyond the US is mill about; things never happen exactly when they're scheduled. But one also learns that this milling about often gives time for haphazard conversations about how old the well is, for watching young women bake thin rounds of *mar'oo'* bread on a rounded surface heated by a fire of twigs, for chance encounters with a story teller one might not otherwise have had.

Finally, the food was ready. "*Sahteen. Sahteen*," everyone said to everyone as huge helpings of food were ladled onto our plates. "Two healths."

A young man unfurled a banner that read "Swiss Agency for Development and Cooperation: Promoting development through culture." Wassim worked part time for this organization and had arranged this collaboration between the SADC, the village, and a Beirut-based NGO called the Association for Development of Rural Capacities. The old folks who'd told their stories, teachers, village officials, the students from the local school, students from our school, and the poet sat in the shade near the banner, eating and chatting.

Just outside the little park, two white United Nations Interim Force in Lebanon (UNIFIL) armed trucks had stopped to talk to the municipal officials. One of their bases was just up the steep hill. From there, they reconnoitered south toward Israel, west toward Tyre, and the surrounding hills and valleys.

I had learned so much. One old man had, in the 1930s, spent the day working on the fields carrying only a handful of figs for his lunch. All the men in one family were long gone, off to Brazil or Canada, or dead. The old women often laughed at the old men, accusing them of inventing stories.

I wasn't hated.

A good day's work, no?

A few days later, I met Wassim for coffee and shared with him my new understandings, emphasizing especially the amazement I felt that I, prodigy of the Great Satan, had been welcomed and accepted. Your allies blew up my house and tortured my cousin, but no hard feelings.

"It's really something, Wassim," I exclaimed. "I'm accepted and welcomed someplace I thought I'd be hated. It's a real lesson in tolerance and people's willingness to forgive."

Wassim smiled. "Sure, Nick. It's a good lesson. But you have to remember…" It was as though he didn't want to go on, didn't want to burst my optimistic bubble. But he went on, nonetheless.

"You've got to remember that if I had gone down there on my own, instead of with the NGO to set up this program, somebody would have said to me, 'Where are you from?' So I'd have answered 'Batloun.' Everybody knows that's in the Chouf. Everybody knows the Chouf is Druze. I would not have been welcomed. I might not have been safe."

He kept smiling.

Layers. One day I had learned that my alleged enemy could become my friend. But the next I'd learned that two sets of my friends could be each other's enemies, no matter how friendly each was with me.

What do I do with this? What do I know that I didn't know before coming to Beirut? What else is there to learn about hatred and tolerance?

* * *

Ah, the politics. So much to learn about the politics. So much the politics have to teach me about myself.

Take today. Everybody's wondering if we're approaching some brink. For some, the possibility of reaching that brink brings back terrifying memories of hiding in apartment hallways while gun battles rage in the streets outside. For others, imagining the brink is impossible—all we can assume is that it would be terrible.

There's a general strike going on: Hizbollah has decided to push harder, hoping the prime minister, besieged in the Serail with his ministers, will capitulate, giving it the cabinet posts and the veto power it wants.

So far all seems well enough. I'm walking along the Corniche, having ascertained that there's no danger—not here, at least—from the roadblocks young Hizbollah supporters have set up a few miles away to keep people from going to work. Young men standing in the roadway to show the government that their leaders have the power to bring everything to a standstill and, by extension, to bring down the government.

It's a bright, clear day. Far in the distance, smoke rises behind the new skyscrapers from the tires burning downtown. Every now and then something with a siren whizzes by, a police car, a caravan of black SUVs, a Humvee.

The Corniche is not as crowded as usual, but people are out, strolling.

Just ahead, two young men and a woman approach. One of the men pretends to kick at the woman. She grabs his foot and holds it, laughing. He hops, laughing. She continues walking, his foot in her hand as he hops. They all laugh together. She drops his foot. They walk on.

The other strollers walk on, some checking the smoke on the skyline from time to time. Others seeming oblivious, following close behind their little boy wobbling on his new bicycle, or jogging, or deeply engaged in conversation.

From the north comes the roar of a decelerating airliner.

"The airport's open," I think, and my spirits lift. If people can get in and are willing to come in, things can't be too bad, can they? If they can get in, I can get out. As long as you can get out, all is well.

There's a womb-like comfort to the bland boredom of airports in situations like this. They're the safety station, the place where you can go when things get too bad—go and maybe wait a long time, then show people pieces of paper, then wait some more, then walk through a long gangway and into the plane, settle into your narrow seat, and depart.

Leaving the bad stuff behind.

I can do that. Some of my Lebanese friends—the ones with two passports, green cards, or an uncle or a cousin who works in the right office—can do that to. Lots of Lebanese cannot do that. No Palestinians can do that.

I remember my visits to South Sudan.

The Mission Aviation Fellowship Cessna would take off from Entebbe Airport near Kampala, zipping into the air above Lake Victoria, then heading north. We'd fly low enough to watch the villages pass below, follow the red-earth track of the roads, wondering all the while, if we were flying over Lord's Resistance Army territory—those crazies who terrorized northern Uganda for decades, decapitating, raping, and kidnapping children..

Eventually, we'd descend toward Maridi's red-earth airstrip cut from the northern edge of central Africa's tropical rain forest. The plane would let us off, usually leaving its propellers spinning, and then turn, drive back to the end of the runway, and fly off. It would be back in four days. You had to book a flight in advance so they'd know whether to bring the five-seater or the eleven-seater.

You'd drive or walk the half-mile to the CARE compound, settle in to your thatch-roofed *tukul*, and head over to the nearby Secretariat of Education offices to get to work.

A few days later a UN plane would drop off more people, turn, and take off. A few weeks later, your flight would come.

Walking the Corniche, hearing the arriving jetliner, I remembered the sense of isolation I had felt in Maridi. What if? What if? I had thought. What if I couldn't get out?

I remembered the time I had been sitting on the veranda of the nearby medical clinic, talking with the director. I was the only ex-pat left at the compound, so I was enjoying this opportunity for an informal chat. The CARE compound radio operator had told me that my flight was due to land at two o'clock. It was almost eleven. Plenty of time.

But then I heard a faint buzz approaching from the south. Looking up, scanning the sky, I saw the little MAF plane, dropping from the clouds.

I leapt up and raced back to the CARE compound.

Damn! I thought. I knew that the 2:00 p.m. was Greenwich Mean Time. Damn.

I grabbed my bag, waved good-bye to the cooks and security guard, and ran back to the airstrip just as the airplane touched down. Had my bag not been packed, or had I been inside somewhere and not heard the plane, I'd have missed my flight. It would have been day before I could catch another—and there might've been no seats.

Maridi—so hard to get into and harder to get out of—felt unsafe.Beirut felt safe, I realized, remembering that feeling, only because I could leave it.

But the airplanes are still landing, so the airport's still open. My passport's valid, my credit card's good, and I have a little cash. And there's more than a flight or two a week.

So I do my best to figure out how to live with the ambiguity that Lebanese politics presents me with—presents us all with.

There are plenty of role models. After watching the girl grab the guy's foot and laugh, I head back up to Hamra, where I pause to watch a little boy riding his little plastic tricycle along a side street while his father chats with friends, watching.

From the far distance, we hear what sounds like gunfire. Several people pull out their cell phones.

Yeah. It was gunfire. It was the army, a man standing next to me explains in halting English. They were shooting into the air to disperse a crowd.

Everyone puts their cell phones away; conversations resume. All the while the kid's been riding his trike back and forth. "Vrrrm! Vrrrm!"

I walk toward Raouche, thinking I'll be able to see to the south from there—smoke, fires, whatever else might be going on. As I pass my old apartment building, I come upon a cluster of young men wearing sky-blue headbands. Hariri supporters. They mill about nervously, carrying long, heavy sticks.

They're looking down the street I was about to turn onto, probably for a cluster of young with yellow headbands, carrying their own sticks.

I turn around. It's now I begin to recognize the truth of the comment I made to my wife a week or so ago, "The real danger, I think," I told her in between her stories of constructive meetings she'd been to and my stories about frustrating students I work with, "is what'll happen when all this gets turned over to post-adolescents filled with testosterone."

She had laughed. The satisfaction of being so right doesn't outweigh the sadness of just what "right" means here.

Funny thing, though. It wasn't fear that turned me around on that street corner. It was just wisdom. There doesn't seem to be any fear: no shot of adrenalin, no back-of-the-neck hackles raised.

Even imagining the worst case—that the streets of Ras Beirut might fill with rampaging twenty-somethings screaming and looking for other twenty-somethings to hit with their sticks, or even shoot with their guns—I just figure, well, hunker down, stupid. The walls are thick; you've got food and water. There are people out there who'd help you get out if you had to. You've got some good books.

I begin to understand what it feels like to be Lebanese. Or Sudanese. Or Congolese. Or Iraqi, Chechnyan, Afghan, Nepali, Basque, or Colombian. It's quite a list. And that's only the list for this year, this week, this minute. Not so long ago I'd have added Laotian, Northern Irish, Watts resident, Chilean...and before that, and before that.

This, I begin to realize, is how people live through things. Well, almost. I have the airport and the money to get me into it and the passport to get me out.

But being here in the midst of this reminds me that the privileges granted to me by the world are precarious and could disappear in an instant. Or, more likely, gradually over time, while I didn't notice, just about the time I was thinking that being able to afford a Starbucks vente every day was a given.

I was reminded of this fundamental precariousness twice recently. Once was on Thursday as we assembled in the teachers' lounge for the after-school faculty meeting and there was some sort of buzz that meant something was going on somewhere.

University students are skirmishing, we were told. Everyone pulled out their cell phones. But that was what everyone throughout the city had done, and there was no place in cyberspace for all the calls, so everyone stood there, punching numbers, hoping to break through the wall of signals, to ask, "Are you OK?" and say, "I'm OK."

Everyone was isolated.

CHAPTER 4

The next day was a beautiful day, warm and clear. School was still closed; the city was testing out normalcy. At the rocky spit of land jutting into the sea just below the American University of Beirut, a few people were swimming. I climbed down the makeshift ladder someone had set up so we could bypass the locked entryway gate.

I walked out to the point and shouted to one young man, asking him how the water was.

"Cold but good," he called back.

"What happened to winter?" I shouted, gesturing to the clear blue skies that are supposed be gray and dull and drizzly this time of year.

"It snowed in Malibu! Everything's changing." he replied. "Are you going to swim?"

"No, not this time. Maybe later."

"Ah," he said. "You should swim now. We never know what later will be like."

* * *

I left Beirut early, before the school year ended.

It was the politics that did me in. In April and early May things just wouldn't settle down. There were flare-ups here and there. Strikes, burning tires. The occasional explosion.

It had to do with visas. When I arrived in Beirut, I was given a one-month visa, which I could renew twice before having to leave the country. Then I could come back to receive another renewable one-month visa. Renewing the visa entailed giving my passport to the ACS courier Imad, who took it to the Internal Security offices downtown. Then, a week later, I had to go downtown to sign for the newly stamped visa.

But things had gotten even more unstable by mid-May, when I needed to renew my visa.

I did not want to be without my passport for a day, much less a week, during such tricky times, when it looked to me as though there was just enough occasional shooting, minor street-brawling, and escalating name-calling among politicians to push the situation toward the brink. I could imagine it degenerating overnight into the surge of dangerous, ubiquitous violence that in fact did develop a year later, in May 2008.

So I told Headmaster George that I was going to leave early. Since I hadn't signed a traditional contract, there wasn't much he could do but bless me for coming, thank me for developing the detailed lesson plans I'd passed along the substitute I had arranged to cover my classes for the last two weeks, and hope—as I was—that the DHL package with the students' final exams would get to me soon enough for me to get them graded and the grades sent to Sana, the high school secretary, before report cards were due to come out.

But I wasn't finished with ACS. When Buffy had visited in March, we had met with George, explaining that we'd like to return together. She could either teach in the middle school or work as a guidance counselor, and I'd teach whatever needed to be taught. George had liked the plan then, and my bailing out early didn't alter his interest in the idea.

So I flew home, back to Newport News, where I'd already lined up work teaching English at a prep school in Williamsburg, twenty miles away, for the coming year.

I would go back to the US. Buffy and I would watch the situation in Lebanon and then, a year or two later, come back to Beirut together.

CHAPTER 5

Watching From America

I'm working in the three-bedroom Boke residence at 7 Pendleton Street in Newport News, Virginia. It's March, 2008.

The scanner component of the photocopier looked easy enough to operate. Seemed likely that I'd just have to connect the machine to my laptop, set the contract face down on the glass, hit the "scan" button, and wait for instructions to show up on my computer screen.

Sure enough, that's how it worked. Once they were safely ensconced somewhere in my computer, I attached the four pages—two for Buffy's contract and two for mine—to an e-mail to George and hit send.

Not quite so simple, of course. The attachment-heavy message turned out to be too big for the school's computer to accept without thinking about it—or something like that.

Fine. I decide to send four separate e-mails, each with a one-page attachment. I explained in the first e-mail that more were coming (though I'm always concerned, when I do this, that the first I send may not be the first to arrive, leaving the recipient puzzled as to what the e-mail's about).

Done.

I'd just finished committing my wife and me to work at the American Community School at Beirut for the next two years. I did this even though the city appears now to be on that brink once again, its government paralyzed, its economy barely functioning, its denizens doing their best to go about their business, hoping the next car bomb won't explode near their apartment, the next street violence not erupt on their street. But most of all hoping that the next whatever won't be the beginning of a slide into something resembling that decade and a half of hopeless, terrifying fratricide. Everybody is hoping that as bad as it might get in Beirut, in Lebanon, it won't get that bad again.

The news on the various Lebanon websites the day after I e-mailed the contracts was not exceptional. The UN is getting closer to setting up the tribunal to investigate the assassination of former prime minister Rafik Hariri, the act that set in motion the current stalemate.

What else? Looks like Lebanon will probably send a delegate to the Arab Summit in Damascus in a couple of weeks. The USS *Cole* is still steaming along the coast of Lebanon, just over the horizon. Israel's preparing for Hizbollah to attack in retaliation for the assassination of Imad Mughniyeh in Damascus a few weeks ago. There are rumors that Hizbollah's been training Hamas fighters. A pro-government Lebanese politician says the Middle East is about to become the Persian Empire again. An opposition politician accuses government leaders of being egocentric puppets of Washington and Jerusalem.

Same old, same old.

* * *

We're reading Conrad's *Heart of Darkness* now in the twelfth grade British Lit class at Walsingham Academy where I'm teaching. Word by word by word. It's too dense, too rich to ask the kids to read it on their own.

We come upon the word "inscrutable."

"Anybody know it?"

Silence.

"It means something you can't know. C'mon, Morgan, write it down. Something you cannot know."

"You mean it's like 'incomprehensible'?"

"Yeah. No. No, it's more than that. See, 'incomprehensible' just means you can't understand it. 'Inscrutable' means…hold on. Here: 'Incapable of being searched into.'"

No matter how hard you try, you can't understand this thing. It is impenetrable to understanding.

Like Beirut.

Like, as Robert Fisk explains in a long article from *The Independent* posted on the *Ya Libnan* website, suicide bombers.

Like things that come from a world where oh so very often the response to a question about politics or the economy or the weather is a shrug of the shoulders, a wistful smile, and "*Nshallhah*."

"God willing."

But it's not like the "God willin' and the crick don't rise" my wife might say, a bit tongue in cheek, to emphasize that you really can't predict anything, anyway. Well, about the crick rising, she's dead serious. About the connection between such a disaster and the whim of some grand puppeteer in the sky, she's not.

Nor does the allah whose will *inshallah* calls upon bear any resemblance to the god they talk about just up the road at the Baptist megachurch—the god who's smiling down on all the smiling parishioners who've paid their dues by saying yes to a smiling Jesus.

No. This allah is less scrutable than the straw-man, crick-regulating deity my wife mentions and certainly a lot less scrutable than the namby-pamby god of whom my neighbors might regularly request lower golf scores.

This god resembles the one Jesus did battle with, the one who might insist you set your first-born atop a stack of firewood to prove your commitment, or with whom you might negotiate the lives of the inhabitants of a city.

This is a god of "acts of god," those incomprehensible natural tragedies that insurance companies don't dare factor into their calculations.

* * *

Inshallah all will be well enough in Beirut for us to board Delta flight 22 to Paris on August 18 (my mother's birthday), to make our connection to this lovely, troubled city.

Just in case, though, I register with a job placement service so we'll have a fallback position if our plans fall through. If war breaks out. Chaos may come to Beirut, but we'll need work.

* * *

Nothing unusual in the news in the few days after we scanned and e-mailed our contracts. The March 14 group (aka the Government, aka the American-Zionist lackeys) accused the March 8 group (aka the Opposition, aka. the Syrian-Iranian lackeys) of reneging on previous agreements in response to the previous day's accusations by the opposition that the government had reneged on its agreements—all of these agreements, of course, being merely agreements to consider possible solutions to the stalemate, not agreements to actually do anything.

In another news item, Hizbollah insists it will avenge the death of Mugniyeh, the official who was recently assassinated in Syria, reputedly by Israel. Israel says it's ready for anything.

Meanwhile, on the school's website, the daily bulletin lists the kids who'll be kept after school for detention, having committed such onerous offenses as lateness to class and, for all I know, overdue library books. Juniors are reminded of the forthcoming meeting about planning for college. In another e-mail, the guidance counselor seems to have smoothed the feathers of teachers who'd been made nervous by some of the questions on the survey she sent around. The middle school teacher's husband who makes and sells tofu will be in the faculty lounge with another batch tomorrow. Spring sports will start soon.

Promises to take out Israel and announcements about volleyball practice. I'm trying very hard to figure out how I'm going to be able to commit myself psychologically and emotionally to living in this bifurcated world. Which should I pay more attention to, the threat of Sunni-Shia riots in the southern part of the city or strategies for getting Omar to turn in his papers on time?

An ACS colleague told me over a beer when I was in Beirut last November that he and his wife have simply stopped following the news. They decided ignorance, if not bliss-inducing, was at least the only way to deal with Lebanon. This sounds like a good idea. The only idea?

But there's a problem here. Intentionally ignoring what's going on in the world around me would go against everything I've turned myself into over the past fifty-some years. Totally. I've always prided myself on knowing what's going on in the worlds of politics, business, the arts and the like. I've prided myself on being able to chat knowledgably with my business-type friends about trends and cycles at work in their world, with policy wonks about who's plotting what, where, and with whom, or with Bangladeshi taxi drivers about the history and prospects of their homeland.

There's been more to it than just knowing things and sharing what I know. I'm pretty sure that keeping up with this kind of information has served me a deeper purpose. I think I've truly believed that knowledge is power. I think I've thought that if I understood something about the world I lived in, I'd be...safer.

Yes. Safer.

But knowledge and power seem pretty disconnected in Beirut. Knowing what leaders are saying and doing—and counter-saying and counter-doing—will not make me safer there.

In Beirut, nothing will ultimately make me safe. If Hizbollah starts launching rockets into Israel or if testosterone-rich young Sunni men start beating up equally hormoned young Shia men (or vice versa) in the street outside my apartment, it won't matter one whit that I could tell you, while sitting in this striped chair in my living room, "Things could blow up at any moment. You see, the resentments of the less affluent Shia, fueled by Iranian petrodollars..."

It won't matter that I know those words. No knowledge will matter at that point. All that will matter will be how effectively my instincts for survival guide the decisions I make about whether to get out of my apartment or hole up.

I am plunging myself into a world that will demand that I make a New Nick.

Oh, sure, it's the Old Nick the school has hired, the loquacious, probing, empathizing, fairly knowledgeable old man who enjoys working with adolescents.

But to survive, I'll have to set part of that self aside, the part that reads several newspapers a day and always—always!—tries to understand what's going on around me and why and what that might mean for my personal wellbeing, as well as for the wellbeing of the world I live in.

Two Nicks. One very familiar. The other, the New one, so different, considering the possibility of intentionally ignoring what he's always paid so much attention to.

The other one, the New one, in other words, living as Lebanese live, striving for blissful ignorance.

* * *

I've already bumped into some indications that my old ways of being just won't work in my new life.

Take what I've thought I understood about government, for example. The Lebanese government—the law-making branch, the parliament, at any rate—has not met since November, 2006. The opposition—whose leader, Nabih Berri, controls the convening of parliament—has refused to call the legislature into session since then, insisting that he will do so only when the Prime Minister (and his March 14 allies) agrees to give the opposition more cabinet officers and thereby a greater say in the executive authority. Meanwhile, the ministers—the executive and policy-making branch, March 14, "the government"—have been holed up in government buildings and the Phoenicia Hotel for months, fearing that if they wander out and about they might be blown up by a car bomb, as has happened to several of their colleagues.

So there's essentially no government.

But I know that I can drop my passport off to get my visa renewed at the Security Office downtown and pick it up a week later. It will have been stamped by a uniformed employee and filed alphabetically by another. I'll fill out a form and hand it to another official, who'll check to make sure my picture matches the one in the document before handing it back to me. Then I'd make my way out past the armed guards into the street.

The government's still at work.

It's like this everywhere. Taxes will be taken out of my paycheck and deposited in some government account. Bridges and stretches of highway that Israel blew up in 2006 are being repaired, meaning that most of the major roadways are choked by construction equipment, big dump trucks hauling chunks of broken concrete away, bulldozers smoothing the new roadbed, traffic coming to a standstill to allow a truck loaded with gravel to cross the highway, back-up signal chiming. Dust, dust, dust swirling everywhere.

So not only do personal lives go on, but the work of the government goes on as well.

I do not understand this.

Who makes what happen?

How are tax revenues turned into officials' salaries? Under whose authority are storm-drainage pipes that line the reconstructed roadways purchased? Who signed for the twenty-two Humvees the US delivered to the government last spring?

How can a stalemated government govern?

You see, I'm already way down the rabbit hole with Alice. And I haven't even budged from the striped chair in Newport News.

* * *

My worldview had been challenged by Beirut in other ways too.

I must begin by saying that I feel more at home in Beirut than I do anywhere else in the world. Period. Trying to deconstruct the affection for this place has stretched my understanding way past the breaking point.

I'm a member of the generation raised on post-Freudian, Skinnerian, Jungian, Rogerian, et al, precepts. As such, I've always assumed that everything I did, thought, wanted, and all the rest—anything anyone did, thought, wanted, and all the rest—could be traced back to a clear cause of some sort. To a Freudian, for example, the links between my desires and my experiences would be rather convoluted, while to a Skinnerian the lineage would be fairly direct, effects causing causes. But all these schools of thought would agree, one way or another, that why I am who I am is ultimately quite knowable. Was it was my parents' divorce when I was five that set the ultimate me in motion, my mother's wanderlust, or my father's just-plain lust? Could it all be traced back to the gene that got both my grandfather and my father fired for standing up for what they believed in? Was that what somehow attracted me to a place that's prone to periodically self-destruct?

No matter what the details, we are all who we are—I am who I am—because of things that happened to and around us. Destiny is determined and, in hindsight, determinable.

That's what I believed.

So when Beirut first began to call to me to return a decade or so ago, I had a ready explanation. Sure. It was clear: I had essentially come of age there, I'd explain to anyone who cared to listen (and, probably, many who didn't).

"I got there when I was eleven, a little boy still playing cowboys and Indians. I left at fifteen, a young man. I was formed there."

Sounded good, didn't it? Made perfect sense.

It made perfect sense, that is, until someone responded with more than, "Ah, I see," one day a few years ago.

"Nick, I came of age in…" Did he say Abilene or Pittsburgh or Greenville? No idea. Doesn't matter. "But I don't want to live there."

Oops.

So there's more to it than just having lived there when I lived there.

But the question remains: why do I wander the streets of Beirut feeling so at home, so happy, so safe and comfortable?

I asked myself this over and over as I trundled around the city last year, smelling thin breads cooking on round metal domes, lemon blossoms on the street that leads to the school, and garbage lightly rotting in green Sukleen dumpsters; overhearing conversations from which I might pick up a word now and then; zigzagging between speeding cars as I hurried across the Corniche to walk by the sea.

Why does this city work for me?

"It's the energy of the place," I'd venture after my coming-of-age theory was demolished. But Lisbon has energy, and Rome, and Nairobi. I enjoy those cities, but they don't draw me to them like Beirut does.

It's the variety, the blending of cultures, I'd suggest, describing two young women walking arm-in-arm along Rue Hamra, one in headscarf and abaya, the other in a low-cut tank top and sequined jeans, chattering about boyfriends. But even the dullest, most provincial American cities have developed pockets of diversity over the last few decades. Our plumber is French Canadian, and the school's custodian is Dominican, married to a Salvadoran. The local Sudanese community is growing daily, and I met a young couple from Sierra Leone the other day.

OK. So it's just that...

It's just that.

It's just.

I like Beirut. I just like it there. Who knows why, or even if there is a simple "why" to it. The place feels comfortable, interesting.

So Beirut has already knocked some of the pins out from under how I see myself living my life.

I've had to accept that in the case of where I want to live, there's no clear cause-and-effect relationship. I'm just stuck with what I'm stuck with.

Like a good marriage, Beirut took me and kept me, no matter that it leaves the toothpaste tube uncapped.

* * *

I'm not alone in trying to figure out why I enjoy this city so much. After all, it only emerged from fifteen years of violent implosion twenty years ago. That was fifteen years when nothing worked and anybody might be killed any day simply for having the wrong last name, living in the wrong neighborhood, talking to the wrong neighbor, standing by the wrong window, or crossing the street at the wrong time. One month this anyone might have been killed by Christians, the next month by Israelis, the next by the Druze, or the Shia, or even by his brother Sunni—or Shia or Druze or Christian—for rumors that he talked to any one of the others.

The city turned itself into rubble. Friends turned themselves into enemies. Trust was idiocy.

So it's no wonder that, in times when it's reasonable to wonder if Beirut is taking itself down so a self-destructive a path again, so many people continue to ask themselves why they love Beirut.

It's no wonder that from time to time I receive e-mails like the one I just got from Wafa, my friend who teaches Arabic at ACS. The subject line was "Why I love Beirut."

The e-mail begins, "Sometimes, more so nowadays, I wonder why I can't get away from this Beirut of ours. Then this came my way...

"I love Beirut because I see a girl in a miniskirt and her sister in a *tchador.*

"I love Beirut because it is neither east nor west. It is both.

"I love Beirut because you can party till six in the morning and not realize that it is Tuesday.

"I love Beirut because in Beirut you can live as if you are going to die tomorrow and party as if you are going to live forever."

The list continues. Some I don't readily identify with—the "how late you can party" ones among them. Others hit home.

"I love Beirut because I can see six thousand years of history.

"I love Beirut because I can smell gardenia and jasmine.

"I love Beirut because of the noise pollution from cars honking.

"I love Beirut because each street is a two-way street even if it's officially a one-way street.

"I love Beirut because I'm the first to call my Muslim friends on Ramadan, and they are the first to call me on Easter."

The list goes on for almost three pages, fifty-three reasons in all.

Robert Fiske, in his heartbreaking history of the Lebanese civil war, *Pity the Nation*, calls this vision of a playful, tolerant, multi-sectarian city a myth, a delusion that actually contributes to Lebanon's inability to pull itself out of its geopolitical morass.

Specifically, he mentions reason number five on Wafa's list, "Because I can be swimming in the morning and thirty minutes later I'm on the slopes skiing, or doing after ski." He notes that this is among the most popular of the country's myths but that he's never known or even heard of anyone who actually swam in the Mediterranean and skied in the mountains on the same day.

To Fiske Beirut is "this city of nightmare," and he has chronicled every group's atrocities against every other group, day by day, month by month, year by year.

To Fiske, lists like Wafa's represent pitiful self-delusions and serve as scant defenses against the realities that undergird Lebanon's appearances.

But this list doesn't ignore those realities. It merely tries to help Beirut-philes find a way to live with them.

Reason number thirty-four reads, "I love Beirut because it has been destroyed seven times in history, and has risen."

I know when the seventh was. When was the sixth? Under the Ottomans' four hundred years of rule? Which destruction toppled the crusaders' bulwarks down by the port? Which one was it that buried the baths the Romans had built not far from there, baths that were uncovered only when the rubble was being cleared away for the reconstruction of Martyrs' Square downtown after the sixth destruction?

Perhaps that's the reason I personally would emphasize. If you pay attention in Beirut, you can be reminded of both how resilient and creative humanity has been throughout its short history and also how likely we are to treat each other horribly and to destroy creations. Of these latter propensities, California poet Robinson Jeffers writes:

> but the race of man was made
> By shock and agony. Therefore they invented the song called language
> To celebrate their survival and record their deeds. And therefore the deeds they celebrate—
> Achilles raging in the flame of the south, Baltic Beowulf like a fog-blinded sea-bear
> Prowling the blasted fenland in the bleak twilight to the black water—
> Are cruel and bloody. Epic, drama and history,
> Jesus and Judas, Jenghis, Julius Caesar, no great poem
> Without the blood splash.

Jeffers wrote those lines on a coastline not unlike Lebanon's, a place of dramatic contrasts, where tall and stony mountains butt up against the sea and the water meets the land abruptly, where rocks jut and waves crash and splash. Rivers run to this sea through narrow, tree-lined ravines. Dust and herbs scent the sun-bright air on that tall coast of California as they do in Lebanon.

But the seventh item on Wafa's list reminds us that here in Beirut, unlike on that other coast, we stand amid and on top of six thousand years of history, of civilizations. We readily see remains left by the Ottomans, the crusaders, and the Romans, knowing that just beneath these, or scattered about in other parts of the city, we'd find a Greek amphora still stained with wine, perhaps Or we might find iron bolts or even cedar ribs from a Phoenician ship. Perhaps there'd be rusted swords and spears left by the Hyksos, the Assyrians, or the Hittites; perhaps spears or scrolls the Hebrews left, or the Philistines, or the Amorites; the rim of someone's chariot wheel.

All the way back to the beginning of recorded time. And beyond, as you might unearth a flint arrowhead just beneath a bronze one.

Stand anywhere in this city and consider this.

Then flip that thought around. Remember that we've been at this business of civilizing ourselves—throngs of us living butted up against one another, transforming raw metals into stronger metals and oils into fuels, writing, sending armored masses of men out to kill other masses of men, building towers toward the sky, and all the rest—for *only* six thousand years.

If the anthropologists and geologists are right, this is less than one-tenth of the time we've been recognizably human, one hundredth the time since pre-people broke with other species to head toward human-hood, a little more than one-hundred-thousandth of the time since the earth settled itself into something that could become a planet we could inhabit.

The blink of a cosmic eye.

But it's what we've got, this little human saga of remaking the world to suit our needs. And it's been taking place on this little promontory jutting into the Mediterranean for as long as it's been going on anywhere on the planet.

That counts for something, doesn't it?

So maybe that'll do, that this city does not simply provide perspective on the human experience. It *is* the human experience, for better or for worse.

That would certainly explain Wafa's reason number forty-four: "I love Beirut because when I explain Beirut to my Western friends, my friends see the passion of Beirut in my eyes."

Maybe I'll even learn how to party.

* * *

CHAPTER 5

So many things seem to have made me, me. My mother's legacy of risk-taking, my years in Beirut, then on to Rio. My studies in international relations and history in college. My reading, both desultory and intentional. It all added up to what I understood about the world: that civilizations come and go; that wealth and power are transient; that people are both very, very different, culture to culture, and also very, very similar; that history happens; that people are predictably unpredictable animals.

With such a background and worldview I thought I might understand events as they unfolded in Lebanon during my time working there the winter and spring of 2007. I thought, for example, that when street violence got a bit out of hand in February, the leaders on both sides would begin to recognize how close to the brink they were. Surely this would send them seriously to the bargaining table.

But no. Nothing improved. Then I decided that once the car bombs and street skirmishes took a turn for the worse a few months later, the end was near, civil war just around the corner. The summer progressed. No war. So I decided that the fact that those hostilities had not degenerated into a larger conflict was a sign that both sides truly wanted to reconcile. Peace, I concluded, was possible.

The closer the country came to the September presidential election by parliament, the stronger my belief that this would give both sides the opportunity to elect a president—and thereby work its way out of the mess—without losing face.

Except they didn't elect a president, and Lebanon would take almost a year to do so, after more than sixteen postponements and another visit to the brink.

There was another layer to my understanding of events in Lebanon. My understanding of history and of human nature led me to believe that there was just so much hostility one group could feel toward another without reaching a boiling point, a point from which there could be no return. How much hatred could one man—or one group—feel for another and still be able to seriously negotiate a workable compromise? How are cycles like this broken? How forgiving could any person be?

Experiences in Kenya had confirmed this, had they not? Just a year and a half earlier, the hostilities there escalated between the Luo and the ruling Kikuyu around a public ballot for a new constitution. I had suggested to my Kenyan friends that the country might have tipped over into circumstances from which there could be no return and that the country could easily degenerate into full-fledged civil war.

"Oh, no, my friend," they told me again and again. "We Kenyans are not like that. We do not fight. We get along."

"I'm not talking about Kenyans," I replied. "I'm talking about the human animal."

They laughed.

They were right. That time. But only two years later the same intertribal rivalries flared up again, this time over Kikuyu President Mwai Kibaki's apparent theft of the recent presidential election. This time the violence was more virulent: over a thousand people were killed in intertribal fighting, and hundreds of thousands were displaced. A fragile power-sharing agreement has been reached. Will it hold? Many think not. Many think the intertribal wounds have been opened too wide to heal.

Lebanon's overt sectarian hostilities have lasted much longer and run much deeper than Kenya's tribal ones, culminating in the almost surrealistic civil war that ended with more or less the same stalemate it began with.

So how can I possibly ignore not what I know about Lebanon but what I think I understand about history, people, and hatred? How can I seriously make plans to pack 1,300 pounds of our goods and go there? To live. To work. With a two-year contract, no less.

* * *

I'm getting better at it, though. I find myself thinking not about what schemes Hizbollah leaders may be devising at a meeting taking place somewhere in southern Beirut but about the view of the sea and the mountains we'll have from the apartment on Rue Jeanne d'Arc.

How can I do this? How can I pretend that all the insights I've spent a long lifetime perfecting no longer apply?

How can I consider boarding that flight to Paris?

This will entail what dramatists refer to as a willing suspension of disbelief. This time, however, I will suspend my disbelief not so I can watch Hamlet or Ernest to Stella strut and declaim, picking up their props, tending toward their long-foregone conclusions. And this time I'll suspend my disbelief more totally than Ionesco at his most absurd ever asked of me.

I will suspend my disbelief—setting aside most of what I think I've learned about people and politics—regarding this city littered with bullets and bones, where automatic weapons and rocket-propelled grenades are stashed in dark closets just behind the mop and the broom. Where having the wrong name as you pass through the wrong neighborhood can cost you your life.

Where people have lost sons and daughters, uncles and aunts, fathers, mothers and cousins to people they sit next to every day on the bus on their way to work.

Inshallah it will turn out well for all of us, and I'll help young Ahmed and Lara, and even the old New Nick, figure out what lines like "This above all else: to thine own self be true," might mean.

All I've gotta do is figure out just who that self is.

* * *

Happy birthday to me.

Today I turn sixty-two years old, and I have given myself—and my wife—a present: I have given myself the present of acting totally irrationally.

Oh, I don't mean I've decided to take the paltry two-thirds of the Social Security check I could get if I waited only another four years. That would be madness, even factoring in the likelihood that the system will run out of money long before I've run out of living.

No, I've decided—we've decided—to stick with our decision to leave for Beirut on August 18.

Even though I was so terribly right in what I thought I understood about both general human propensities and Lebanese specifics.

You remember what happened there in mid-May. Everything collapsed into gunfire and burning tires, into battered trucks dumping huge piles of red earth across the highway to the airport and the one to Damascus, eliminating the possibility of an easy escape from Beirut.

Stranded in their apartments, our friends listened to the gunfire stuttering in their streets and to rocket-propelled grenades launched at apartment balconies, trucks, and armed young men huddled angrily in alleyways.

For five days there was no safety in Lebanon. First in Beirut, then in the Bekaa where Shia and Sunni clashed, and in the Chouf where revitalized Druze militiamen stood up to Hizbollah, and finally in the north, where infuriated Sunni sought out Shia and killed them. The Christians, this time around, just lay low.

Buffy and I went online the first thing every morning: to Ya Libnan, Alnahar, Aljazeerah, BBC, Menasaat, Lebanon Now, and the blogs, occasionally following the link to a new, obscure site.

We got a few brief e-mails from friends in Beirut. They didn't have much to say. What can you say when you're clicking at your keyboard, maybe sipping a cup of lightly sweetened tea, with CNN or the BBC in the background, while every now and then something would explode—who knows how far away?. What could you write?

"Damn, something just exploded, and I almost spilled my tea on the keyboard"?

"I'm terrified, but I'm writing anyway"?

"I'm not scared. Really. It'll blow over. Everything will be all right. Hang on. I've gotta reheat my tea."

What would you write while the electricity continues to flow, your cell phone rings from time to time with news of fighting from a friend who lives in another part of the city, and you check the same websites I'm checking—only the amateur video of the fighting in Ain el Tineh means something very different to you, three miles from the shooting, than it does to me, safe in my little study on Pendleton Street where the azaleas have just gone by?

Was the marching of Hizbollah fighters down Hamra Street in Sunni Ras Beirut—two blocks from my old apartment—truly a culmination, the ultimate act of assertion, or did it just seem so to me, coming so close to where I'd have been if I'd been in Beirut?

My first reaction to the fighting was, selfishly, one of relief. At last, I thought, we don't have to wonder if it'll get violent. It *is* violent. Now we know: we cannot go to Lebanon.

We have clarity.

From there, the clarity and relief of those first few days, it's all a blur. When did it end? Was it Monday? Wednesday? When did the shooting stop in Beirut and Hizbollah pull back from the streets it had taken? When did talk of Italian and Egyptian officials making plans to fly into the city imply that the airport was on the verge of reopening?

When did the possibility that the various leaders might go to Doha, Qatar, arise? When did we hear that the road to Damascus was open?

That was just about the time George W. Bush touched down in Israel to help that country celebrate its sixtieth anniversary, wasn't it?

His arrival was almost simultaneous with my reading Ibn Saud's 1943 memo to Roosevelt in Michael Oren's *Power, Faith and Fantasy: America in the Middle East, 1776 to the Present*:

> "Jews have no right to Palestine," Ibn Saud insisted, and warned of harsh backlashes against American interests through the Middle East if, "God forbid...the allies should, at the end of their struggle, crown their victory by evicting the Arabs from their home." (469)

Meanwhile, the likelihood being that all was on the verge of collapse in Lebanon, Buffy and I had set other job-hunting wheels in motion. The principal at Walsingham gave me until early June to make a final decision about the recently opened English position. Having learned of opportunities with two Unitarian Universalist churches in the Richmond area, Buffy had formally expressed interest in both. We had finalized our files at Search Associates and had begun to seriously review the e-mail listings of international teaching openings that arrived each day.

* * *

Oh, how things change once you begin to see things through Lebanese eyes.

After the shooting had stopped, I found myself feeling the same feelings I'd felt last year in Beirut when bad things had stopped happening, when the two bus bombs in a Maronite village were not followed up by more bus bombs, the city reopened, and the residue of burnt tires were cleared away after the general strike.

I remember stepping out of my apartment building onto narrow streets that had seemed, during whatever trouble we were going through at the time, so threatening.

I remember thinking, "Hey, this isn't so bad!" as I made my way down Rue Sadat to Bou Khalil supermarket, hoping the corner vegetable stand would have some ripe avocados.

Then I remember watching the streets fill up with chattering people and irritated drivers and thinking, "Hey, it's Beirut again."

It felt so good to be back at school the next day, seeing teachers and students make their ways to their classrooms, groggy from staying up too late on those "political turmoil days." Zalfa excitedly told us how frightened she'd been by a car bomb that had gone off near her home, and Rita explained that she couldn't get out because her neighborhood was blockaded by flaming tire barricades.

We all greeted each other as enthusiastically as though we'd been apart for months.

"Good morning. Sabah al Kheir. Maybe the worst is over. *Mumkin maa fii mishkeleh lyoom.*"

"*Nshallah maa fii mishkeleh yoom.*" Maybe there'll be no problems today.

The guys from Sodexo would set up for lunch. I would print out the daily bulletin with its news of the adjustments we'd have to make because of the day or two we'd been away from school.

Then, "Come on. We're back. Get your books out, please." And they'd grumble and get their books out.

There's something extraordinary about this sort of relief. The worst being over, the normal feels wonderful.

But there I'd been, all set to send an e-mail to Headmaster George, reluctantly tendering our resignations. "I'm sure you'll understand…" and so forth.

Buffy suggested asking if we could talk with him by phone instead.

OK.

So much for clarity.

We made e-mail arrangements to talk on Saturday.

* * *

Meanwhile, I began to imagine ambling along the Corniche on a sunny afternoon, the surf breaking on the rocks just below the promenade and the breeze tousling my hair, couples walking arm-in-arm, street vendors selling time with a water pipe or oregano-filled rounds of bread or plastic demitasses of thick Turkish coffee.

I looked up from my writing, out the plate glass living room window, and see not a weedy lawn that could use a mowing but the rolling green of the trees of the AUB campus and the red-tiled roofs of its hundred-plus-year-old buildings all perched on the steep hillside leading down to the sea. Beyond lies the Mediterranean, rich with white caps and the glinting sparkles of sunshine, the water a deep blue.

So Buffy and I started talking again, discussing what we should do. She—having imagined what it might be like to serve as interim minister at one of the churches that had expressed interest in her—seems upset that I seem to be backsliding, reconsidering Beirut.

I explained that I had thought she had suggested I not send the e-mail offering our resignations because she had been having second thoughts about staying in the US. I take her in my arms and try to explain what I'd thought, while she explains that she had merely meant we should not act precipitously, though the situations still seemed dangerous.

Sighs. Forgiveness.

Well, she'd go ahead with the conference call interview with the church's search committee Friday night, we decide, and then we'll talk with George on Saturday.

Sighs.

And we got on with our lives.

* * *

Things stay calm in Beirut. The various leaders take off from the reopened airport, bound for Doha, where they're to meet with other Arab leaders and, ostensibly, craft a lasting solution.

A small crowd attends their departure, bearing signs that read, in English and Arabic, "If you don't agree, don't come back."

The city remains peaceful. The dead are buried, but this time—unlike what had happened only a few days before—no angry Sunni mourners are shot by an equally angry Shia shopkeeper as the cortege passes by his store. The fighting dies down in the Bekaa and the north.

The city begins to come back to life, people out shopping, first for the food they used up during the clashes, then for shoes and hats and magazines.

Friday night Buffy has her interview and is offered the job.

Saturday we talk with George. Buffy explains the vulnerability she feels because of her recent back surgery.

"I couldn't run. I couldn't get away if it got dangerous," she tells him, going on to acknowledge the irrationality of the fear.

George explains that nobody runs anyway. Most of the time it's pretty clear what's going to happen and where and when it's going to happen. So you just make sure you've got food and water, batteries and candles, and do your best to stay busy reading or whatever.

George explains that the school doesn't rely on the embassy. "We'll get you to Syria," he tells her.

George explains that nobody wants a civil war. Everybody agrees on that. And so on.

We're comforted.

It's a beautiful day outside, bright and clear and breezy and blue, so we drive to the ocean at Virginia Beach. We lunch overlooking the bicyclers, walkers, and brave souls testing the chilly mid-May waters and, farther out to sea, container ships heading east.

The sun's so bright, the air's so clear, how could you not feel hopeful on a day like this?

A beautiful day spent on the heels of having decided. What the hell! We'll go! Unless it all falls apart again, let's take the risk. Let's go.

Buffy calls one of the women who had interviewed her the night before. Thanks but no thanks. We're still going to Lebanon.

Happy birthday.

* * *

I find a website that runs the editorial that Michael Young had written for yesterday's Beirut *Daily Star* but that the paper had decided not to run.

> There was never a way for Hizbollah to emerge successfully from the conflict it created...the Shia community is obeying a leadership that cannot be said, in any way, to have understood the essence of the Lebanese system, who never had any liking for the Baroque but necessary give-and-take of the Lebanese order.
>
> What kind of party places its community in such dire straits? Certainly not one that can ever hope of finding itself at peace with its fellow Lebanese.

Lebanon's conflict makes it above the fold in the Sunday *New York Times*, right next to a terrifying photo of a Chinese man and woman running past collapsed buildings, hurrying to escape flooding rivers.

"Hizbollah's Actions Ignite Sectarian Fuse in Lebanon," the headline reads.

The lead describes the torture inflicted on a young Sunni man by young Shia fighters, concluding that by the time of his release he "had gained a whole new way of seeing his Shiite countrymen and his native land.

"'We cannot go back to how we lived with them before,' he said as he sat with relatives and friends at home here. 'The blood is boiling here. Every boy here, his blood is boiling.'"

My wife picks up the paper and reads the article.

"Not so good," she says.

"No, and they seem to be bogging down about Hizbollah's weapons at the talks in Doha," I reply.

"But we go anyway, if we can, I guess." It was more a question than a statement.

"Yeah." Mine was too.

Happy birthday.

* * *

I don't believe in miracles. Never have.

So I have no idea how to describe the fact that the talks in Doha worked.

I'm firmly convinced that the leaders would sneak out of Qatar in the dead of night, having made only vague promises to keep on talking, to eventually arrive at the solution they'd been unable to arrive at since November—notwithstanding the Qatari emir's insistence that they couldn't leave without a settlement and the threat of streets lined by protesters should they return empty-handed.

I'm firmly convinced that they'd return prepared to hunker down, stock up on arms, figure out what the powerbrokers outside the country expected of them, and get ready for the big one.

Wednesday morning. Daybreak. I get dressed, turned on my computer, then go into the kitchen to prepare Buffy's coffee and get the paper while it booted up.

Log onto the Internet. Opened Naharnet.

And there it is.

They'd reached an agreement at 3:00 a.m. Qatari time, just as I'd been getting ready for bed.

They *would* elect Suleiman as president. They *would* give the oppositi0n another cabinet position, thereby giving it veto power. They *would* revise the electoral laws and redistrict Beirut.

I stare at the computer screen, my vision blurred by tears of relief and joy. Yes, we could go. And, yes, we could go with a modicum of certainty that we would be fairly safe.

I hear Buffy coming down the hallway from our bedroom. The story led the news on "Morning Edition."

"They did it!" she cries out. We hug.

I did not want to stay here, nor did I want to teach history in Durango, Mexico, or English in the RKP International School in Mumbai, which had just offered us jobs that would begin August 2.

I wanted to go to Beirut.

* * *

But would they mean it, I wonder.ed, when the initial euphoria had worn off? Would they follow through, or would they just return to Beirut and pick up where they left off, shouting at each other, making speeches that sent their supporters into the streets to fire off their automatic weapons in shows of support.

I got a little nervous when I read, a few hours later, that parliament wouldn't convene to elect Suleiman as president till Sunday. That left a lot of days for some leader or the other to shoot off his mouth and collapse the whole thing.

That afternoon, however, something happened to convince me that they meant it.

The opposition took down the tent city they'd erected outside the government offices at the Serail. The tent city had caused the government to surround its buildings with rolls of razor wire, soldiers, and armored personnel carriers. It had crippled the renovated shopping area just a few blocks off, as people stayed away from the fashionable restaurants and tony dress shops, causing two hundred shops and restaurants to shut their doors permanently.

Downtown could breathe again.

The next morning, my wife forwarded another news story to me at work, an even more encouraging one.

Prime Minister Fuad Siniora had spent the past eighteen months holed up in the Serail to avoid being assassinated. His apartment building on Rue Bliss was protected by a squadron of armed guards, while strategically placed concrete blocks and steel girders turned the street into an obstacle course so anyone intent on doing his family damage would have to slow down enough that the soldiers could get a clear shot at them.

It seemed that Prime Minister Fuad Siniora took his wife out to dinner.

Then they went for a walk.

Saturday we called Huda in Beirut. She's the community service coordinator who lives just around the corner from the Mustaqbal television station that the opposition set fire to only—how long ago was that, anyway?

"Allo? Allo?"

"Huda, it's Nick. How are you?"

"Nick, Oh my god, you wouldn't believe it!" Her voice was vibrant. "Downtown they have taken away all the tents. And they are putting down—what do you call it?—grass, rolls of grass in the square. It is like tent city was never there. You wouldn't believe it, Nick."

"Yeah, we've been following it, Huda. It sounds great."

"They have done this because they know you love it here so much, Nick. They've done it for you. Now you can come back."

* * *

Sunday they elected their president.

Monday Naharnet reported that tourist bookings were up 75 percent over the past two days.

* * *

And yet, people are shot and bombs go off in Tripoli, still.

And yet. The government still is not formed, and the squabbling continues over what faction gets which ministry, still.

And yet. The tourists trickle into Beirut, while ex-pat Lebanese return home for the summer.

While I sit in this backyard, beneath the dogwood that grew beneath the canopy of sixty-year-old oaks. Sturdy trees. Cool shade. Sunday morning silence.

While I think about staying here and going there.

Staying here seems less and less an option.

Only yesterday I burned another bridge as I went on a rant about SUVs, taking a break from a softball game with friends in the shade of a tall sycamore. Mason sat to my right. Next to him was Rich and then Greg and Tanya. Chris stood off to the side.

I have no idea what set me off or exactly what I said, but I'd imagine my tirade included adjectives like "stupid" and "immoral" and "short-sighted." You know, all the standard ones you'd use to refer both to those who build SUVs and to those who buy them.

Out of breath, or out of insults, I paused. Only to remember that Rich had, just an hour before, proudly pulled up in his new, silver SUV, having given up his panel truck and spending, I suppose, some of the money his wife inherited when her father died on this brand-new near-relic.

I felt, of course, bad. Had I remembered that Rich was there and had driven up in his shiny new SUV, I'd not have carped so publicly.

Or would I? Or should I have done just that?

I find I'm a bit more publicly outspoken than I used to be about the decisions we have made as a society—to diversify beyond imagination the varieties of yoghurt and chocolate bars we produce instead of building humane and human-sized schools for our children; to ramp up the power of our leaf-blowers instead of competing viciously to create more fuel-efficient cars and trucks; to fill the pockets of misogynist rap singers instead of demanding more poets "who'll solve the depths of horror to defend a sunbeam's architecture with his life," as e. e. cummings put it. All that. All those decisions. All those votes in the marketplace of public opinion, the ones that the sensible, humane side almost always seems to lose. Hands down. Sensible options usually don't even appear on the ballot.

Jesse tells me that when he tells people he has a friend who's moving to Beirut, the people he tells seem almost to condemn him for having such a friend.

I tell him that when I tell my friends who've worked overseas that we're moving to Beirut, their eyes glisten with envy.

And that Sue, who just returned with her husband from several long-term working stints in Haiti, notes in an e-mail that being back in the US—even in human-scaled Vermont—is more difficult than she had anticipated, that she understands the decision my wife and I have made as we seek a friendlier place where people matter more than things but that she is sure that, in the long run, she'll adjust.

People who have seen what else there is in the world understand our decision to leave the US.

People who haven't? An acquaintance told me how difficult it was to visit San Francisco, confronting the homeless sleeping on cardboard next to luxury townhouses, watching the homeowners step over the sleepers as they pushed the little mechanism that makes their Lexus welcome them.

"But that's the world," I replied.

"Yeah, well—and I know I shouldn't say this—I remember how happy I was when Mayor Giuliani cleaned up New York. 'Course, I don't know where all those homeless people went, but..."

And I lay in bed that night thinking that at least in, say, Nairobi, the poor are allowed to build shanties for themselves, to put roofs over their heads, walls around their shopping cart full of possessions, a lock on their makeshift door. That shantytowns are an improvement on what we in the US allow the destitute.

I was as embarrassed to have this thought—my little midnight ode to the Kibera slum—as my acquaintance had been to admit being pleased with Giuliani's handiwork.

The same one who went on to admit that he liked the suburbs. The safety.

"The illusion of safety," I replied.

"Sure. The illusion. But it'll do."

* * *

I am an American. I had learned that fact almost half a century ago, when I first returned to the US on home leave from Lebanon. I remember recognizing, way back then, my fundamental Americanness.

I could not then put a name on it or explain it. But I was—I am—more akin to my friend who'd prefer to live in the suburbs than I'll ever be to whomever my next-door apartment neighbors turn out to be in Beirut. I'll have more in common with Rich and his SUV than I'll have with Rima, the dynamic math teacher at ACS.

I certainly have reached some conclusions about who we are, about what it means to be an American. Many of the characteristics I have identified are not particularly attractive: we do not know much about what's going on in the world, even the world right around us. We take our affluence and our security as god given, something we simply deserve. We have highly individually refined preferences for things like how French fries are cooked, which grass seeds to plant where and when, how supermarkets should be laid out, and lots of other irrelevancies.

That seems to be who we've become. That's what our affluence has made of us. We're a people so profoundly skewed by our wealth and status in the world that are virtually blinded. We sport bumper stickers that read "freedom isn't free" while protesting violently against tax increases of any sort. We pack our Wal-Mart shopping carts with Malaysian running shoes and Chinese dish-drainers as we complain about the loss of American manufacturing jobs.

We don't get it. Even those of us who read Edward Said and Rashid Khalidi and blog with Kurdish dissidents seem barely able to see how truly isolated and deluded we've become.

Is that what makes an American? Is that what we have in common, a vague "I've got mine, and I deserve it, so get outta my way" attitude?

No. Surely it's not that bad.

But sometimes it seems awfully close.

Doesn't it?

* * *

Deep in the dark of the morning of the Fourth of July I dreamed I was a journalist, present at the conclusion of a skirmish between a Hizbollah squadron and some ragtag enemy. Hizbollah had called everyone together, victors, vanquished, and whatever observers happened to be in the area. All of us were armed with hand grenades. The leaders sat behind a table on a dais, while the rest of us sat in rows of chairs, facing them.

Whose side were the Filipinos on, the ones who turned to watch us take our seats? Were those camp followers, the pair of young women who sang "We're so happy!" as they made their ways through the aisles, or were they simply part of the Hizbollah victory experience?

I'm awake. The streets are quiet this morning as most of us sleep in, all but the lucky ones who work at places that promise blow-out Fourth of July sales of SUVs and couches and mattresses.

A year or two ago our neighbor Darryl strongly recommended one of the many local sites for watching Fourth of July fireworks where they played patriotic music.

"It's really an experience," he enthused. "You'll really be deeply moved."

Not being in one of my more charitable moods, I responded from the heart.

"The day I'm deeply moved by a bunch of colored gunpowder exploding in the sky is the day I'll really begin to worry about my sanity."

Darryl's a kind man. He still speaks to me.

But Charis just got in from Nepal, so we'll probably take her somewhere—not close enough to hear the booms and bangs, but close enough to watch the colors streak across the sky.

Both John McCain and Barack Obama have been talking about American values a lot lately. And now Obama's wearing an American flag pin, perhaps calming those same people who'd be upset if they knew that when I stood with my hand over my heart throughout last year when the Walsingham Academy students and faculty had stood and recited the pledge to the flag, I pledged "allegiance to the United States of America. One nation, indivisible, with liberty and justice for all."

No flag. No god. I'm not so sure why my countrymen feel that I need to reaffirm my loyalty to *anything* every day, but if I'm going to go along here, I'm going to go just so far. No flag. No god. Just liberty and justice. The good parts. The values.

I remain, however, awfully unclear as to exactly what America's values are. Oh, I know the basics: my right to speak freely and the right to write what I want. I suppose those two are the most important to me.

And then there's tolerance and acceptance, values less well honored than one might hope but certainly more respected than in many societies: that a person of color and a woman can become serious contenders for the American presidency is testament to this society's evolution toward decency.

Moreover, there are few other places on the planet where I'd have been granted professional permission to exercise my talents in quite so many ways, jumping from this place to that and from this job to that.

Trial by jury of one's peers. The right to confront one's accusers.

There's certainly lots of good stuff.

It's these values that Tereza, a friend in Recife, Brazil, alluded to in a recent e-mail. Buffy had concluded an online posting about our move to Beirut by saying something about wanting our lives to entail more than listening to leaf-blowers and getting season tickets to the local symphony orchestra.

Noting the many difficulties Tereza and her husband face every day—violence in the streets, theft, economic instability, political corruption, and all the rest—she explained that these small pleasures were exactly what she and Henrique longed for.

This was, of course, embarrassing to us. It was like having real grownups come along and say, "Someday you'll get it. You'll outgrow your little dream world and see what's really going on around here."

Meanwhile, Lebanon still doesn't have a government. Squabbles over the distribution of ministries continue, with Michel Aoun, the Christian leader who's aligned with the Hizbollah-led opposition, insisting on the ministries of communication and justice for his people and Prime Minister Siniora unwilling to grant him these. Aoun then insists that Siniora is reneging on a promise he had made in not granting him these posts.

And so on.

* * *

The Fourth of July came and went with the usual amount of fanfare.

We stopped by for dinner at a friend's house on Buckroe Beach. A little chitchat, then a walk on the beach with Charis past acres of people for whom the pursuit of happiness seems to entail purchasing a wide variety of colorful plastic items to bring to the beach and consuming far, far too much fat and sugar.

Charis chides me for being too hard on people (as does my wife).

But it's the unrealized promise that irks me so, Americans' apparent belief that whatever we do is right because we are who we are. Where we are and what we do must be good because we are there, doing it.

A man pulled a blue and red plastic wagon along the path through the beach grasses to the water's edge. Women and children clustered around as he rummaged through the wagon, pulling out a Roman candle, setting it in the sand, and lighting it. A sputter of random sparks was followed by bright glittering shafts of sparks that silently rose in high arcs, then a flurry of crackling sparks—the finale. He reached in for another Roman candle and lit it.

The glitter and sparkling, even though dusk was a long way off, attracted the attention of the authorities. A policeman on a motorcycle pulled up on the cement walkway fifty yards south of this small fireworks display. He pulled out his bullhorn.

"Fireworks are illegal in the City of Hampton," his voice boomed. "If you want to observe fireworks, there will be a public display at the southern end of the beach at dusk."

Then he drove off.

The man at the water's edge waited a minute or two, then pulled another Roman candle from his stash, set it in the sand, and lit it.

About halfway through its cycle, a municipal dune buggy carrying two uniformed officers sped along the sand to the small crowd.

Women and children clustered around the officers' machine while, at their backs, the Roman candle began to shoot its larger glitter higher and higher.

The man who had lit it stood there too, listening to the officers, I suppose.

What was he thinking? What was he feeling? What did he say to the officers? What did he say to his friends when the officers drove away?

Somehow it seems as though knowing the answer to these questions would help me understand something about America, something important.

* * *

August has almost come. Almost. The days pass as slowly, demarcated by the tick-tock of the old mantle clock whose continued functioning, the clock repairman told Buffy, is something of a miracle.

Still time to decide whether to bring the clock to Beirut. We've done all the visiting we could think of to do, having traveled to gentle, familiar Vermont where the bumper stickers suggest we should find peaceful ways of getting along with the planet's denizens and keep its waters clean and pure.

Vermont is a little island of sanity. When Burlington's cable television provider considered dropping Al Jazeera because of complaints from some subscribers, it did the only logical thing and called public hearings. The voices of foolishness were few, spouting nonsense about letting the enemy into our living rooms and complaining of the channel's supposed anti-American bias. Most speakers raised issues like the importance of access to information from many sources. Most denounced the closed-mindedness of the few who believe that to hear something you don't like is akin to sin and should be shunned. Most denounced the myth that Al Jazeera is anti-Israel or anti-Jew. Some even raised the point that Al Jazeera is usually in trouble with Arab governments.

Sanity and faith in humanity's ability to sift through nonsense won out. Meanwhile, Fox News is still trying to convince British officials that it is indeed fair and balanced.

One cool Vermont evening as we sipped tea, looking out on George and Julie's sheep pasture, talking about our children's plans, Lebanon, two-thirds of a world away, finally appointed a cabinet. Alluding to the likelihood that it would offer little but acrimonious debate, one commentator called the accomplishment "a tower of Babel."

The interesting thing is how little I feel that this—and all the other complexities of Lebanese politics—will affect me. Obviously, if things get too bad, even without descending into actual civil war, the school will have no clientele, as those who are affluent enough to pay the ACS tuition head for Kuwait, Abu Dhabi, Montréal, or Dallas. But there are levels of incompetence and inconvenience above that bottom line that will be deeply disruptive of and disturbing to the lives of those we serve but whose direct impact on the school, and therefore on us, will be minimal.

This must sound ridiculous, given that Lebanon has a history of internecine violence that has periodically made the streets and shops unsafe for natives and foreigners alike.

But such potential for outright violence in the streets aside, my sense is that we'll be safer from some of the contemporary world's economic and political vicissitudes in Beirut than we are in Newport News.

After all, we will be visitors. Granted, we'll be employed visitors receiving monthly paychecks, but beyond needing the electricity to stay on with some certainty, the water to keep running, and the economy to remain healthy enough to support the families who'll send their children to the school, not much will matter to us.

Lebanese politics will not be my politics. Puzzled as I may become over the ins and outs of sectarian alliances and international plotting, my wife and I are not members of any of these sects, and our daily doings will be far removed from the daily doings of foreign ministers and secretaries of state.

I've often joked that one of the benefits of living abroad is that news of the US—until we invade someone—is buried on page fifteen of the local paper. And even then, we're spared the details of every Washington corruption scandal and Congressional wildfire.

Consider the current situation. I'm gnashing my teeth over John McCain's support for extending the Bush tax cuts and find myself flabbergasted that he doesn't know how to use a computer. I'm secretly wondering if maybe Hillary Clinton wouldn't have been a more effective president after all as I wait for Barack Obama to come down off his cloud. I wonder how long Virginia's legislature can remain so ignorantly hardheaded, denying the fact that addressing the state's traffic problems will cost a lot of money, most of which will have to come from taxpayers. A lot of taxpayer money.

To say nothing about nagging fears that Wachovia Bank, where we keep our money, will collapse and that the house we own in Newport News and the one we're buying in Richmond won't regain their values.

And so on.

In Beirut I'll be a spectator. A concerned and interested spectator certainly, but a spectator nonetheless.

Lebanon is not my country. I will have no deep investment in the outcome of anything that goes on there, beyond keeping a job and not getting shot.

It will probably never occur to me to write a letter to the editor, carry a sign at a demonstration, or call my municipal or national representative.

Because they are not my representatives.

My representatives are back here. On the Newport News city council and the school board, in the Virginia legislature, and in the United States Congress.

But I will be removed from their doings, physically distant from them and from the direct impacts of their decisions. Far removed from the shouting matches that politics can easily degenerate into.

Here in Newport News, when I watch workmen painting the artificial slates on the new buildings at nearby Christopher Newport University, I grumble at the stupidity of such an expenditure of public funds in the face of a likely recession. I consider a letter to the editor or even an e-mail or phone call to the president of the university.

In Beirut, I mildly wonder at the source of the funds for reconstructing the sidewalks along the Corniche. But it's not coming out of my pocket. And if a tidied-up Corniche brings in more tourists, I say to myself, the expenditure's worthwhile.

In Beirut, lacking citizenship, I gain distance and perspective.

But at the same time I lose something. I lose that sense of belonging. My wife and I become a man and a woman without a country.

Oh, it's not that we really have no country, of course. We'll still have those little blue passports that'll open almost any door anywhere. And we'll still vote fervently in this coming election. We will pay property taxes on two homes, contribute to—and in the not-too-distant future, withdraw from—the Social

Security Trust Fund. We'll read the *New Yorker* online and worry about the San Andreas fault.

We'll be Americans.

But if the past is any indication of what's to come, we won't feel quite so American. Our citizenship will become something of an abstraction, not something quite so tangible, so gut-level, so day-to-day. Nor, as I have pointed out, will be feel Lebanese.

I'd like to think we're about to turn ourselves into citizens of the planet, belonging nowhere and everywhere, in a sense homeless and in another sense more at home than we've ever felt by virtue of our not being able to pinpoint a home.

(But I find myself wondering if, being so distant and emotionally removed from the downsides of being an American, I'll finally *want* to salute the flag.)

* * *

The first of August. Eighteen days before we leave.

"Not so long," my daughter tells me. She who barely staved off madness during her last month in Nepal by visiting everyone she'd ever met in Kathmandu and its environs and drinking more butter tea in that month than she'd drunk in the previous year.

And we also visit. Lunch with Patricia and Mason to celebrate his landing a job teaching at-risk kids in Hampton. Dinner at Jesse and Carole's house with Alan and Michelle Sheeler. Jesse and Carole who'd just returned from almost a month hiking 130 miles in the Sierras through rain, hail, heat, mosquitoes and immeasurable beauty. Alan and Michelle who'd just returned from hiking the Inca Trail with their son, Jesse, who'd been adopted from Chile a decade ago, and their teenaged daughter, Carrie, who trooped on through the fogs and the air-thin passes far, far ahead of the rest of the family.

Coffee at Panera with Hussam, my Lebanese friend who teaches Islamic Studies at CNU.

"How does this work, Hussam?" I asked. "I just don't get it about whose idea it would have been for the Sunni to start shooting at Alawites in Tripoli. Or was it the other way around? I mean, does someone in Damascus make sure he's got enough bars on his cell phone, then call someone in Tripoli and say 'OK. Go ahead and shoot some Sunni. But quit shooting when the army pulls up'? Or does a young Sunni independently decide to take revenge because he saw the cousin of a cousin of a prominent Alawite key his car? How does this work?"

Hussam looked as puzzled as I felt, eyes wide, brow furrowed.

"I don't know, Nick. They say that before Hizbollah took Beirut there was a call from Teheran to the Iranian ambassador."

"They say! They say!" I barked. One of the wonderful things about talking with a Lebanese—maybe with anybody from any Mediterranean country—is barks, wild gesticulations, and deep groans will be understood by your partner in conversation to be merely part of the way we make our points. "Who's 'They'!? And how do 'They' know what 'They say' they know?"

"I don't know," Hussam said, a bit dejected. "I don't know how any of this happens. They say—oops, sorry. Some people say Lebanon is merely a pawn in the hands of Syria, Saudi Arabia and Iran."

"And the US," I added.

"And the US."

"But what does this mean? Text messages telling Nasrallah it's time to start talking about retribution against Israel again? Faxes with diagrams of Sidon to show which police barracks to target?" I was getting worked up again.

"I don't know."

"I wonder if anybody does."

We paused.

"So how's your wife adjusting to life in the US?" I asked.

"Oh, well enough. But she misses the people. She asks me 'Where are the people?' whenever she goes anywhere."

Indeed. Where are the people? Not walking the wide sidewalks along Warwick Boulevard as I make my way to the dentist's office. Not on the footpaths winding along the shoreline of Lake Maury.

Too hot. Too muggy.

About as hot and muggy as Beirut is now, but that won't keep families from enjoying a stroll along the Corniche in the afternoon or businessmen from sipping coffee at a sidewalk table at Costa Coffee on Hamra Street.

I wonder if those businessmen ask the same questions that I asked Hussam about what makes things happen in Lebanon.

Probably not, if my understanding of the culture is at all correct. More likely each will have a theory, which each will vehemently defend. Nasrallah never makes a move without a word from Ahmedinejjad. No, it's Assad who pulls his strings. No! No! Nasrallah is his own man—when he called for Arab support of Sudan's President Bashir, accusing American-Zionist plotters of forcing the International Tribunal to issue an arrest warrant for him, it was his decision and his alone. No one pulls his strings.

So much for one Lebanese journalist's theory about the impact of the arrest of Radavan Karadic for ordering the slaughter of Bosnian Muslims. The journalist posited that arresting a Western leader for killing Muslims might convince some people that the human rights folks were more even-handed than they had suspected. Seems not to have affected the way Nasrallah thought about it.

I'm still trying not to pay so much attention to what's going on in the news.

* * *

We leave tomorrow.

I rolled out of bed at 6:18. Just wasn't going to be able to get myself back to sleep.

The Sunday paper tells me that Michael Phelps won his eighth gold medal. Russia plans to begin pulling its troops back tomorrow. Obama's people want him to start telling us exactly what it is he's hoping for. John McCain's response to the 2001 destruction of the World Trade Center was to start talking about taking out Saddam Hussein.

It also tells me that nothing has happened in northern Lebanon since the bus was blown up in Tripoli on Thursday, when eighteen people, mostly soldiers, were killed. They say this might have been an expression of displeasure by Al

Qaeda types for Lebanese president Suleiman's agreement to reopen diplomatic ties with Syria. Or it was retribution by Fatah al Islam for what the army did to its ranks. Or...I've forgotten what else they say it might have been.

But somehow all this—the bus bombs, the farewells to friends, the wondering what in the world makes anyone do virtually anything—has got me reading stuff like A. E. Houseman and Thomas Hardy beneath the dogwood in the cool of this almost-last morning in Newport News.

Maybe it's the safety that lies in the steady, predictable lines:

> Others, I am not the first,
> Have willed more mischief than they durst:
> If in the breathless night I too
> Shiver now, 'tis nothing new.

Or maybe it's the sense that everything means something; that everything makes, somehow, the kind of sense we thought possible a century or so ago:

> I leant upon a coppice gate
>   When frost was spectre-gray.
> And winter's dregs made desolate
>   The weakening eye of day.
> The tangled bine-stems scored the sky
>   Like strings of broken lyres,
> And all mankind that haunted nigh
>   Had sought their household fires.

But I couldn't read long, not matter how soothing I found these anachronisms. Time to finish packing.

PART II

Back in Beirut

CHAPTER 1
Arrived

Sunday morning. The breezes haven't picked up yet. The damp sky hangs heavy over the calm sea, hazing the horizon; dark blue water and light blue air meld wetly in the far distance.

The quiet of a Sunday morning, I've learned, may be as close to a universal as we have on the planet. Now and then a car passes along Rue Bliss, four floors below. A solitary workman moves some lumber across the rooftop of the new Pizza Hut next door. A Sukleen worker in his light-green uniform ambles along the sidewalk, picking up bits of trash with his long picker-upper tongs.

There are no pedestrians for taxi drivers to tap their horns at, calling out "*Teksi?*" No mother leans from the window of an apartment in the building behind us to call for her children. No cell phones chime. No call of "Ali!" or "Mahmud!" or whatever might be the name of the construction worker the other construction worker is looking for.

Air conditioners hum. It's hot. It's been hot since we arrived on August 19, ranging from the low nineties to the low hundreds. Hot and humid.

I begin to sweat the moment I step from the Barakat Building onto Rue Jeanne d'Arc, and I am soon soaked. I am chilled the moment I enter an air conditioned building.

This chilling is not a problem in our lovely apartment with its balcony views of the lush green of the American University of Beirut and the sea beyond. We have two AC units, one in the bedroom and one in the living room. Running both of them, we have found, throws the breaker switches.

So we run the one in the bedroom and drop in there for a cooling off when the spirit moves us.

Running electrical equipment in our apartment is something of an art. It seems we can safely run one air conditioner, one refrigerator and one other piece of equipment, like the hot water heater or the electric kettle (but not, you will remember, the other air conditioner). But if we add to that load, say, the washing machine, once it hits its high-demand spin cycle, POW! I guess that's all, since we don't have any other appliances, other than the set of speakers Buffy bought so we could play all the CDs we loaded onto our computers before we left or the wireless Internet setup, but neither takes much power.

We don't know what turning on the television would do to this delicate balance. Not long after arriving, we found out that under the apartment's antenna-based arrangement we could only faintly pick up only two stations, both in Arabic.

I went to Ibrahim, the physical plant director at the school. Unfortunately for Ibrahim, his responsibilities include every physical aspect of all five school buildings, as well as the seven or eight apartment buildings where ACS ex-pat staff members live.

So when we encountered a couple of minor problems after moving we in, Ibrahim sent Ahmad and Mohammed over to check them out. Next Ibrahim asked his assistant, Mahdi, to arrange for a washing-machine repairman to pay us a visit. But the repairman had an automobile accident on the way over on Thursday, and then, Mahdi explained, he said he couldn't come Friday because his assistant had broken his arm.

"Ibrahim, how do I get cable TV at the apartment?"

"Well, there's sort of a gang of guys who control setting this up in different neighborhoods. No, I don't mean like a gang with guns and stuff, just that each guy has a territory and so we have to find the right one."

He riffled through his Rolodex.

"Here, it's Maan in your neighborhood. Call him and arrange for someone to come hook you up." He jotted the number down.

I called. Taking the call on his mobile phone in a noisy café, Maan was polite and businesslike.

We agreed he'd send someone at four o'clock the next afternoon. OK. I'd be out of my meetings by three.

The next day I walked the half-mile (horizontally) and two hundred feet (vertically) home when my meetings were finished. Approaching my turn onto Rue Jeanne d'Arc from Rue Bliss, however, I heard an ominous sound.

Generators.

Ah, damn. I'd forgotten that today's daily three-hour power outage runs from three o'clock to six o'clock in the Hamra District.

This created two problems.

First, Maan's man might not be able to do his work without the electricity on, and our building does not have a generator.

Second, we would have to walk up four flights of stairs (actually, by American measurements, five, since the ground floor, the *rez de chaussée*, is not included in the counting).

Problems one and two, of course, bring problem three into being: I really should wait downstairs for the TV guy so I can arrange a return visit with him if, on arrival, he decides, "To hell with it. I'm not going to walk up all those stairs and not be able to do my work."

So I grabbed a book, walked back downstairs, and set the battered chair in the foyer by the doorway to the street, hoping occasional breezes would cool me a bit.

New problem: there's quite a bit of foot traffic into our building. In addition to eight other apartments, Malik's accounting firm takes up two floors, and Books and Pens has a second-floor office as well as its sidewalk storefront.

So how was I going to know which was the TV guy?

No idea. I sat, opened my book, and figured that *Inshallah* it would work out.

As you may have intuited, if you've been following the thread of this narrative, it didn't. As far as I could tell, no TV guy arrived. Maybe he knew the power would be out. Maybe he misunderstood "Barakat building" and went to the "Makram building," or some such. Street names and addresses mean nothing here—only building names and city districts. We live on the fourth floor of the Barakat building in Hamra District. Not 401 or 402. Just "the apartment to the left of the elevator". I have no idea if the building has a street number, and Rue

Jeanne d'Arc is irrelevant—most taxi drivers have never heard of it, though most are familiar with Rue Bliss.

But something else worked out.

Wordsworth had just met Southey in the fascinating Wordsworth/Coleridge biography I was reading sitting in the doorway, hoping for a breeze while watching for a TV guy, when a tall, balding man about my age stopped to ask what I was reading.

Turns out that the friendly man, Bakr Barakat, was the owner of the building.

"But I'm moving," Bakr informed me. "If you know anyone who wants to rent my apartment, let me know."

"Why are you moving?"

"I've had it with Lebanese politics."

But everybody's had it with Lebanese politics, so we talked books for a while. He showed me the one he'd just picked up about the history of the Arab world from 1248 to 1948. He wasn't clear on the significance of the first date—something to do with Saladiin, he thought. The last date is horribly significant for Lebanon, signifying the creation of Israel and the influx of what has turned out to be over half a million refugees and what is considered to be a permanent state of war with "the Zionist state" in "occupied Palestine."

Then Lebanese politics reintruded.

A decade ago, Bakr explained, he and some friends had invested in a piece of property in the mountains not far from Beirut.

"Now it's worth a lot on paper, but nothing's been realized yet. We can't rent it or sell it."

A few years later, he had another plan to build, this time in Beirut itself. But then, in 2005, Rafik Hariri was assassinated, and that project too was put on hold.

"Politics!" he said. "None of it means anything. I am a Muslim, but I can't understand what the leaders think they're doing when they murder people to send a message."

"But isn't that the point about the politics?" I asked. "That everything that happens is intended to do just that, to mean something, to send a message."

"Yes, but so many bloody messages. And they're so hard to read. Who knows what's going on? Who knows what people are trying to say? And there's that little skinny guy in Teheran who's directing so much of it."

"And the stupid guy from Texas in Washington," I added.

"And the stupid guy from Texas in Washington."

So Bakr will leave Lebanon.

In the meantime, however, he gave me the name of an electrician who, if I would buy a decoder, could connect my television to his satellite dish on the roof if I decided not to work with Maan. "Tell him I said you could borrow my service."

It's four days later. I haven't called Maan or Bakr's friend. We still don't have television.

But we're learning about the sort of dance around electricity we have here. Here's how it works. Aside from the generalization that you can never run many things at once, there are specifics, such as the fact that a little while before you think you might want some hot water for a shower or to wash the dishes, you throw that switch. But don't start the electric tea-kettle until you think you might have heated enough water for whatever you had in mind and can thus safely shut that off, because starting the electric tea-kettle will probably throw the breaker switch.

This is slightly simplified by the fact that we can't use the washing machine at the moment. It turned out that somebody had left water sitting in the front-loading machine for several months, so the clothes we washed came out smelling worse than when we'd put them in. Even after two washings. And the machine did not smell any cleaner after Buffy did everything she knew of to clean it: she ran it through another very hot cycle, then through two cycles with white vinegar (whose purifying powers she swears by).

This was why Mahdi had arranged for a washing machine guy to come last week—he had the accident Thursday, and his assistant got hurt Friday. We decided to take a load of clothes to the launderer's down the street.

Two days later, I returned to pick up the laundry.

"I'm sorry. It's not ready yet. Come back in one hour," the owner said deferentially.

"*Sa-aa Libnaiya, ow sa-aa Americaniya?*" I asked. A Lebanese hour or an American hour?

He laughed. His assistant laughed.

"*Sa-aa Americaniyya*! Come back at five fifteen. It will be ready."

I waited till five thirty. It was not ready.

So I did what one does here. The same thing I'll do when I drop my shoes off at the cobbler's around the corner and when the baker tells me the bread is almost ready to come out of the oven. The same thing I did with Bakr while waiting for the TV guy.

I started a conversation.

"I'm only here because our washing machine is broken," I told him.

"Ah, that is good news for me then. I like it when your washing machine is broken."

Then he told me a proverb that translates loosely as one man's loss is another man's gain.

There was a word, however, he couldn't quite translate.

"'*Qowm,*'" he repeated. "It means … um, it means, *yaani* [*yaani* means 'well' or 'um' or 'I mean' (which is what it literally means), and is used two or three times per sentence] larger than your family. The proverb means that when one group has bad fortune the other group profits."

I looked up the word in my Arabic-English dictionary back in the apartment. Looking up a word in Arabic, however, can be pretty tricky. I had to figure out if the "k" sound was a "caff" or a "qoff," and then I had to figure out if the "ow" sound was a "wow" or just a little diacritical mark above the "k." You see, you don't look up the word; you look up the two–, three–, or four-letter root that forms the verb. When you find the right root, it'll give you all the related nouns, adverbs, adjectives, and all the rest. Sometimes they go on for pages.

Turned out it was a "qoff," and that there *was* a "wow."

How appropriate a phrase in Lebanon.

It's not one *man*'s loss and another *man*'s gain. That would be Western. That would be you and me with our hard-won, jealously-guarded little fiefdoms of individualism: our fenced-in front yard, our place in the checkout line, our right to a-little-lettuce-but-no-tomato-and-don't-put-too-much-mayonnaise-do-you-have-a-little-Dijon-mustard? for our hamburger.

No. In Lebanon the proverb says that one *qowm* benefits when another loses.

One tribe.

I stopped by the laundry shop the next day to give him the translation. After all, he had taught me *qowm*. I taught him "tribe."

Now we're even.

* * *

The sun's risen well above the mountain ridge a few dozen miles to the east. The traffic's picked up a bit. A couple of workmen have shown up at the Pizza Hut building. The Sukleen worker has returned with a broom, sweeping the leaves from the sidewalk.

A heavy-laden container ship appears from the west, a quarter of a mile off the coast, heading for the Port of Beirut a few miles east, just before the coastline curves northward.

The ship is loaded with things like those we've bought since arriving: our Spanish coffee filters, Italian pasta, Chinese electric kettle, Liberian strawberry jam, Egyptian corn flakes, and Linksys broadband wireless router from Cisco Systems, made, of course, in China.

I find it comforting to watch the arrival of ships like this. They symbolize stability and hope.

Who would risk sending a piece of equipment so expensive and vulnerable as a ship like this, carrying such irrelevancies, unless they were fairly certain that the ship would make it safely into and out of the harbor?

What merchants would risk ordering the goods if they were not fairly certain that there'd be somebody like me on the other end, affluent enough and secure to buy the corn flakes, or like the technician at Cyberia Internet Services, savvy enough to know how to temporarily bypass all the Norton features that were in the way of connecting my computer to their system?

But beyond the freighter, almost hidden in the haze, another vessel. Sleek and serious-shaped, it's clearly a warship. I believe it's German and has been assigned by the UN to pace up and down the coast, looking for bad guys doing bad things.

A Sunday morning reminder.

* * *

In America, I know what things mean. Or close enough. Republican insiders, for example, selected Sarah Palin to be John McCain's running mate for a variety of relatively comprehensible—and reasonable—reasons. As a woman, she'll take away some of the Democrats' thunder for having nominated a black man; as an ultra-conservative, she'll bring some wavering right-wing back into the fold; as a person in her forties, she'll assuage some doubts that it's an old man's party.

Oh, I'm sure there are other reasons. Who knows what Governor Ted Stevens' situation may have had to do with the decision? And that pregnant daughter—was that a case of inadequate vetting, or was even that unfortunate situation considered a way to reach some constituency that's traditionally voted Democratic? Unwed teenagers hardly seem a likely target. Maybe social services professionals?

But maybe the fact that I'm even considering such a possibility indicates that I've been paying too much attention to Lebanese politics for too long.

See, here in Lebanon, almost everything *means* something, as my new friend Bakr suggested as we chatted in the foyer of my apartment building. Nothing is ever just what it is—it's always something else too. Or some things else. The problem is that nobody's ever quite sure exactly what these some things might be.

On the other hand, trying to figure out what signal anyone might be sending at any given moment with any given gesture is part of what's fun about living here. That is, if your idea of fun is putting together a jigsaw puzzle when you are: 1) not sure what the final picture is supposed to look like; 2) not sure if you have all the pieces; 3) not sure if instead of working with one puzzle, you might not have been given a box full of pieces from a dozen puzzles, the remnants and scraps of all the unfinished puzzles in the neighborhood, picked up at a yard sale.

I mean, compared to what goes on around here, Vice President Cheney's trip to the Republic of Georgia is positively transparent in the meaning it conveys. Unfortunately, of course, the trip conveys a secondary and unintended meaning: it signals that once again this administration really can't see what it has done to America's status in the world and still doesn't understand the concept of "political capital"; moreover, the political capital is finite and easily squandered. The ignorance and foolishness of our leaders aside, however, it's clear that we meant to send the signal to Russia that we remained Georgia's friend and supporter, by god! Unfortunately, that being said, about all that remained to be said out loud was something like "Put that in your pipe and smoke it, Putin!"

A far cry from a dire threat.

Take what's going on with Syria. This country, recently among the most likely to be bumped onto the Bush administration's axis-of-evil triad once North Korea got demoted to "not-so-bad-after-all," Syria now stands front and center in regional politics.

Oh, that doesn't mean that the US is in there mixing it up with Bashar al Assad. The nearest anybody's gotten to this part of the world recently is Condi Rice's visit to Libya, where she made nice with Muammar Ghaddafi, who was once referred to by everybody's favorite Republican, Ronald Reagan, as a "mad dog." In case anybody missed the message Rice wanted to convey, she has explained that she's really trying to show "other countries" (read "Iran") that the US will get along with countries that change their ways, no matter how much they may have previously irritated us.

She didn't mention, of course, Libya's oil and gas reserves, but what the heck, that wasn't part of the message to the world anyway. That part's just in case McCain doesn't win in November.

Anyway. Syria.

Here's what's going on there now.

1) Lebanon's president has recently returned from a visit to Damascus, one result of which is the agreement to open formal diplomatic relations between the two countries. See, Syria thinks the West stole Lebanon from her when it granted Lebanon's independence as a separate country

in 1943, so Lebanon and Syria have never exchanged diplomats or set up embassies.

2) Syria and Israel have, through the good offices of Turkey, begun to discuss formal peace. Lots of tricky parts to this, of course, including whether Israel will return the strategic Golan Heights that it took from Syria in 1967, and whether Syria will continue to arm Hizbollah, the anti-Israeli Lebanese militia/political party that promises to kick the Israelis out of what is referred to here as Occupied Palestine, as well as to retrieve the so-called Shebaa Farms for Syria.
3) Then Qatar—whose emir brokered the deal that brought Lebanon back from the brink of civil war in May of this year—and France decided to join the fun, so they, along with Turkey, are now in Damascus trying to see how many of these situations they can help smooth out. Although Saudi Arabia, Egypt, and Jordan aren't taking part in the meeting, they'd like a hand in this effort to make lemonade as well—it's always better to be at the table rather than getting the handouts at the end of the meeting as you try to read between the lines to figure out what the big kids have decided.

This is all well and good, isn't it? It looks as though there's movement on lots of volatile fronts. Or is there? Can Syria really make a deal with Israel without totally undoing its crucial relationships with Iran and Hizbollah? Can Syria really accept an independent Lebanon, giving up any future right to reclaim it as part of Greater Syria?

And what about the fact that while Syria's chatting about getting along with Israel over cups of strong Turkish coffee in some meeting room in Damascus, Hizbollah's leader Hassan Nasrallah is announcing that even if Lebanon gets its land back from Israel as a codicil to some deal, it's not about to lay down its arms—its missiles said now to total around fifteen thousand. And in response to Syrian president Assad's suggestions to French President Sarkozy that the Lebanese army really needs to straighten things out in the north of the country, where Sunni and Syrian-backed Alawites keep shooting at each other, the pro-Western Lebanese Forces party flew off the handle at the very thought of Syria meddling in Lebanese affairs again.

Posturing and counter-posturing. Messages, right, left, and center, there to be read by any and all. But who's saying what? And to whom? And to what end?

And do they mean it? Whatever *it* is?

* * *

Now I remember how this works. It's about getting lulled.

Only a few weeks back and I've learned so much. On a Saturday morning stroll through the Hamra district I discover that if I want eggs from the egg store near the Commodore Hotel, I'll buy them in multiples of five, not six. They come in packets of six and twelve at Bou Khalil and Idriss (I wonder why it's decimal-based in the traditional market and duodecimal in the modern stores. And who decided? When?) If I buy only a few here at the egg store, I'll not be given a container to protect them and will have to carry them home gingerly in a little black plastic sack.

A few blocks on, I carefully jot two new words, comparing the English with the Arabic on the poster advertising *Not for Public*: *masrah* means "theater" and *masraheeya* means "play."

It was probably a mistake to bring my camera on this walk. I'd decided a few days earlier that it might be interesting to take photos of some older buildings before they're torn down.

In this part of Beirut, two– and three-story houses that date back to the French period between the World Wars or even to the Ottoman period stand utterly crumbling next to half-century old, mildly crumbling six– or seven-story apartment buildings, both of which stand next to brand-new fifteen– or twenty– or even thirty-story shining apartment towers.

The oldest buildings have an Escher-like quality to them, exterior staircases winding their ways around the outside of the house, leading to a doorway facing the street on the first floor and another on the side of the building on the second. Bougainvillea climbs roof-high trellises, shading patios and terraces. Tall windows are shuttered against the sun.

The older buildings are, for the most part, left to crumble, because property in this part of the city is very valuable, and everyone knows that someday some wealthy Kuwaiti or Qatari (or Lebanese, if Bakr can round up enough partners) developer will approach grandma with an offer she can't refuse. In the meantime, why fix it up?

So I wander the narrow streets snapping photos, reading advertisements, stepping into an egg shop and a shop that sells tubs of hummus while I wait for the Tourist Information Bureau to open to see if they still have schedules for the dozen or so Lebanese Commuting Company bus lines that will get you any place in the city—or even twenty-five miles up the coast or into the mountains—for sixty-six cents.

All is well.

And indeed all seemed well when I picked up last Wednesday's *Daily Star*. The headline wasn't about bombs or assassinations, but about newly—and miraculously—elected President Sleiman's setting Tuesday as the day for Lebanon's various factions to begin the national dialogue they promised to engage in back in May, when they met in Doha after a week's fighting in the streets.

Just below that there was an article outlining the General Labor Confederation's criticisms of the new minimum wage. The GLC argued that the parliament's hike from 200,000 to 500,000 Lebanese lira per month ($125 to $350) was "offensive and insufficient."

Yes. No doubt. But at least there's a parliament. At least it's meeting and it's passing legislation. At least Lebanese labor unions have something to complain about other than the fact that there's no parliament, passing no laws.

All seemed well.

At school no mobile phones had rung wildly during any faculty meetings with warnings about what parts of the city to avoid on the way home. At break the boys had wrestled playfully—"He's my cousin, sir. We were only fooling around!"—while the girls giggled in the corner. Mo had explained that he was late to because his art class was on the other side of the campus. Dania had lined up all her colored pens on the desk so she could write important notes in red, ordinary notes in blue and… who knows what her little plan is.

CHAPTER 1

I stopped paying attention to anything but the things one pays attention to in a normal world: What's for lunch? Can I get my papers graded on time for the next class? Will Buffy and I walk home together, or will she have a late meeting?

You know. Life. Regular stuff.

Then Lebanon reintruded.

Not in the sort of way that jammed the mobile phone lines or even got people mumbling in the halls between classes.

An assassination. A car bomb. It happened Wednesday evening—the day I had been so comforted by the quality of the news in the morning's *Daily Star*.

Saleh Aridi, "a senior member of the Lebanese Democratic Party was assassinated in a car bombing…in his hometown of Baysour, southeast of Beirut."

Southeast of Beirut is the highland area known as the Chouf. It's mainly Druze, a thousand-year-old rather secretive offshoot of Islam that makes up 10 to 20 percent of Lebanon's population.

So who killed this guy? Who would've wanted to kill this guy? Who could've gotten into the village to set the bomb, since everybody there knows everybody there?

Aridi had been working to reconcile differences between his Druze boss, pro-Syrian Youth and Sports Minister Talal Arslan, and the very prominent anti-Syrian (but not particularly pro-Western) Druze leader Walid Jumblatt—at this point, at any rate; Jumblatt has a reputation for unpredictably shifting allegiances with some frequency.

Aridi had been, in other words, laying groundwork within the Druze community for the kind of larger reconciliation that President Sleiman was hoping to generate through the formal national dialogue set to begin Tuesday.

Why kill him?

The only suggestion I've read so far is that it was the work of the old standby, Israel, on the premise that Israel doesn't want its northern neighbor to settle its differences and stabilize.

Well, maybe.

Or maybe it's something closer to home. Maybe it's related to some longstanding Arslan-Jumblatt clan quarrel that we know little about, something between what the laundryman had explained as one *qowm*—one tribe—and another?

Or maybe not.

The photo on the front page of Friday's paper is a familiar one: a young woman carries one child and leads another by the hand past an area cordoned off with yellow tape, at the center of which is the hulk of a burned-out car. Maybe a grey Mercedes.

So I find myself wandering the streets of Hamra two mornings later, learning about eggs and how to say "theater" and bemoaning the loss of the city's architectural heritage. I pass a soldier talking on a pay phone, his AK-47 hanging off his right shoulder as cavalierly as a schoolbag. If he's not on any special alert, why should I be?

There's nothing on the news websites this morning about the assassination. After all, he wasn't a minister or even from a particularly prominent political family.

I note that they've decided that the table they'll use for the National Dialogue meetings among the fourteen political groups will be rectangular, not round, and am reminded of the interminable discussions between adversaries around table size and shape during the lead-up to negotiations near the end of the Vietnam War—maybe that Lebanon's leaders resolved this so quickly is a good sign.

The dialogue, one article begins, entails "an effort to resolve deep differences, particularly over the defense strategy."

Ah, there it is. There's the euphemism, and there's the rub.

That's what finally has to be resolved: how to create a stable nation when one group maintains an arsenal of (probably) tens of thousands of rockets and untold other weapons, has created its own army and mini-state in the southern part of the country, and has vowed to drive "the occupiers" out of Palestine. While the rest of the folks worry mostly about what time the power will be out in their part of the city today, how to upgrade their TV reception, and where they'll live if their building gets sold to developers.

But oh how beautiful the house on Rue Nehme Yafet is, trees and bushes spilling over from the terrace garden, the tiles of its steep roof crimson in the morning sun.

CHAPTER 2
Settling In

It *was* a pretty terrible experience. Terrible for me, terrifying for Buffy, about whose claustrophobia I had learned thirty years ago when she had almost savagely clutched my arm and began to hyperventilate while we made our way through the dark, narrow passages of Rome's catacombs.

But what could we do? We *had* stepped voluntarily into that elevator, each of us silently considering the possibility that the erratic flow of electricity might be severed on our way down. Neither had suggested, "Maybe we ought to walk."

I was explaining that the elevator had gotten stuck during a power outage two days earlier, and as I said, "And then the elevator stopped," the elevator stopped.

The lights went out.

The power was gone.

It could've been worse. We might have been stuck in a modern metal box of an elevator instead of our seventy-year-old model with frosted glass in its doors to let in light and slanted slats above the doors to let in air. And at least the night watchman scurried up the stairs to see what was going on when he heard us banging on the door. Kicking at the door, actually.

The good part was that we knew the power would come back sometime within the next three hours. We would neither suffocate nor die of starvation or dehydration, cramped as the two of us were in an elevator that holds, at best, three, on the floor of which we had set Buffy's purse, my backpack, our lunch bag and, of course, the bag of trash we'd brought to drop in a Sukleen dumpster along the way to school.

It could've been better. We might've stopped on a floor with an interior door handle to pry open instead of on the first floor, from which the handle had been removed in some sort of gesture toward security for Books and Pens. There might've been a concierge who lived on the ground floor, charged with helping residents who needed things like help resetting the air conditioning or getting freed from elevators.

And how nice it would've been if, determining that he couldn't open the door from the outside, the night watchman had said, "I'll be right back with some tools to pry this open."

Instead, he said we'd have to wait till the maintenance man at Malik's (owners of Books and Pens, whose accounting offices are on the third floor of the building) showed up.

"How long might that be?" I asked.

"*Nus sayah*," he said. Half an hour.

"*Nus sayah*?!" I replied, knowing my wife—who was remaining remarkably calm for someone who wasn't sure whether crying hysterically, screaming at the top of her lungs, vomiting, or peeing in her pants was the most appropriate response to being trapped in this little box—might blow at any moment.

"*Naam. Mumkin sayah*."Yes. Maybe an hour.

Uh-oh.

What do you do? Two approaches here. For her part, Buffy is working as hard as she at not doing any of the things outlined above, all of which have become more likely since I've translated what I've just learned about how long we might have to wait in the elevator. One factor in her ability to do something—anything—other than the above, she told me later, was her realization that none of these would neither improve the situation in any way or help me deal with whatever I had to deal with.

For my part, I'm trying to figure out what to say and not to say to help Buffy not do any of the things I guessed she was considering. I didn't know about all of them, but I could guess at the crying and yelling options. If I was afraid, my fears were buried beneath my knowledge that any fear I might feel paled in comparison with those of the woman who had dug her fingernails into my arm back in the catacombs.

So I did my best.

"This is the kind of time prisoners of war design their dream houses," I suggested.

"What?"

"They draw the plans in their minds and figure out how much lumber they'll need, where they'd buy it, and all that. Lots of details."

"Oh."

Her turn.

"I got an e-mail from Sally. David has told Chris he won't serve on the Library Board, but he's willing to run for justice of the peace."

"Oh."

My turn. No, wait. I have to explain that our conversations are punctuated by one or the other of us pounding periodically on the door, buzzing (runs on a battery, apparently) the alarm buzzer and, once, chatting with a woman who was walking up the stairs to Malik's.

"Are you all right?" the sympathetic female voice coming from a blur on the other side of the glass asked.

"Yes, but we would like to get out of here." Buffy told me later that she was trying to decide whether communicating real panic might help. She decided against it.

"I am sure they will get you out soon." Everybody wants to help. Her high heels clicked up the stairs toward the third floor.

Mid-September and the heat hadn't let up a bit. We'd been hot when we'd left the apartment. Now we were really hot and sweaty.

Whenever we heard the rumble of voices downstairs, we tried to determine if they sounded like they might be talking about how to help the poor people trapped in the elevator or if they might just be discussing how bad the traffic had been on the way to work.

"In the States, every guy for miles around would've been here trying to figure out how to get us out," Buffy said. "They'd have loved the macho part of the challenge."

"Yeah."

"They'd have all wanted to be the one to figure out how to take the door off."

"But they'd all have had a full tool kit in the trunk of their cars," I added, "and they wouldn't have been afraid to piss off the owner of the elevator by busting a bit of glass or something." Whoever, in this convoluted system of owned and rented apartments, the owner of the elevator may have been.

I fiddled intermittently with the door handle, trying to feel for innards that might be manipulated in such a way as to unlatch whatever latch was keeping the door shut. Nothing, though. All I got was greasy fingers.

"Don't keep messing with that," Buffy grumbled at one point. "Oh, well, I guess if it makes you feel better, go ahead."

I went ahead.

"Teach me to count in Arabic," she said.

OK. We went to five.

"That's enough."

"Two more. They're easy."

"No. Oh, OK."

"*Sitta. Sabaa.*"

"Six and sabbath, seven; I see. *Sitta. Sabaa.*"

"One more time."

"Sure. But I'm not gonna remember these when we get out of this mess, you know."

And just about the time she finished counting, just about the time we were both at the ends of our tethers, we felt the elevator begin to drop, slowly and unevenly.

Somebody's upstairs winding us down.

Street floor. Throw the door open. Out.

"Want to go upstairs and change?" I asked.

"No. I just want to get to work." Translation: I've gotta get out of this building!

So she headed down Rue Bliss while I zipped up to Malik's. I just couldn't leave without thanking the maintenance guy for springing us from the elevator. For existing, for being born.

Making our way along Rue Bliss as the morning traffic picked up, we took small stabs at talking about being stuck in the elevator.

"I'll need to cry sometime," Buffy said, "But one thing that helped me keep it together was thinking about everybody out there. I mean, this wasn't a great way to spend part of the morning, but I was thinking about what they'd been through just last May when there was shooting in the streets."

"I have to confess," I said, "sometimes I was thinking about what I'd write about it."

* * *

Everyone at school was more than sympathetic.

"A whole hour? You were stuck in the elevator for an hour? I couldn't take that! I don't know what I'd do," Paul, the high school principal, said.

"What! An hour? That's terrible," said Sana, the administrative assistant.

"You were in an elevator for a full hour?" asked Mahdi, deputy director of physical plant, whom I help with his English while he helps me with my Arabic.

And it made a good story, a nice way to start my classes: "OK, you know how adults are always giving you advice? Well, I have a different kind of advice today." Long pause. Survey the audience…oops, students. "Never start your day by spending the first hour stuck in an elevator," I began, rolling into a five-minute riff about heat, darkness, and trying to communicate in patchwork Arabic with people who were only vague silhouettes on the other side of a frosted glass pane.

In the creative nonfiction class I teach to a small group of seniors, as my riff wound down, I had an idea for a writing assignment, which I gave at the end of the period.

"For the next class, please write an extended paragraph."

"On what, sir?" asked Dani, wanting me to move on quickly so they could get to the front of the lunch line.

I paused and glared. "How about you let me tell you?"

"Sorry, sir."

"On 'my most frightening experience.'"

"*Your* most frightening experience, sir?" Zalfa asked.

"What do you think, Zalfa?

"Oh. Ours. OK," she said as she slapped her notebook closed.

The next few days were not too bad for Lebanon. A little fighting around Tripoli, but not much. The National Dialog hit a snag as soon as the question of Hizbollah's weapons came up. Rumors surfaced that the power cuts would be extended to six hours a day. Yipes!

But school moved along well. Students did their work as well and as enthusiastically as it makes sense for students to do, so in my history classes we moved Rome toward its fall, and in my English classes worked on replacing weak verbs like "gets" and "has" with stronger ones like "grabs" and "holds."

Creative Nonfiction meets only twice per week, so the students had plenty of time to finish their writing. They ambled in and took their seats. First a free write to loosen up our writing juices, followed by discussion of sentences they liked. Then to what they'd written about their fears.

"OK, let's hear what you wrote about your most frightening experience. Raquel, will you read yours?"

"I'd rather not read it out loud, sir."

"OK. Who? How about you?"

I was addressing a tall young man, his hair cut almost to the scalp, usually dressed in neat jeans and a t-shirt. He always looked mildly sardonic, as though he was willing to tolerate all this stuff but really knew that there was much more out there and that school was just a game one plays until they let you out.

"Sure. I'll read."

He opened his notebook, flipped through the pages, paused, and then began to read.

"'*Salam aleykum*,' were the last words out of Hassan Nasrallah's mouth before the bullets began to rain down on us."

He read on. I listened, hearing what he was saying, but, on a different level, being hit—once again, dammit!—by the realization that I'm not in Kansas anymore.

I knew they might write about their experiences last May, when Sunni and Shia started fighting in the streets of Beirut and Shia and Druze in the mountains.

Sure.

But to hear this handsome, pleasant young man reading, "So I got my pistol and my AK-47 and hurried downstairs," now that's different. He was sitting here between Zalfa and Firas, his copy of Bloom's *The Essay Connection* on the desk in front of him, reading about spending the week on his street corner with his friends in case Hizbollah entered his neighborhood. He was reading about this as matter-of-factly as one of my Williamsburg students last year might have written about riding the new roller coaster at Busch Gardens.

That's different.

"Wow! Nicely written," I said when he finished. Not "Wow! How does it make you feel to you to assume that this may go on for the rest of your life? That this is your life? That this is your home? That…" I wouldn't even know where to begin with the real questions.

This is a writing class, I kept telling myself.

"Hey, reread that first sentence again, please."

"OK. '*Salam Aleykum*,' were the last words out of Hasran Nasrallah's mouth before the bullets started raining down on us."

I'm at the board now. "Who remembers what you call the literary device he has used really well here? It has to do with the way he has juxtaposed ideas."

The students did what students always do, randomly tossing out literary terms, hoping they might hit a good one.

"Personification?"

"Metaphor?"

"Oh! Oh!" one of the two Danis in the class said. "Irony. It's irony!"

"Great, Dani. And what's irony?"

"Um, it's when you put two things together that don't fit. And he began 'Peace be upon you' were the words before the shooting started. That's ironic."

I wrote "irony" on the board, defined it.

"So what does juxtaposed mean, sir?" Saif asked.

I explained. Then I watched him, his broad back hunched over his notebook as he wrote.

Irony.

* * *

It had been quiet around here since that day.

My sister Sara sent a wonderful response to one of my musings about what makes Americans American, saying:

> What makes me an American is one single fact—that I live in a country where most (but not all) can make plans, can assume that tomorrow will be here and I can implement the day and take care of things, go to work, call my son's teacher, take the car in to be fixed, have a decent supper, take a walk in the evening. I can go on for a day—maybe months, maybe years—making certain assumptions about life. Probably one half of the world cannot do this because of terror and survival and poverty and survival. What will tomorrow bring? I guess that in many West European countries people can do this also. So what makes me different from the Parisian or the Londoner or the non-Turkish German? Except for our highly materialistic life—I think Americans in different parts of the country are vastly different.

Juniors and seniors are coming in to talk with Buffy, "Miss, we need a freak-out! Can we come to your office?" two girls asked the other day. By the time they came, the freak-out was over. But the conversation still mattered.

Friday after school Buffy and I walked over to Raouche, where two 150-foot-tall columns of limestone called Pigeon Rocks rise from the sea to the level of the land. We sat on the shaded veranda of Le Petit Café, looking out on the surf crashing against the rocks far below, and at the white caps on the sea beyond the cove.

"One white wine and an Almaza beer, please."

"I'm sorry, sir, but we do not serve alcohol during Ramadan."

Orange juice and lemonade then. The cool breeze blew in from the sea as the sun dropped toward the horizon. We talked. Shaded our eyes against the bright flash of the sunset. Talked as darkness fell.

That evening Buffy put on a Simon and Garfunkel CD as we sat down to dinner. The song about going to "look for America" had just reached the poignant part where they sing that they are "counting the cars on the New Jersey Turnpike."

The evening call to prayer began, breaking the day's Ramadan fast.

"*All-a-ah akbar*!"

"They've all gone to look for Ame-rica."

"*All-a-ah akbar*!"

Irony.

Again.

* * *

My friend Jawad reflects on the fighting between the Shia Hizbollah and the less well-organized Sunni militiamen that filled the streets of Beirut in May. Jawad is Druze. We're walking along the Corniche.

"I did not fight then, sir. We were waiting for orders, but they never came. They told us not to go to the mountains, where Hizbollah was attacking our people. He was destroyed there, sir. They did not need us. They told us to wait in Beirut.

"If something happened now. I would call," he said, pulling out his shiny mobile phone, "and in a minute we would have one hundred Druze here to fight. We are ready.

"Hizbollah he knows that. He will not attack us again."

Jawad is short, wiry. Occasionally he smiles broadly, but usually he frowns, constantly surveying, watching for what he might need to do. During the civil war he was sent—"Twice, sir! Each time I returned a hero!"—to Cuba for military training by the PLO, Yasir Arafat's Palestine Liberation Organization that moved to Beirut in the 1970s and was driven out by the Israelis in 1982, reluctantly relocating in remote Tunis.

"Ah, the snipers in the war, sir. They were not Lebanese. They were Korean or Philippine. They were deadly. We were not trained to be snipers. One shot—pow!—and they have killed. We did not have that skill.

"But when we found one, we would circle behind and trap him. One they cut up in pieces and threw the pieces around."

So Jawad fought with the PLO. The PLO fought against the Maronite Christians, then against the Shia Amal Militia, which was later replaced by Hizbollah as the primary Shia party.

Today Jawad thinks the Shia are Lebanon's main problem because of their desire for a Shia-dominated world. Today the leader of the strongest Druze faction, Walid Jumblatt, whose legendary father, Kamal, was well known to Jawad's own father, he boasts, is closely allied with the Sunni and several Christian parties.

"Me, sir, I don't know much about my god. I don't care what you believe. I believe what Jumblatt tells me to believe. It is not my job to question. It is my job to protect my people."

He thinks John McCain would be a better president than Barack Obama.

"I do not have much learning from books, sir. I learned what I learned in the streets, carrying my weapon, in prison where I was beaten. McCain is a man like me. You know what he says and what he means.

"Obama is an intelligent man. But he has not learned things in his heart, the way a warrior learns them. He cannot know what McCain can know. I cannot trust him the way I can trust McCain."

Jawad turns left off the Corniche just a mile from the school.

"Here, sir. I want to show you my building," he says. We turned onto a narrow side street, heading toward a small apartment building.

His mother was sitting in front of the building. She greeted Jawad and called for the nanny to bring the baby. She stood, took the baby, smiled a toothless grin, and handed the baby to Jawad.

Jawad cooed at the child, offered her a finger to hold, and introduced me to his mother. The mother and I exchanged greetings.

A few days later, Buffy and I went to dinner with Sharon, a drama teacher who was here to fulfill a lifelong dream of working in the Middle East. And, she added, to honor her father, who had worked for USAID in Pakistan and Tunisia, where she had spent several years as a child.

We'd found a seaside fish restaurant at the western end of the Corniche—not far from Jawad's home.

The restaurant was packed. We squeezed into a table near the window, looking out on the waves that were crashing high against the seawall below.

The waiter suggested that instead of ordering from the menu we could simply order a fish and split it three ways.

"*Soixante mille liras, ou quarante mille dollars, le kilo*," he told us. Forty dollars a kilo that we'd split three ways. Fine. He brought a large sea bass for our approval, followed by hummus, tabbouleh, and a bottle of Lebanese white wine.

As our mezze arrived, the restaurant began to clear out, and we realized that we had come at the end of Iftar, the small meal that marks the breaking of the fast each evening during Ramadan.

Everyone was going home to get ready for dinner, which would begin at ten or eleven. Only one other couple remained.

Sharon's husband, who taught music in the same school in Napa, California, where she had taught drama for twenty years, had not accompanied her to Lebanon. As much as he loved travel, he wasn't ready to give up the music program he had created. "It's a monster that demands everything from him, but it's a monster he loves," she said.

He had, however, understood her need to fulfill this dream.

"How will it feel going back?" I asked.

"I'm already dreading it. I know that this is changing me. I'm already thinking about what it's like there and what it's like here. This—as much as I love my husband—is better."

The fish came. We talked. As we neared the end of our meal, the tables slowly began to fill.

Sharon and Buffy and I talked about our children and our parents, about civil wars and suicides, about shopping malls and what Buffy and Sharon might do on their trip to Cyprus next week, when the school sent them out of the country so they could reenter to get their residency permits and work visas.

It was almost ten when we began our slow walk home along the Corniche, passing children riding their tricycles on the wide promenade, parents watching to make sure they didn't plunge into the roiling surf below, lovers walking arm in arm, old men playing backgammon, and families setting up camp for the evening, complete with folding chairs, hookahs, and small gas stoves to heat their thick coffee.

All so familiar. All so strange.

* * *

I wondered how much trouble we were going to be in for the little end-run we just performed around Electricité du Liban?

Well, it wasn't really around the electric company. It was around the guy who came by once a month to collect our payments.

Friday he'd stopped by, sticking a little green form saying we owed thirty-five thousand lira in the door. It also said, though I couldn't read his handwriting, that he'd be back on Monday.

When I got back from work on Monday, there was a bigger white form stuck in the door. I could read that it was from the Electric Company of Lebanon and that we still owed the money. But I couldn't read it well enough to determine if it contained a threat. So I went downstairs to the guy who owns M'Lords, the clothing store next to the entrance to our apartment building.

I'd stopped by to chat a number of times. We'd talked about this and that: the uneven flow of electricity and the best place to buy a cheap generator, the foolishness of Lebanon's politicians and the occasional wickedness of America's. The usual.

"Don't worry," he said after reading the white paper. "You won't have to pay this till Thursday because of the holiday."

I went back upstairs, somewhat comforted.

Buffy and I sat discussing the day, talking about kids and teachers, frustrations and triumphs. You know, the kind of thing two people who work together and live together talk about.

We were waiting for the power to come back on at the end of the three-hour outage. I heard the AUB clock tower chime six and went to see if the little light on the front of the refrigerator was on. Nope.

Oh well. Sometimes the power's a little late coming back on, or even a little early.

We continued talking. I went back to check the refrigerator a few times. Then I thought I heard the elevator. Stepping into the hall, sure enough, the power was back on in the rest of the building.

Tried some lights in our hallway. Flipped the breaker switch in the kitchen up and down a couple of times. Nothing.

Downstairs again.

"The son-of-a-whore has cut off your power," the shopkeeper said. Actually, he explained to me that my power had indeed been cut, in English, but referred to the guy who collects the fees as an "*ibn charmouta*" in a brief rant to his friend.

"We will go turn it on," he said.

Huh?

I followed him back into the building, where he opened a door under the stairway and then stepped into a dark room lined with switches of all shapes, sizes, and colors, some buried behind bundles of wires.

He found one near the front that was down and flipped it up. "Go try your power."

The elevator was busy, so I ran up the stairs—all five flights. Nope. Got my flashlight and hurried back down.

I made my way into the little room, shining the flashlight on the switches. I flipped everything that was down up.

Ran back upstairs.

Nope.

New problem. Now the elevator didn't work, nor did the light in the hallway.

Oops.

I must've cut everybody's electricity. I wondered which one that was. Searched, messed with some, still couldn't find it.

Back to the clothing shop. Back to the dark little room with my friend.

"Here. This is the elevator," he said, flipping the switch up.

Yup. I could see the light come on through the frosted glass.

He found another, a small red one, way in the back of the room, and flipped it.

"I tried that before," I said, but I was game for anything, so I ran back upstairs, where Buffy stood waiting, proudly pointing to the shining overhead light.

As I scurried downstairs, I realized that when I flipped the red one before I had also flipped the bigger one that had cut all the power.

"Thanks so much," I said to the shopkeeper.

"No problem," he replied. "These bill collectors make a commission on what they get from us, and he didn't want to bother coming back again. Just go downtown on Thursday when the holiday is over. Anyone can tell you where the offices are."

* * *

Of course, paying the electric bill was not simple.

Understanding how likely it was that this seemingly uncomplicated act could easily complicate itself in ways I couldn't even imagine, I took the bus to the Electricité du Liban offices the day before they'd be open, once the holiday marking the end of Ramadan, Iftar, was over. A scouting run.

I'm pretty sure Lebanese Commuting Company drivers are under the strictest of instructions to stay under fifteen kilometers per hour. Given the speed at which most Beirutis drive, the company must've invented a pretty sophisticated screening process to find so many men willing to essentially dawdle their ways along, slowing for everyone who looks at all interested in catching the bus (but not, like taxi drivers, tooting their horns at everyone they pass), stopping to chat with the regulars, coffee vendors, policemen, and shopkeepers sitting on plastic chairs in front of their shops, but always poised to snag a customer.

So the number two bus made its way from sector to sector, briefly east toward Sanayeh, south along the edge of Verdun, and east and up onto Beirut's crest in Ashrefieh. Then it turned abruptly northward through Mar Nicolas and east again toward the edge of Beirut and Dora, the end of the run.

Slowly, slowly. I certainly wasn't going to be whisked past my stop.

Well, there aren't really stops. You just say, "*Hone*," "here," to which the driver responds, "*Hone?*" "*Naam, hone.*" And he stops. You get out, and then you walk back the block to the Electricity Company office which you've been told you passed. Which is closed, as you had expected. But now you know how to get here, your dry run successful.

And you walk back the four or five miles home—as the crow flies; who knows how far the forty-five-minute bus ride took you home. Through various *secteurs de caractère traditionelle*, lined with two– and three-story, tall-windowed, filigree-balconied buildings, shops at street level, apartments above; past

Martyrs' Square, where the blue minarets of the new El Amine mosque rise high above the steeple of the old Maronite cathedral; past the empty thirty stories of the Holiday Inn, pocked with bullet and rocket scars; and on into the Hamra district.

The next morning you set off early. Find the end of the line where you pick up a number two bus, pay your sixty-six cents, seat yourself, relish again as the bus plods along and you try to fathom something of Beirut's architectural and cultural complexity. Then, "*Hone.*" "*Hone?*" "*Naam, hone.*"

Only problem is that you've come to the phone company, not to the electric company.

No big deal. It's back a half mile or so, and the cashier—"*Vous parlez anglais ou français?*" "*Les deux*," you respond, "either one," pretty sure she'd rather speak French—explains that it's a huge building you can't miss: Electricité du Liban. Even though you already did miss it. Three times: twice while driving by, once while walking by.

No problem. Any excuse for meandering on foot.

There it is. Twenty-story building with offices on the ground level, and more offices downstairs, which you'd reach by walking down a rather grand, wide staircase that winds into a broad courtyard, then through any of a dozen glass doors.

Lots of windows, some marked *caisse* for cashier, some "remissions" for maybe payments, some *arrières* for past-due bills. Start with *caisse*.

Show the cashier your bill. "Where do you live?" she asks. "Hamra." "Go to number eighteen over there."

At number eighteen the agent looks at your bills—the little green slip telling you in Arabic that the collector would be back Monday and the white slip he left Monday explaining he was cutting off your power—and shows them to another agent. They confer.

You've decided to stick with French, so he explains in French that you go over there, through the little doorway, to the right, then to the left.

You do so, and now you're no longer in the high-ceiling, public-friendly wing of this building but in a dingy, long box of a room filled with tables and lined with fuzzy-glass-walled offices.

Step into one. Show the young woman standing near the door the documents.

"Go to the fifth office, Hani Khaldy."

One. Two. Three. Four. Five. "Hani Khaldy," the sign reads in Arabic.

A middle-aged man wearing a (for Lebanon) fashionably wide, purple necktie sits, debating with a customer.

The customer leaves.

You hand Hani the bill and explain your problem.

"Ghassen Youmanyi," he replies as he writes, first in Arabic, then in English, a name and phone number.

Name and number of the guy who had dropped off the bill in the first place.

"Call him," Hani tells you.

So you go home, and you do so. Three hours later he comes by and you pay the bill—no late fine or anything. Then he goes downstairs to flip up the switch to turn your electricity back on. He discovers it's already up, mumbles, "*Ibn charmouta*—son of a whore," under his breath, and goes about his business.

Now I know that many readers are thinking that all this was an awfully long, complicated process that could easily have been streamlined at any number of points: sticking a note in the door explaining we should just leave the money in an envelope, leaving a phone number, not using Electricité du Liban forms, even—from Ghassen's point of view—figuring out a way of effectively shutting off our power, rather than just flipping a little switch downstairs that I could just as easily flip back up.

But somehow I don't mind. In fact, I began to understand that I've come to see this kind of complexity not only as part-and-parcel of living here, but that I've even to expect it, almost to relish the challenges it will pose.

Take the question of depositing the $160 insurance refund we'd gotten in the mail from the US a couple of weeks ago.

"Oh, just drop it in the ATM at the bank," Buffy had suggested.

"Won't be that simple," I replied. "I'd guess they'll want us both there to sign it in their presence."

Little did I know. One lunch period I zipped up the hill to BLOM Bank—well, not exactly zipped; I huffed and puffed up more quickly than I usually huff and puff. I handed the teller the check.

"It's too late to deposit."

"But you don't close for half an hour."

"Yes, but we don't accept deposits now." Then he looked more closely at the check. "And you need to have signed the international check form. Did you do that?"

"We signed papers for almost an hour when we opened the account. I'd imagine we did."

"Probably not." He checked my records and then turned to speak to a senior officer, who came around to the front of the counter.

"Sir, you have not signed the form. And even if you had, you would leave the check here and it would take around ninety days to clear. We have to send it to the States, then they authorize us to pay. But because we use another bank, it would cost something, maybe around forty dollars, though I'm not sure exactly how much, to cash the check."

"There's no other way?"

"No, sir. I'm sorry."

I left the bank elated and realized I had turned some sort of corner.

"Buff," I called as I walked into her third floor office at school. "It's even more complicated than I thought to cash the check. Listen to this!"

CHAPTER 3
Making Adjustments

I've been reading too long, getting stiff. Maybe I'll get up and fix myself a cup of coffee.

I glance out the window. The grey-and-black urban camouflage-clad policemen stationed in the street below look bored. They lean their AK-47s against their leg or the back of the tattered black chair where they slouch, guarding the corner of the street that leads to the Hariri residence, two blocks away.

Every car that drives within a block of that tall, beige building is checked for suspicious objects, the driver's and passengers' faces scrutinized for signs of nervousness—or perhaps for hints of serene commitment.

The red-and-white striped barricades farther up the street, near the home of the family of Lebanon's most controversial car-bomb casualty, Rafik elHariri, are much sturdier and the security more serious and ongoing than the security by current Prime Minister Siniora's apartment on Rue Bliss, near our old apartment.

No armored personnel carriers down there. No machine guns. Nothing like these thick barricades that are raised to let cars through only after careful examination.

But even here the soldiers seem to be going through the motions as they check cars and briefly scrutinize me as I walk by with my two bags of groceries from Bou Khalil.

Two days ago, nobody bothered to stop Bassaam, Hisham, and several others as we ferried our belongings from our apartment in the Barakat Building on Rue Jeanne d'Arc, where nothing quite worked, to the Adel Building on Rue Commodore (or Baalbeck, depending on whom you're talking to), where everything does.

No wonder. What a picture we presented, the tiny two-ton flatbed piled high with beds, chairs, boxes of books, a basket of clean laundry, a mattress draped over the roof of the cab, and three guys draped over the whole shebang to make sure none of it bounced off as we made our way the six blocks from Jeanne d'Arc to Commodore—from a street dominated by the university into this more residential and politically charged neighborhood.

Actually, only two guys remained on the truck bed, after Yussuf almost toppled off, and Hisham told him to clamber down and grab the driver's-side window for the last four blocks. In and of itself, this would pose no problems, but cars in Beirut often squeeze tightly together to keep others from scooting in, so Yussuf had to suck it up and in as much as he could several times as Hisham made sure not to lose his place to some little Renault cutting in from a side street.

This little journey was after we'd lugged our four rooms' worth of furniture and personal belongings down five flights of stairs because, of course, the power was out in Hamra.

But we got here. Everything got unloaded. Most of it got unpacked.

And now we're settled in, Buffy working a crossword puzzle downloaded from the Internet, and me, having graded a stack of papers and tired of *Genghis Khan and the Making of the Modern World*, thinking about last week's events and our new apartment.

This apartment—or this apartment building, at any rate—evokes a pretty powerful memory.

One afternoon when I worked here in 2007, I ran into Andrea, the ACS librarian, on the way home from school. She invited me over for a glass of wine.

As we approached her building—the Adel Building; now our building—I thought it seemed familiar.

The closer we got, the surer I became.

Yup. This was it.

CHAPTER 3

Let me go back.

It was 1957. I was in the first month of my seventh grade year. It should've been my sixth grade year, but when we arrived in Beirut the principal told my mother that sixth grade was full. Did she want to put me in fifth or seventh?

Seventh. Seventh would be fine.

So there I was, a little boy still wanting to play cowboys and Indians, amid a bunch of kids experiencing just enough new hormones to keep them reaching for their comb every five or ten minutes, preferring talking to members of the opposite sex to poking them.

OK. I'd do my best, I figured.

One night the phone rang. My mother answered.

"It's for you, Nick."

For me? I don't get phone calls in Beirut. Hell, I hadn't gotten phone calls in Bethesda. Phone calls are for grownups.

"Hello?"

"Hi, Nick? This is Priscilla."

"Priscilla?"

"Yes. Priscilla Thayer from school."

"Oh. Hi."

"Nick, what are you wearing right now?

Oh, jeez, what kind of question is this? And how do I answer it? You don't say words like "pajamas" to a girl. You don't even admit that you wear pajamas to a girl. You don't even acknowledge the existence of pajamas to a girl.

"Umm." Long pause. "I'm ready for bed."

"But what are you wearing?"

"Ummm. I'll be going to bed soon."

This back-and-forth went on for a while. I finally cracked.

"I'm in my pajamas," I said, shamefaced, shame-hearted.

"Good. I'm having a come-as-you-are-party next Saturday. You'll wear your pajamas. OK?"

Oh god.

"OK."

"Bye. See you at school."

"Bye."

So Saturday night my mother called a taxi and gave the driver the name of the building, and we meandered around Hamra as he tried to pin down the building. The Adel Building.

So I came to my first boy-girl party here. In this very building.

If its significance was only that it was my first party, I'm not sure I'd have remembered it so vividly. But there was more.

Arriving at the party, I was comforted. Priscilla had waited to make her phone calls until pretty much everybody was in their nighttime attire. The boys were all standing around in our little striped suits and the girls in ankle-length and very modest night gowns.

OK, I thought, I could do this. Everybody looked equally dumb.

Uh-oh. After a few minutes, everybody disappeared. Boys went into one bedroom, girls into another.

"Where are they going?" I asked somebody, probably Priscilla's mom.

"Oh, they're going to change. Didn't you bring your regular clothes?"

Nope.

I spent the rest of the evening learning to jitterbug, to sip punch between dances, to chat about whatever you're supposed to chat about when you're a pre-teen in Beirut. But I was doing all these things in my pajamas, while everybody else was dressed normally, the boys wearing khaki pants with little buckles at the back, button-down shirts, and cardigan sweaters, the girls in skirts and petticoats and sleeveless blouses. As I recall, the girls took pity on me, paying me a bit more attention than my looks or my personality merited.

At any rate, our new apartment is a three-bedroom one, on the same side of the building as Priscilla's. When I step onto the balcony, I look down on the same street that I looked down on when I asked Gail Chandler how she liked our French teacher, Mrs. Parker.

Woo. That's a full circle, no?

* * *

CHAPTER 3

There's no milk anywhere. No milk on the cluttered shelves of cluttered little corner markets. None in the big stores like Bou Khalil and Idriss. No milk Monday. Or Tuesday. Or Wednesday.

No Dairyland. No Candia. No liters or half-liters.

Of course, having milk in Beirut was new, given that the closest thing we had years ago was a wretched powdered milk. There was a brief period when we did drink fresh milk. It was toward the end of our stay, probably 1961, when my mother announced that a new dairy had opened, one that was regularly pasteurizing its product. The only problem was that it couldn't get a license—the bureaucrats' assumption being perhaps that the company would have an unfair advantage over the other producers, the ones with *wasta*, the Lebanese term for influence—so we'd have to buy it, and the wonderful ice cream products that it also produced, through the black market. For some months unmarked containers of milk were regularly smuggled to our door. No more Klim.

There's pasteurized milk everywhere in Beirut these days. I wonder if that clandestine company is among those we find on the shelves.

But there was no milk anywhere last week.

One afternoon, having struck out again at Bou Khalil, I decided to take a circuitous route home, one that would allow me to hit as many small markets as I could, hoping to come upon somebody hoarding a small stash.

No milk at the first shop, but a garrulous shopkeeper explained why he hadn't received any.

"The price is going up, so they're holding it back until it's been decided."

"How long will that be?"

"A few days."

Makes sense. Fair enough.

No luck at the few other markets I stopped at, so I gave up for the evening.

After school the next day I headed in the opposite direction. No milk at Idriss yet, so I tried my dipping-in-along-the-way-home tactic again.

One shop had no fresh milk but did have a few boxes of irradiated milk, the kind that'll keep for a few months until you open it.

"The problem," the shopkeeper told me, "is Saudi Arabia and Egypt. Lebanon has no milk. It comes from those countries and is bottled here."

"How long will it be before it starts to come again?"

"One or two months."

"One or two months?"

"Maybe more."

Uh-oh.

I bought several liters of the irradiated stuff and went home.

Over the next few days I dropped into every store I passed. Still no milk.

Finally, Petit Marché across the street from our apartment had milk. Not just a lonely container or two, but a shelf full: *écremé, demi-écremé*, and high test, both Dairyland and Candia.

"So why was there no milk?" I asked the clerk.

"It was in France. It was worldwide. There was no milk anywhere. Not even any irradiated milk from Europe."

"Why do we have milk now?"

He shrugged. "It was only one day, anyway."

Huh?

I paid. I had milk, *alhamdillah*.

* * *

All it takes is a day of not checking the news and you find yourself really out of the loop.

Oh, I don't mean about obvious stuff like the stock market plummeting—once you see it heading steadily down from eleven thousand you can figure that it's gonna drop below nine thousand before it gets any better, if then. And once you hear that Iceland's banks are taking their hits, you can figure that this financial mess is taking its toll just about everywhere.

I'm talking about closer to home. To my home.

At the end of September we got another Warden Message from the embassy. Well, some people got it, and one of them forwarded it to me. When I e-mailed the embassy to ask why I hadn't gotten it, I was told that I was on their list and they were surprised that I hadn't received the message. "Please," I replied, "make sure I'm on the right list."

Anyway, the message warned Americans to be careful:

> The US Embassy is concerned about the potential for groups or individuals to exploit the end of the holy month of Ramadan to undertake violent actions targeting Americans. US citizens in Lebanon are reminded to maintain a high level of vigilance and to take appropriate steps to increase their security awareness.
>
> The period of highest concern is the first half of October. In light of this concern, the Embassy is reviewing its own security.
>
> The Embassy strongly urges Americans residing in Lebanon to review their planned movements and to remain vigilant during this time. American citizens should also carefully assess the need to visit popular gathering spots or other public places where large numbers of people are present.

It went on to suggest that Americans who didn't have to come to Lebanon shouldn't, but that's boilerplate.

OK. I'd keep my eyes open.

But I didn't. I don't mean to say that I was snatched by hooded jihadis pouncing from a dark alley where Rue Makdissi runs into Abdul Azzis. I mean I just stopped paying attention to the news. I dropped my guard.

Tuesday morning I walked to school, checked e-mail, greeted kids and colleagues, and headed to the Café Vendome on the Corniche to get the $1.30 double espresso that would rev me up for the morning's work.

Usually the younger of two women is on duty first thing in the morning. This time it was the older woman, the one who insists I shouldn't bother learning Arabic and should just stick with English.

Usually I approach along the sidewalk and one or the other walks toward the coffee-making apparatus beneath the awning and starts stuffing the espresso filter as soon as she sees me. Not today.

"Come! Come!" she beckoned, walking into the café, furtively scanning the street and sidewalk.

I followed.

"Do not go into the streets. Stay off the streets. It is dangerous."

"What? What happened?"

"They took two Americans. The dogs took two Americans hostage. Stay away from the streets. They are worse than dogs."

But that's all she knew.

Coffee in hand, I hustled back to school to check the news on the Internet.

It turned out that just about the time the embassy was issuing its warning, a couple of American journalists had disappeared from Beirut.

Initial reports—the ones my café-friend had heard—were that they'd been staying in the Hamra district, where I live. The reports read as though the two had, in fact, been snatched from a dark alley just off Makdissi.

Reading this, I tried to figure out how one protects oneself if there are hooded guys lurking in alleyways looking for guys who look like me. So they can grab me and...

And what?

Maybe that's the worst part. The "and what?"

Maybe that's the part that grinds you to a halt as a wave of something vaguely akin to fear surges through every part of your being.

But it's not fear.

Fear is clear. Skin prickles. Hair bristles. Everything you look at comes into sharp focus. Your breath runs shallow, rapid.

Staring at the computer screen contemplating whatever it is you're forced to contemplate by the news you've just read, wondering how to walk home safely, what to tell your wife when she comes back from Cyprus and how to keep her safe (and how to apologize for bringing her here in the first place), what it'd be like to hole up in your apartment till you got an all-clear...then realizing that you're overreacting.

But how much are you overreacting? And how would you know that?

And then realizing that it's almost time for class. So you log off, shut down, and flip through your papers to consider how you'll approach the two readings about Justinian the students compared for homework last night.

The news trickled in over the next few days.

The reporters had come to Beirut from Jordan, where they worked for *Jordan Times*. They'd come for a holiday.

The next reports indicated that they'd taken a bus north—to Jbeil or even all the way to Tripoli, perhaps. The same bus Buffy and I had taken? Charis and I? The same bus I had recommended to Abbie just a few days ago. "Hey, don't spend fifty dollars getting there when you can do it for less than a dollar, three if you want the fancy bus with the Arabic action movie playing on the screen above the driver."

What about the report that they'd missed an appointment with a reporter from Reuters, or was it the *Times*? Not much comfort in either case. But at least I could still walk down Rue Makdissi.

On Thursday we learned that the journalists were in a Syrian jail and had been there for a few days.

A Syrian jail?

"Yes," a colleague at work told me. "The Syrians say they were trying to sneak into Syria illegally."

"Do you believe that?"

"I cannot believe that Lebanon is taking hostages again. That would be too much, too bad for my country. I just hope that it was this, that the problem is with Syria, not with Lebanon. *Nshallah* they just made a mistake."

Reports followed that they had arranged an interview with the leader of one of the feuding factions in Tripoli. Other reports indicated that they had wanted to see the Syrian troops settling in on the northern border.

Finally the report came that they'd been released.

Finally a report from them.

> [Reporter] Luck said the two had hired a taxi driver to take them from Lebanon to Syria. But instead of driving to an official border crossing where they expected to get an entry visa for Syria, the driver went off the main road, then "locked the doors" and demanded their money.
>
> Luck, of Oak Park, Illinois, said they refused to give the cab driver anything.
>
> As they drove on, a military car showed up and pulled the taxi over, then moved the Americans and their luggage into their vehicle, Luck

> recounted. "We did not know we were in Syria until we saw a sign for Al Hosn Castle after twenty minutes of driving." He said they remained in the Syrian jail for eight days. Syria's Foreign Minister said they were detained Thursday, a day after the U.S. Embassy put out an alert that they were missing.

Questions remained. Surely they knew that Americans can't get into Syria without arranging a visa before arriving at the border. Surely they knew that it wasn't wise for unauthorized journalists to be snooping near the military bases along the border. Surely they knew....

But they were safe.

A greedy taxi driver had just tried to shake them down. Then they'd come upon some soldiers in a country where didn't belong. And then, and then.

So we're safe.

Nobody's any more likely to drag me off Rue Makdissi than they were a week ago, a year ago. The guys driving the bus to Jbeil and the passengers you ride with are just as likely to help you get where you want to go as they were last year.

Lessons? Nothing new, I suppose. Oh, right. If we want to leave the city, go see if Moussa's still hanging out over on Sadat, in front of Smith's grocery store. A couple of years ago he drove us to Zahle over in the Bekaa and back for fifty dollars. It'll probably cost a bit more, since prices for everything have gone up since then. Even for milk.

But maybe when he brings us home he'll open his trunk again and hand us bags of fresh apples and zucchini like he did last time, fruits and vegetables he'd bought cheaply in the fertile Bekaa while he waited for us to finish our lunches above the little brook that burbles down the mountainside into the Litani River. The Litani that breaks westward through the mountains to flow to the Mediterranean just north of Tyre. The Litani that Israel used to demarcate the northern reach of its incursion into Lebanon back in the '80s.

CHAPTER 4

Juxtapositions

"What's happening in Tripoli? Is Lebanon OK?" my brother asked as soon as he heard my voice on the line. He sounded a bit frantic.

"What're you talking about, Richard?"

"In the news. All the violence in Tripoli. Rioting, I think."

"Gee, not for a long time. Nothing for a few weeks, Rich." My Internet was open. I clicked on Ya Libnan, then on Naharnet, then Al Jazeera. "Nothing new. I'm not sure what you mean. What're we missing?"

"It was in the paper, about what's going on in Tripoli."

"Well, it's been quiet for a while. I wonder what you were reading." I paused. "How's the pacemaker working out?"

A few days later, I boarded a Cyprus Air flight for Larnaca, Cyprus. I had to leave Lebanon for a few days so that, upon my return, I could be issued a residency permit and a work visa.

* * *

I've discovered that the only way to begin to understand anything is by juxtaposing it with something incongruous, something with which it seems to have no affinity.

To wit. I've almost finished Judith Palmer Harik's *Hizbollah: The Changing Face of Terrorism*. Harik teaches at AUB, just down the road from ACS. She's been paying attention.

The guy who loaned me the book is the one who recommended ignoring the local news. "It'll just frustrate you," he told me.

I'm still not very good at following his advice. After all, if I don't know there's been shooting in the southern part of the city, maybe I'll make bad decisions about where I walk. That's what really puzzled me about Richard's concern—I've been paying attention; what had I missed?

I don't seem to have this problem regarding news about the US, especially these days. Oh, I'm pretty clear on whether the Dow's heading up or down (and the Nikkei, and all the rest of the stock exchanges, whose workings I only slightly understand), and I paid enough attention to the recent presidential debates to know that McCain recently lit into Obama's friends and acquaintances.

But mostly I get my US news more indirectly. I know, for example, that Richard's partner Mikki may have to close his new hair salon if business doesn't pick up. I know that enrollment's down at Springside Academy in Philadelphia because the head of the ACS French Department, who used to work at Springside, tells me that parents who were counting on cashing in stock options to pay their tuition have seen their stock options vanish into nothingness. I know that a gay Republican acquaintance who can't see the contradictions between his lifestyle and his politics also hasn't figured out that Democrats got the idea to personally attack their opponents from the Republicans.

But that's about the extent of my current knowledge about American politics. I have no idea if Virginia, where we still own a house, has begun to face up to how many billions of dollars it'll take to fix its roads and that these dollars will have to be raised as taxes or how California, where I was born and where my sister lives, plans to deal with its monster deficit.

In short, I know a lot more about Lebanon's politics than I do about America's.

I knew I'd have lots of downtime during my three days in Larnaca. Maybe I'd take my wife's advice and head out for some of the amazing Greek and Roman ruins on the western end of the island. Or maybe I'd take a bus to Nicosia and wander aimlessly about the capital. Or maybe I'd just hang out here, visiting some churches and ruins in Larnaca itself, swimming in the Mediterranean at the beach right across the busy, palm-lined street.

Yeah. That's probably what I'd do.

Probably I'd walk and explore, stop for a coffee from time to time, and read *Hizbollah*.

After all, it promises such marvelous juxtaposition.

The Sun Hall Hotel's sidewalk café is flanked by another two dozen sidewalk cafés. I could pick up a couple of large pizzas, some garlic bread, and chicken wings at Pizza Hut for €34.95 almost $50—enough, the colorful poster tells me, to feed six people.

Or, a little closer, at Café Evento, for ten euros I could order a lightly lemony pastry drizzled with mocha sauce and garnished with a mint leaf. Sandwiches and kebabs, burgers and pasta. It's all here.

I stick with the Sun Hall Café.

A slim, dark-haired mother pushing a stroller passes, her white flounced skirt rippling in the light breeze. A pale-skinned young couple in shorts and sandals walks by, holding hands—he has a crew cut; she wears a ponytail. At one nearby table a heavyset, middle-aged Greek woman holds forth to a group of friends. Her gold bracelets jangle emphatically as she waggles her finger at a wryly smiling, silver-haired man. The matron's golden hair holds its wave perfectly as she leans back, bursting with laughter. Next to them are three very dark African men and a woman. One of the men wears a black baseball cap that reads "FBI." The woman—her lime-green top dropped from one shoulder—takes the ringing cell phone from her seat-mate.

It's late afternoon. The beach across the way is emptying. Shiny tour buses pull up to drop off their charges. The tourists—exhausted from a day of Corinthian columns and Byzantine relics—head to their rooms for a rest and a shower. In an hour or two all these cafés will fill, first with holiday-makers looking for a glass of beer or wine, then, long after the sun's gone down, with hungry diners.

Light spackles of cloud pass overhead. Palm fronds ripple in the breeze. The sea is calm. I open *Hizbollah*, picking up on what Speaker Nabih Berri has to say about Israel's use of "rumor mongering" to chip away at Hizbollah's credibility. He writes, "Despite its use of massive force against Palestinian citizens, Israel still needs to promote its image as a small country besieged by Arab terrorist hoards."

At the table next to the Africans, Gramma, Grandpa, and little Andreas have settled in. Andreas begins to wander from table to table. The boy is called back and quieted briefly by the bowl of ice cream as only a three-year-old can be. But then he's off again, roaming around the restaurant, clacking each little wooden table-number block against the glass table-top. Gramma stops him. He finds another. Then he zips off to chase some pigeons. Then he comes back to clack more tabletops. Grandpa spends most of his time watching for Mama and Papa. Will they ever show up?

In *Hizbollah*, I learn that "Israeli General Schlomo Gazit, former commander of military intelligence...observed that Hizbollah did observe 'the rules of the game' for a long period. They refrained from shelling Israeli territory and from infiltration...[only after Israeli airstrikes in Lebanon] did Hizbollah retaliate by shelling some Israeli localities—with no casualties."

The young Africans have left. Grandpa has called for the bill—Andreas's parents still haven't arrived. A tour bus pulls up, disgorging Spaniards. The sun's gone down.

I look up from my book, over the sea. A couple of hundred miles to the southeast—just beyond the horizon that's just beyond the blue-and-white sunbeds and umbrellas—scattered throughout Lebanon, people are plotting. Smart people who know how the world works, who know a lot more about the likes of George Bush than he knows about the likes of them. People who understand nuance and subtlety. Survivors.

I turn back to my book.

* * *

I'd never done anything like that before.

Hell, I'd never even thought of doing anything like that before.

But standing in front of that marble stele capped with gently arcing leaves I suddenly found my hand reaching out toward the stele, hesitating a few centimeters from the surface, and then touching that twenty-five hundred-year-old stone.

This stone was sculpted by some long-long-dead craftsman who never imagined I'd stand here in this little museum, awed by his still-vibrant handiwork. And I never imagined that I'd violate the canons that govern these institutions that no one had even thought of when the sculptor tapped his chisel, finding the grain, raining bits of marble onto the floor of some long-disappeared workshop.

I ran my fingertips along the curve of each leaf he had drawn from the stone. Encouraged, I dropped my fingers to the bust of the long-dead young Greek he had carved below the leaves. I felt the smooth contours of his eyes and eyelids, his nose, his lush mouth.

The stone was cold.

The face was familiar.

This young man probably lived just down the road in a mid-sized house in Kition, the three thousand-year-old city that stood just to the north of downtown Larnaca, its partially excavated ruins now surrounded by modest suburban homes. Theirpatios, probably like the young man's, cooled by the shade of grape arbors, their western windows, like his, shuttered against the glare of the sinking sun.

He probably lived not far from the sculptor he modeled for.

That's probably why I felt impelled to touch these stones, then to run my fingers over the thin Phoenician letters carved into a small memorial, letters explaining the lineage of the person who had commissioned it, to reach into a waist-high amphora, feeling the inner ridges of the vessel's wide lip, leaning over to look for stains from the gallons of wine or olive oil it once held.

Maybe I felt so emboldened to try to feel what someone else had felt as he shaped a vase or carved a lip or chiseled a letter because I knew that the person who had done these things had done them so close to where I stood.

Millennia ago he too must have run his fingers over the face as he sculpted it, standing, perhaps, where I stood. Standing alone in the long hall of Larnaca's Archeological Museum, I tried to touch the person who had touched these stones, this pottery.

But there was more to consider, to marvel at.

Gazing at the ten-thousand-year-old bone sewing needles and stone ax heads unearthed from the Neolithic Village just up the hill from Kition, you wonder how they got here. Not the items. The people, all those years before the Phoenicians had set out to do business with anybody who had business to be done, before Odysseus might've dropped anchor here, looking for Lotus-eaters, before the Egyptians sailed for Punt, and before the Gilgamesh author recounted his version of the flood myth.

Who came here, and when, and how, bringing those artifacts, those little crafted items that say humans were here?

The barista at Costa Coffee, a block and a half from the museum where I—alone in the silence of the deep past—caressed the forgotten, is employee number 306. Her name is Kyriaki.

Did I just touch the stone image of the forehead of one of her long-dead ancestors? Did those bronze hoop earrings or that gold necklace so artfully displayed in that long glass case belong to Kyriaki, heirlooms of long-dead intestate ancestors?

Or did her ancestors come later, wielding the jagged bronze spear-points and swords? Is Kyriaki descended from some invading sixth century Assyrian nobleman or fourth century Greek warrior? Did her genes come with the Romans around the time Jesus wandered Palestine? Or with the Ottomans when they toppled what was left of Byzantium? Is some silent part of her heritage quietly celebrating the reconstruction of the Kebir mosque near the sea front, the one the signs tell us is being rebuilt with help from the Libyan government?

And if so, would that ancestor be Sunni or Shia? Would its radicals side with Al Qaeda or with Hizbollah? How would they feel about Larnaca's quiet cosmopolitanism, where gay men come from Lebanon to breathe freely for the weekend and northern European girls bare their breasts on the beach, relishing the bright Mediterranean sun?

It all seems so peaceful here, so tolerant and accepting, seated at this little table at the corner of Grigori Afxentiou and Lordou Vtronos streets. But then you remember the chain link fence surrounding the other mosque just up the street. The one that's been left to crumble since Greek Cypriots won control of the southern part of the island, pushing Turkish Cypriots and Turkish troops into the north. Until you remember that negotiations to re-unite the island are always stymied by the fact that the angry leaders usually refuse to appear in the same room with each other.

* * *

As I often do in Beirut, I wander the streets reading the signs. There's tau-rho-alph. Oh, yeah. *Trapeza.* I remember that from our visit to Greece years ago: "bank." And fa-far-farm. Sure, pharmacy. The sign that begins ph-o-t-o- just above a store window filled with lamps and chandeliers reads "photo-something-or-other": a lighting store. Photo. Light.

What's that one? E-x-omicron. Oh, of course. Exodus. It's where you get out of the supermarket. The entrance is on the other side. The entrance to the hyperagora.

Sure does a number on your worldview to watch a frumpy old couple carrying bags of corn flakes and carrots through the exodus from the agora. To understand that these green-handled shopping carts are lined up in front of the modern descendant of the agora, that mythical place where Socrates expounded on the nature of truth and justice while Plato took notes? And that all the grand majesty of the Moses's biblical exodu*s* boils down to "exit."

Still, young boys rumble their skateboards across the concrete platform, flipping the boards into a spin as they launch into the air, hoping the board will land on its wheels and they'll land on the board. For now most don't. Eventually they will.

Young girls strut by the boys, harboring vague premonitions that the way they strut will one day—long after the boys have learned to land on their boards—devastate the boys, who'll set aside their skateboards, set aside anything the girls might ask them to set aside, just to stand near the girls, breathing the air the girls have breathed, imagining the unimaginable.

Is the correlation a direct one between the amount of flesh modern Western young women are willing to reveal and the fervor with which modern Muslim young women choose to put on the headscarf? My faithful companion, *Hizbollah*, tells me, as I sip a cup of coffee at Costa:

> [The Lebanese political game requires] interaction by moderate members of various communities—individuals who have no difficulty in allying with ideological opposites. In this situation, Hizbollah members feel no constraints at all in going with communists and even cooperate with those implicated in the Sabra/Shatila massacres [by Christians of Muslims, egged on by Israelis]. Acting like everyone else certainly convinces many Lebanese today that Hizbollah is not like to supersede the limits of the system it has work so hard to join, while at the same time broad interactions with Christians appear to have greatly reduced the threatening image with which Hizbollah began (77).

I returned to Beirut, picked up my resident's visa and my work permit, caught a taxi back to the apartment, and decided it was time to figure out what had worried my brother. I googled "Tripoli violence" and came upon several things that had gone on in Tripoli, Libya, before finally finding the brief piece *The New York Times* had decided to run next to a photo it'd probably been sitting on for a while. The caption read:

> The crumbling streets of Lebanon's ancient northern city of Tripoli are starting to resemble a battleground. A string of bombings over the past two months has left at least 20 people dead and scores wounded. Left, a Sunni man shooting in July toward a source of mortar fire by Alawite forces, whose faith is an offshoot of Shiite Islam.

This was not new news. A fairly accurate summary of events and tensions in that part of the country over the past couple of months, ever since the army blasted Fatah al Islam out of the Nahr al Bared Palestinian camp.

However, Beirut is, for the moment, no battleground. Far from it. I called my brother to tell him all was well. Even in Tripoli.

* * *

This, I knew as I stood on the sidewalk listening to the strains of Handel or Haydn pouring from some unknown apartment, is what you've come here for.

Only you don't know it's what y0u've come for until you've found it. You didn't know to look for it, to listen for it. You never quite know what it is.

So all you can do is find it and marvel.

It's late Friday afternoon. You've braved the rush-hour traffic to cross the wide avenue, wanting to get closer to the little mosque that's just begun to broadcast its call to prayer through the tinny loudspeakers set high on the minaret. You stand on the corner, listening. Somewhere inside the unkempt old stone mosque, someone intones, imploring the faithful to remember that there is no god but god and calling them to come humble themselves before this faceless force that has given us the universe with all its grandeur, all its woes.

The call finishes. Which way home? Left or right? They'll both get you there. Reveling in the marvel of randomness, you choose the road to the left, and continue on your way home from the Monot Theatre, where you just picked up your tickets for tomorrow night's performance of *Sharon and My Mother-in-Law*. That's "Sharon" as in Ariel Sharon, not dear little Sharon Jenkins or Sharon Jones. It's a play—adapted from a memoir by Souad Amiry—about life in Ramallah, when that West Bank city was besieged by Israeli soldiers.

I had set out for the theatre to work the kinks out of my mind and body after a hard but satisfying week. I'd selected a major thoroughfare to start with but had soon found myself turning onto narrower and narrower streets, their sidewalks filled with old men playing backgammon and cluttered with shop front displays of shoes, potato chips, toiletries, and all the rest spilling almost into the street. The balconies above were hung with laundry and young men leaned against whatever young men find to lean against. Women—some wearing headscarves, others not—toted plastic grocery bags home, maneuvering around the tightly packed cars and scooters, through the traffic. Posters of Hizbollah's Hassan Nasrallah were pasted to the walls of buildings alongside photos of the bright smiling faces of men martyred in the struggle against Israel.

I bought the tickets and checked out the menu at a Lebanese takeout place around the corner and the Chinese restaurant above that. Then I headed home by another route. Always by another route.

I walked along busy Boulevard Fouad Chehab's narrow sidewalk till I heard the call to prayer begin from the small mosque, and I zigzagged my way through the traffic to listen.

The call ended. I selected my street.

I walked past the German Institute for Oriental Studies, set in the deep shade of a wide old tree behind a high iron fence and past several open-fronted metalworking shops, long strips of aluminum, iron construction rods, and sheets of steel stacked here and there, leaning against the dark walls. I moved out of the Bashour Secteur and into Patriarcat.

The street narrowed, bending to the left not far ahead. A heavyset old woman walked ahead of me, her gray hair hanging disheveled to her shoulders, the white sleeves of her blouse rolled up above her elbows. She wore a calf-length black skirt and white running shoes.

"*Masa al khair*," the middle-aged man walking toward his black Honda Civic said to her, nodding and smiling. Good evening.

"*Masa innoor*." Good evening to you, she replied as she walked on.

"*Allah maak*," he said, setting his key in the car door. God be with you.

"*Allah ya salmak*," she replids. God give you peace.

Who is she? I wonder. Unlike many women of her age in this part of the city, she is not fashionably dressed, her hair tidy and tinted and all the rest. Unlike some others, she is not covered; her hair lies free, and her forearms and ankles are bare.

Is she, perhaps, French, her parents remaining behind after the Versailles Treaty "mandate" was returned to its rightful owners at the end of World War II? Or maybe even white Russian, like "Madame" who tutored me in French after school in the dark living room of her tall-ceilinged old house on the Corniche, a room full of knickknacks and faded photographs, its overstuffed chairs protected by antimacassars?

She turns the corner. A young man in a t-shirt and jeans leans against the first-floor balcony railing of the building straight in front of me.

I wonder what he's doing at this time of day on that balcony. I imagine him wondering what this old white-bearded Euro-American guy in his plaid shirt and khaki slacks is doing wandering his street at dusk.

I slow, noticing several interconnected turn-of-the-century buildings to my left, a single exterior staircase leading upward from the street, then splitting halfway to the first floor, one stairway going left, another going right. The right-side staircase splits again on the way to the second story, one stairway going left and another right, up to the third floor. Tall, narrow, wood-shuttered windows face the street, while the stairways lead to French doors. Floor plants—palms, ficus, and bamboo-like things—are set here and there on the landings.

The two-meter-high wall surrounding the complex is pocked and scarred, violence from the Civil War left unrepaired. Higher up, some of the walls of the buildings also bear these reminders.

I was about to move on when the music came from somewhere amid this complex of stairways, doorways, greenery, and windows. A flute. Then a harp. An eighteenth century piece by one of those composers you'd choose if you were hoping to tinge your evening with wistful serenity.

I stopped, searching for the source of the music. But no window seemed any more likely to open on a room that would produce such a sound than any other.

So I gave up trying to understand anything and just stood, listening to the gentle music some composer hoped might be of interest to this French count or that German baron, might keep the wolf from his family's door for another couple of weeks.

Listening to the gentle music that was interrupted by the br-a-a-a-at of a motor scooter zipping by, loaded with grilled chicken and samosas from nearby Barbar's take-out grill. Somebody's dinner.

Listening to that gentle music, studying the bullet gouges in the wall across the street. Wondering where that woman had lived when those bullets were fired.

Wondering if the young man on the balcony was listening to the music.

Wondering what the old man from the mini-market who'd stepped out to watch me standing there listening to music might be wondering about me.

The little concerto drew toward a close, repeating its theme in that friendly way little pieces like this do when they want to make sure you know they're almost finished.

Then it finished. A voice came on, explaining in French that this was the end of the classical music hour.

I turned from the building and started home again. Two young men stood talking on the balcony now. Neither seemed to notice me. The old man stepped back into his mini-market, comforted, I suppose, that I was on my way.

I wondered briefly where the old woman had gone.

* * *

I'd been quietly dreading this. The irony was just a bit too much to handle: This aging American agnostic was about to teach a bunch of mostly Muslim Lebanese fifteen– and sixteen-year olds about the rise of Islam.

The big day came. My students had read the photocopied readings on "Arabia Before Muhammad" and "Muhammad, Prophet of Islam."

We set to work.

How come it takes me so long to figure anything out?

How come, knowing what I know, I was so surprised to find that most of my charges knew about as much about the roots of their religion as most American teenagers know about the roots of theirs?

Oh, sure, they could translate the call to prayer. And they were familiar with the basics about the five pillars—acknowledging the oneness of god, alms-giving, prayer, fasting during the month of Ramadan, and pilgrimage.

But about those early days in Mecca, about the hostility manifested by the powers that be toward Muhammad, and about the way Christians, Muslims, and Jews initially coexisted in Medina they knew almost nothing.

It turned out to be a very interesting class, defining "animism," mixing geography with theology, and investigating the reasons religious reformers are almost always met with hostility.

Then we took a detour. I had noted a comment in the reading that, "Islam, like Christianity but unlike Judaism, became a world religion with a missionary spirit."

"Hmmm," I thought. "Wonder where we could take that one."

So.

"OK, everybody. There's an interesting paragraph on one ninety-two. If you had read it at all carefully, you'd have written a question mark next to a sentence because there's something there that I know you don't understand. Please find it."

Long silence. Then shoddy guesses, my response to which was to ask if they actually knew what that meant.

Finally, from Rami, "This sentence about 'universal religion with a missionary spirit.' I don't know what that is."

Great. Now let's see what happens.

"Please, everyone, jot in your notebooks what you think a 'universal religion' might be, given what the sentence says."

Long silence as they wrote.

Almost everyone decided that this meant a religion that had spread all over the world. But somebody—I forget who—suggested, tentatively, that it might mean a religion that sees itself as exclusive, as the only true religion, valid for everyone.

Great. Backtrack to a review of the way the Romans didn't much care what you believed just so long as you worshipped in state-approved temples with some regularity and that this would have been the case in Egypt, Assyria, Greece, or any polytheistic society, except perhaps India after the BJP decided that dammit, if Christians and Muslims could be intolerant fundamentalists, so could they (I decided against going down that particular path).

We agreed that followers of a universal religion believe that theirs is the right way and all others are wrong. Paradise/heaven for believers; hellfire and damnation for others. Moreover, you're supposed to get others to believe in your religion.

Yup, said the Muslims in the room, Sunni and Shia. Yup, said the few Maronites, Roman Catholics, and Greek Orthodox (the Druze didn't comment).

Got it?

Got it.

"What about the rest of the sentence? There's one last bit of the sentence. Yeah, Marwan."

"It says Judaism isn't a universal religion."

A word about Israel. While a significant portion of the population of this part of the world has come to accept the idea that Israel will probably continue to exist, most do so grudgingly. From their point of view (and it's hard to argue with) Israel exists because Great Britain promised European Jews a homeland during World War I in exchange for their help financing the war. Then, following the next great war, the Western powers (reluctantly) supported the creation of this Jewish state but without actively protecting the rights of those non-Jews who lived there.

The vast majority of the people in this part of the world do not speak of Israel. They call it "Occupied Palestine." You are not allowed to enter most countries in the Middle East—Lebanon included—with an Israeli visa in your passport.

On a visit to Beirut some years ago, the concierge at the Berkeley House Hotel explained that Gore had been lucky to have lost the presidency.

"Why?"

"Because the Jews would have assassinated him so Lieberman could become president."

So here I was, having realized that my affluent Muslim students were just about as knowledgeable about their religion as my affluent Lutherans, Catholics, and Presbyterians had been about theirs back in the US.

But was I really ready to talk about Jews and Judaism here?

Yup.

Another major surprise.

The students were fascinated.

Now I have to admit I structured the presentation in such a way as to make it fascinating. But that's my job, isn't it?

So after going over some of the basics of Muhammad's teachings, we turned to several pages way back in the textbook I keep for use in the classroom. A unit on early Judaism.

They read, "Thou shalt have no other gods before me."

"That's like 'There is no god but god'!"

They read on.

"And the Torah regulated many aspects of daily life, including personal activities such as marriage and the treatment of women, as well as broader questions such as the punishment of crime."

"Here, Mr. Boke. Wait. I can find it. Here. Here it is. Look, in the other reading on page one ninety-seven it says 'Islamic law, then, permeates all levels of activity, from personal and private concerns to those involving the welfare of the whole state.'"

Paragraph after paragraph. Comparison after comparison.

But I knew what was coming. Ali had already mumbled the words during one of our discussions.

Something about, "Yeah, but they don't act that way."

No, Ali, they don't.

But we don't have time for that right now.

Someday soon I'll have to set the textbook and supplementary readings aside and we'll stop talking about how Mary and Jesus and Moses and Abraham all appear in the Koran, about the split between the Sunni and the Shia, about the gradual retreat of the Byzantine Empire in the face of expansionist Islam.

Someday soon we'll just have to talk about people, won't we? We'll just have to set aside all this history stuff and theology stuff and ask ourselves, "What would it take to make the world a place we could be proud of?"

After that, we'll get back to our studies.

My guess is that the topic will come up about the time we begin to study the crusades. You know, when the Christian jihadists decided to come do their raping and pillaging in this part of the world.

All in the name of God.

Now that—with my nice little German name, fair skin, and affection for all the wonderful things Europe brought to the world—is something really worth dreading.

CHAPTER 5
New Beginnings

How many times over the past eight years have I been asked, "Where are you from?"

How many times have I had wanted to say, "America, and I apologize. I'm sorry for what we've been doing to the world. I'm sorry for the kind of people we seem to have become."

I joked with Kenyan friends who'd just about had it with their own president, Moi Kibaki. I'd offered a trade: "I'll take Kibaki and give you George Bush with Dick Cheney thrown in for good measure."

Lots of laughs, but no takers.

So many people in so many countries had so patiently explained to me that they did not hold America's insane foreign policy against me personally but had then gone on to ask how so powerful a nation could so badly misunderstand the way the world works.

How many times I had wanted to avoid the whole conversation by responding, "I'm Canadian."

I was not alone. Almost to a person, Americans living abroad share these sentiments. There's something about watching your country from a distance that clarifies things, and so much of what had been clarified since 2000 was how ignorantly, brutally, and arrogantly we had stepped into the world and had been stepping into the world for decades. And about how shortsightedly we were treating our own internal problems.

But not today. I have no apologies today.

Not in this little bookstore on a side street half a block from Rue Makdissi on this early November morning.

"So where are you from? The UK?" the young man asked me.

"Nope. I'm American."

I answered without a pause or a glitch, proudly maintaining eye contact through every syllable.

Not because my country's about to fix everything and do everything right or because its leadership will never embarrass me again but because for the first time in eight years the American people have done something we can be proud of. We've done something about the part of our heritage that emphasizes equality, the "of, by, and for the people" part of our heritage. Not the "live free or die" part or the "taxation without representation is tyranny" part or any of those aggressive, in-your-face parts of our heritage.

No. It's the part of America's heritage that starts off with assumptions of human decency and dignity. The parts of our heritage that could, in the long run, truly help make the world a better place.

I told the same story in each of my classes the day after the presidential election. I recounted going to rock and roll concerts in Greenville, South Carolina, in 1956 with my cousin Chuck. We heard The Coasters, Little Richard, Bo Diddly, some of the greats of early rock and roll.

I described how the white people sat downstairs and the black people sat upstairs and how if a black person had come downstairs, the police would have arrested him, as naturally and as legally as if that black person had just held up a liquor store or hit me over the head with a baseball bat.

The students' eyes grew wide. Just as wide as the eyes of my students had grown last year in Williamsburg, Virginia, when—asked whom I would vote for in the upcoming presidential election—I had told the same story.

Because this story of flagrant, institutionalized racism is the story not of America's distant past but of a past I can remember and a past that everyone, black or white, who experienced the American South until the mid-'60s, recalls. Including my cousin Chuck, who, my aunt tells me, retired from working as a public school gym teacher in North Carolina a couple of years ago. This means that Chuck, unabashedly racist as a teenager, had taught the black children of some of those black rock-and-roll-lovers who would've been relegated to the hot, sweaty rafters of Greenville's concert hall decades before.

Oh, there's more, of course, to my newfound pride. At the first "debate" back in 2006, every Democratic candidate, when asked what the first thing he or she would do if elected president, had replied, "Try to mend our relations with the rest of the world."

And maybe the Democrats will actually have the guts to ask American citizens to pay enough taxes to fund some of the services those citizens expect—like unclogged roads and safe bridges and maybe even public transportation to lighten the load on the roads and bridges, to say nothing of health insurance for the uninsured and at least halfway-decent schools for everyone.

Perhaps we can run a foreign policy that will not result in my Lebanese friends being taken aside for questioning by stern-faced security officials when they visit the US. Perhaps people like Hizbollah's Hassan Nasrallah won't have such good reason to feel so much animosity and fear toward the United States.

Throughout the day on Wednesday people waved to me and said, "*Mabrook*, America." Congratulations, America.

To which I responded, "*Mabrook aal aalam*." Congratulations to the world.

* * *

It was Saturday, so I had got time to just goof off. I picked up James Reston, Jr.'s *Warriors of God: Richard the Lionheart and Saladin in the Third Crusade*.

Richard had just left Famagusta, Cyprus, where I spent a holiday with my mother in 1959, and sailed to Acre, just north of Haifa. My mother and I had visited there decades before, taking a round-about route through Syria and Jordan in 1960, visiting the "Holy Land." Richard, however, had come to help newly arrived Phillip of France finish "re-conquering" that port city in 1191.

Here. The subchapter entitled "Spoils."

> It is certainly true that only through the arrival of the overwhelming English and French forces had the city of Acre fallen. But after the city

> was taken, Richard and Phillip proceeded to gather the spoils entirely to themselves with breathtaking high-handedness, as if they felt they and only they had been involved in some heroic enterprise. Blithely the two kings ignored their lesser allies, oblivious to the fact that much of the loot belonged to their own people. They scoffed at the claims of the local barons of the Kingdom of Jerusalem who had lost their property to Saladin four years before, who fought and starved and toiled to preserve a Christian toehold in the Holy Land...not surprisingly, this arrogance evoked considerable resentment. (215)

Breathtaking high-handedness. Blithely ignoring their allies. Scoffing. Arrogance. Considerable resentment.

One can only hope that over the next few years, reading something like this won't send such chills of recognition down my spine.

Wednesday's *Daily Star* headline read: "Yes, He Could: Obama Wins in Landslide," and beneath this, "Despite euphoria, 'The challenges that tomorrow will bring are the greatest in our lifetime.'" The cartoon on the editorial page came from the November 5, *Asharq al-Awsat* (The Middle East). It depicted George W. Bush as a rotten tooth being extracted from a grateful world.

Oh, I'm sure there are those outside the US who'll miss him. These will include my southern Sudanese friends, who correctly acknowledged that Bush was the first American president to pay any attention to that region's fifty-year long civil war. Of course, Bush was also prone to get involved wherever there was oil, of which there is plenty between north and south Sudan, although China's got a pretty sound foothold there now, as it does in many African oilfields. And Bush's taking notice of this region was largely payback for evangelical Christians in the 1990s who had discovered the abuses their cobelievers were suffering from the Islamicizing government of Sudan. I never got around to asking any of my evangelical American acquaintances if they knew that this incredibly syncretic region included many self-identified Christians who had several wives. Oh well.

And I'm sure Vladimir Putin will miss Bush. Imagine, Russian leaders will now have to deal with an American leader whose analysis will more than likely involve a bit more than peeking into an ex-KGB good-ole-boy's soul.

Indeed, Barack Obama is a character of the twenty-first century, not a throwback to the days of TV westerns.

Well, maybe if our foreign policy shifts a bit from cowboy-ism to a recognition that the rest of the world does truly, matter, we might even see a change along the façades of some of Beirut's hotels.

See, almost all the hotels in this part of town regularly fly a few flags out front. So if some Iraqis, Italians or Jordanians are staying at the Embassy Hotel or the Napoleon or Marble Tower, their respective flags will be hung out of respect for the country.

Most of the hotels have several standard flags that never change. Certainly the Lebanese flag, usually the Saudi. Most keep the EU's circle of stars up all the time, and some hang the Union Jack.

But never—not once—have I seen an American flag flapping in the breeze in front of any of the nearby hotels.

Not once. And Lebanon's as pro-Western an Arab Middle Eastern country as you'll find—Hamra's as Westernized a part of this region as there is.

So I'm watching now, hoping to see the stars and stripes hanging in front of the Embassy Hotel. *That* will tell me that things are really getting on track.

* * *

Time to go. Downstairs, out the door, into the narrow street. The men working on the Commodore Suites across the street have started mixing their concrete; saws whir and whine through marble and granite; a generator rumbles.

Left, then right up past the Hariri's heavily guarded six-story residence—some call it their palace—in front of which hangs the black banner with white letters reading, in Arabic "*Al Haqiqa*," and in English, "The Truth," referring to the demand that Rafik Hariri's assassins be brought to justice. A UN commission has been looking into this for some time now and is set to issue a report soon. Will it directly blame Syria, as many assume? What about the four Lebanese generals who are still in jail, awaiting the Tribunal's revelations?

Up, up I walk. Past Lebanese American University, scrambling to take its place alongside the American University of Beirut as one of the country's leading post-secondary institutions.

Up. Up. Past Diab's Home Furnishings and Appliances. The young man in my creative nonfiction class who had stood guard with other young Hariri supporters during the fighting in May lives up here, just behind Home Furnishings, which is owned by a relative.

The terrain flattens, and I walk along a narrow street lined on one side with seventy-five-year-old two– and-three-story buildings laced with filigreed balconies and tall, shuttered windows, set behind wide-spreading magnolia, eucalyptus, and ficus trees.

Brand-new twenty– and thirty-story buildings rise on the other side of the street, cranes lifting bundles of rebar as the hum of machinery is occasionally broken by the rattle-crash of debris shooting through wide blue tubes from the upper floors into dump trucks.

Busy. Busy. Busy. So much building.

We've had three months with nothing but a bit of sectarian shooting in Tripoli, one family firing a few shots at another family in the Bekaa, young Sunni and Shia whose neighborhoods border each other a couple of miles from here in Corniche el Mazraa getting into a ruckus that sent a few of them to the hospital. Wasn't there something else? Oh, yeah, the Druze aide-de-camp whose car was blown up and something in the Ain el Hilweh Palestinian camp in Sidon.

But, all in all, peace.

So the new marble and glass apartment buildings go up. About two million visitors came to Lebanon this year. Many were Lebanese, coming home to see family, and many were visitors from other Arab countries, coming to enjoy Beirut's openness and diversity. There were a few Western tourists—the other day, over by Pigeon Rocks I helped a northern European foursome find their way to the restaurant that'd been recommended to them.

What a difference this political calm makes at ACS. We've not had to cancel school on account of "Political Turmoil" even once this year. The Student Council has not had to conduct a "Safe Sects" campaign, as it did a few years ago when things got pretty touchy between our Sunni and Shia students.

And it's November, so everyone has basically figured out what's going to be going on in their classes. My students understand that I won't be asking them to memorize—"Oh, thank you, sir. Open-book tests will be so much better!!"—and that every time I test them, I'll be asking them to stretch their thinking—"Oh, sir! This is so hard. Can't we just go back to memorizing for multiple choice tests?"

But they know how it works now, pretty much. They know how far they can push me. They know that from time to time the class will be a lot of fun, when their brains get set on fire. They know I don't wait for them to raise their hands and that I might call on any one of them at any moment. They know I expect them to treat what other students say seriously.

They know there's no such thing as a dumb question.

So Ali recently felt free to ask, "Sir, if they're Muslims, why were they fighting each other?"

Ali is an interesting student. He's been pleasantly surprised by how well he's been performing in this class—turns out he's got a good mind, but it's never been called upon to do what it does well, which is to connect this dot on this page with that one way over on the other side of the next page.

I smiled at the question.

We'd been studying the astoundingly rapid spread of Islam from 632, by which time most of the polytheistic/animistic/Christian/Jewish Arabian Peninsula had been overtaken by the new religion, to 750, by which time Islam had spread to India in the east and Spain in the west, only being kept out of France by Charles Martel at the Battle of Tours in 732.

Along the way, however, the empire had begun to fragment, until by 900 there were four major Muslim dynasties governing various parts of these lands, to say nothing of the split (or "schism," as the students insisted on calling it, to connect it with the more or less simultaneous split between the Roman and the Byzantine Christian churches) between the Sunni and the Shia.

Ali's question had come from the heart, not the head.

I doubt he's particularly observant, but comments he has made now and then have made it clear that he feels that same implicit chauvinism about his religion that most of us have about ours, no matter how lapsed we might be.

"Why do you ask the question, Ali?"

"Well, sir, they're Muslim. They all believe the same things. Why would they fight each other?"

"OK. Why?" I turned to the class. "Why would they fight each other?"

"For resources."

"Sure."

"For territory."

"OK."

"For power."

"Yup."

"Because of religious disagreements."

"Yes."

They had run out of possibilities.

"Don't you know?" I asked. "It's something more basic than that. Think about it. Why were Muslims willing to fight other Muslims?"

Silence.

"Oh, my friends. They fought each other because they're people. It seems to be what we do. Eventually every group seems to fragment and turn on itself. Doesn't it? Isn't that what we've been seeing?"

Stunned silence.

"Think about all the history you studied last year and all the stuff we've studied so far this year. Don't we human beings just seem to be prone to fight, for whatever reason?

"Imagine this was a classroom in America and many of you were Christian. What if we were—as we soon will be—studying the European Middle Ages when one Christian kingdom fought another Christian kingdom? What would you have asked?"

Pause.

"We'd have asked why Christians would fight other Christians," Samer said.

"Right. And," I went on, knowing I had to find a spin for this that these young men and women could safely carry out the door with them, something positive to ponder, "we're all hoping that maybe someday we can find a way to keep this part of our humanness from doing what it does. That's our hope, isn't it?"

Nods.

"OK. Let's take a look at the map."

* * *

Sometimes things happen to remind me of why I'm here, teaching this strange, often strained mix of people at the American Community School at Beirut.

Ali's question—and the fact that he felt comfortable asking it, and the fact that it gave me a chance to step far, far from the "curriculum" and talk about the kinds of things that history lets one talk about—reminded me again of why I'm here.

And so did the question a young Southeast Asian student's father asked at the brief conference I had with him and his wife yesterday afternoon.

I'd spoken with them earlier in the year about what seemed to be some anomalies in their daughter's writing. There were some grammatical and syntactic problems I couldn't recognize. I asked if they'd mind if she spent some time with our English as a Second Language specialist.

They were hesitant. Their daughter had always been an A student at the English-language international school she had attended for years. But they agreed, just so long as we didn't do it in such a way that she lost confidence in herself.

The student been able to resolve most of the issues that had concerned me, and now the parents were here for a more general discussion. It was a pleasant enough conversation, though they were still mildly puzzled that this formerly excellent student was now doing only "B" work.

We were about to wrap up our conversation when the father hesitated and then asked, "Do you rank students here?"

"Rank? Oh, you mean will you find out how your daughter compares with other students in her class?"

"Yes."

"Well, let me begin by telling you that I hate grades. I give them, and I understand that they're important. But it usually comes from my gut," (I patted my belly), "not from some mathematical formula. So a 'B' really means 'Hey, this is pretty good!' and an 'A' is 'Wow! Astounding.' When I actually do the formal average, it's just about the same as what my gut—or is it my heart?—had told me."

The parents listened intently, nodding but still puzzled.

The mother interjected, "We have come from a system where everyone was ranked in order of their averages, so this is a little confusing to us. We're accustomed to knowing exactly where our daughter stands among her classmates."

Ah. Now I got it. Not about them, but about us. I didn't know this before they asked these questions.

"Ma'am, this is an American school. I'll admit that there are lots of problems with the American system. But at its heart, the American system is working on a very different premise from the one you described.

"What we do here—when we're doing it right—is we pay attention to the person we're working with, not to the scores that person achieves. When schools like this are doing what they're supposed to be doing, what we care about is the human being, the whole thing, and we're mainly trying to help that human being become the best it can become, step by step."

I stopped. They looked at me. Puzzled? Sure. Convinced? Probably not. Willing to think about what I had said? Undoubtedly.

The father thanked me and offered his hand. I shook hands with him and his wife. They left.

Probably on the way to their car, they agreed that I had their daughter's best interests at heart, however I did my business. No lasting harm, they probably agreed, would be done.

The conversation was very helpful to me, though.

I'm not sure I'm any closer to understanding what being an American means. But I'm a bit clearer about what I'm supposed to be doing here and why it matters that I'm teaching at this "American" school.

Yes, this is a good place to be, good work to be doing.

* * *

Some things stay the same.

Well, relatively the same. For a little while, at least.

Take the Manara Palace Café. Set on the rocky westernmost point of the city, just below the lighthouse (*manara* in Arabic), it's an amazing little restaurant.

We often stop by for thick Turkish coffee on a weekend morning. But you have to get there early—the little playground off to the side makes it a favorite for young families.

That and the fact that it sits less than two meters above sea level.

So when Buffy and I wandered into the sunset along the Corniche for a bite to eat before the seven o'clock performance of *Lend Me a Tenor* back at the high school, we knew, watching the surf crash against the rocks, we'd be in for a treat.

Indeed, the waves smacked at the rocks, the spray scattered in the light breeze, and the whole thing whooshed and grumbled and made all those other wonderful noises that the world makes when it tosses piles of water against big lumps of limestone. We ate our *mutabal*, tabbouleh, and hummus, along with the side of pickled beets, cucumbers, peppers, and cauliflower that comes as routinely as a basket of bread and a bowl of butter in an American restaurant.

It's hard to get up from a meal like this and from watching people watching the water slap against the land.

The Manara Palace is like that. You just want to sit there. Everybody seems to feel this way, and the restaurant seems to understand this. Sometimes it'll take half an hour for a simple meal to make it to your table. Sometimes you'll have to get up to track down the waiter who's ensconced himself on the jam-packed terrace at the far end of the restaurant out at the tip of the peninsula.

But this evening all went relatively smoothly, so we watched, ate, and chatted and then walked back to school, where an intricately timed and broadly staged production wrapped up a wonderful evening.

Buffy rode home with Rima and her sister. I couldn't resist another evening walk along the sea and then up to Rue Hamra, where I engaged a young Lebanese man wearing a University of California-Berkeley sweatshirt and his girlfriend in brief conversation (they'd graduated three years ago and then come home to look for work), past the sushi place, Nando's peri-peri restaurant, the vegetable stand, and home.

All these strange conversations keep popping up. How do these conversations unfold, anyway?

Well, it starts when I discover that I can get a double espresso at from the sidewalk operation in front of Le Vendome just down the street from the school, on the landward side of the Corniche. Two thousand Lebanese lira. A dollar thirty. Hard to pass up, no?

So I stop by before school some mornings, or during a free period.

The young woman who serves up the coffee tells me she's hoping to go to the US soon. Sure. So is everybody. No, really. Turns out her husband is there now, and her visa's in the works. OK. Maybe.

Also turns out her husband's a writer.

"Oh, what does he write?"

"I'll bring you one of his books."

"OK."

A few days later, after handing me my coffee, she tells me to come with her and heads for her parked car. Opens the back door. Reaches in. Takes out a copy of *Globalization and the Manufacture of Transient Events* by Bilal Khbeiz.

Hey, this is really cool. The left-to-right part is in English, and the right-to-left is in Arabic, so I can practice my Arabic with it.

Cooler. Listen to the beginning of the first chapter, "The Body Manufactured with Letters":

> The practice of modern living is toilsome. It requires spending a substantial part of what is perhaps a short existence in preparation before commencing it. This living requires nothing short of long and unavoidably exhausting years in educating the mind and acquiring a variety of techniques for caring and hiding, whilst in contact with others, the persistent and cumbersome traces of the body. According to G. Canguilhem, a proper, healthy and therefore viable body is a silent body (11).

Hot damn! Poststructuralism

Which means that, unlike the biography of Genghis Khan I finished a couple of weeks ago, the one of Richard the Lionhearted and Saladin I'm about to finish, and the *Histoire de Beyrouth* I'm plodding through (French dictionary close at hand), *Globalization and the Manufacture* will wander hither and yon, and I'll be allowed to—expected to—take my own detours as I manufacture whatever meaning I feel like manufacturing from the meanings Khbeiz has been messing around with.

I make my way through the sixty-nine-page book over the next few days, frequently turning to the other end of the book to see how one would actually say in Arabic, for example, "Today's Holland is punctuated with natural preserves, which figure as the emblems of devoted ecologists." Turns out the translation's pretty loose, but it's a lot of fun to try to put together those pieces of the puzzle I am able to puzzle out, anyway.

Monday morning. Just enough time to scoot down for a coffee.

"*Sabah al khair.* How're you today?"

"*Sabah innoor.* Fine. You?"

"Great. Could I have a double espresso, please?"

"*Akeed*."

"I really enjoyed that book by your husband."

"You read it?"

"Yeah. Lots of interesting thoughts."

"Would you like another book?"

Another book? "Sure."

And so the next day she handed me a copy of *Tragedy in a Moment of Vision*, which is about Lebanon. Same arrangement with the languages. Same PoMo approach to the relationship between what the author's put together and what I get to do with it.

Over the next few weeks, while my coffee's hissing from the two spouts into the little brown plastic cup, we talk about her husband. He used to write for the *Al Nahar* newspaper here and is trying to figure out what to do with himself next in the US. He didn't finish college but has a lot of credits from AUB.

We talk about his need for formal training and how academia's just about the only place anybody's interested in letting you mess with your mind the way he wants to mess with his. We get more specific about subjects he might study, places he might apply.

Then, one day, as she hands me my coffee, "Well, we're leaving tomorrow."

Oh, no. So that's where all these conversations were taking me.

"You're really going?"

"Yeah. We've already sold most of the equipment."

What do I say? "Don't go"? "I've really enjoyed talking about your husband's career"? "I was hoping for more books"? "This is the cheapest espresso in the universe"?

"Well, good luck."

"Thanks."

Le Vendome's all closed up now. I can go next door and get a Turkish coffee for about the same price, with about the same zip.

But it's not the same. Is it?

* * *

Directly across the street from our third-floor apartment, the neo-neo-classical ten stories of the Commodore Suites make their way toward completion, day by day. The eleven columns that grace the veranda of the top floor await their cornices, and then the roofing. The rust-proofed balcony filigree is being painted black. Beige sandstone tiles are cut, then mortared into place on the exterior walls.

A block past the Suites, on Rue Hamra, I can see the grey stone of the twenty-story Crowne Plaza Hotel. There's a shopping mall on the lower floors where you can get a hamburger and fries at the Roadster Diner or Schezuan fare at Noodles.

But mornings on my balcony begin with something simpler than all this. The sun rises. I get up, make my coffee, choose a book, and settle into a white plastic chair.

A rooster crows from the roof of a run-down three-story French Mandate-period house between the Crown Plaza and the Commodore Suites. Another rooster answers it from somewhere to the right, maybe from the abandoned upper floors of the Maktabi building.

Roosters.

In the heart of the city.

I think I'll read Eliot today. It's always a bit frightening to consider reading Eliot. For all his flaws, he knew so much and knew so well how to say much about what he knew. Reading most of what he wrote, I am humbled.

But we crave that humbling, don't we? Isn't that craving what I saw when I stepped into the Mohammed al Amine mosque downtown a few days ago? It's one of the mosques that Hariri funded before his assassination. Modeled on Istanbul's Grand Mosque, it's said to be the largest in Lebanon.

When I first visited Beirut in 2000, nothing stood at this building lot just off Martyrs' Square, just tall fences postered with huge architects' drawings of what the mosque would look like surrounded the several-acre site that abutted St. George's Maronite cathedral to the south and, to the northwest, the second-century CE Roman ruins that were unearthed during the reconstruction after the civil war. On the far side of the ruins stand the Greek Orthodox St. George's church and Ansour Assaf mosque.

When I brought Buffy to Beirut in 2004, construction on the new mosque was well under way.

And when I came to teach here in 2007, it was at the finishing-touches stage. However, with Hizbollah's tent city right next door and the prime minister holed up in the Grand Serail just up the hill, the new structure was surrounded by rolls of razor wire, an occasional armored personnel carrier, and plenty of soldiers to protect this Sunni building from Shia animosity.

Now it's finished, and it is indeed a grand building, the four sleek minarets surrounding its sky-blue dome towering tall and thin.

The mosque is open now, the razor wire and weaponry removed, the soldiers mostly gone. But I'd not yet visited.

Well, this Saturday was as good a day as any. I'd arrived downtown after the Independence Day celebrations were finished, though I didn't learn that till later, thinking, on reaching the empty streets and reviewing stand, that I'd come too early.

The mosque is so different from the Capuchin Church I'd visited a few days before. That church, like most Christian churches, has a focal point: a crucifix hanging at the far end of the long, narrow chapel. Rows of seats face the crucifix. The pulpit stands a bit off-center, near the focal point, not obstructing it.

Mosques are different. There is no main thing to look at, only an open, wide expanse. A grand expanse of space beneath the high ceiling curving up toward a heaven. A short stairway for the imam to mount, from which to give his sermon.

But mainly space. Open space, surrounded on all side by calligraphy: "Allah," "Mohammed," and verses from the Koran.

There is, of course, a focal point, but it's outside the mosque, far away. It's a focal point on the planet, in the universe: Mecca. The holy center of all things, not the specific holy center of this building.

So all there is to do here is what people do when they come here. Find a spot, any spot on the floor since there are no pews—and no turning round to chat with neighbors before the sermon begins. Stand. Center yourself. Recite. Kneel. Pray. Prostrate yourself against the earth. Stay very still. Rise. Stand. Again. Again. Humble yourself.

Submission—that's what Islam means.

Humility in the face of the magnificent power that is everything.

I stopped by the mosque and took off my shoes. I entered, sat, and contemplated things like this for a timeless while. Then I left and walked through other parts of the city still under reconstruction, toward the Corniche, and back to school for another volleyball game. The ACS girls won that round, against Sacre Famille too.

Sunday begins, as every day begins, with roosters.

And, this Sunday, with daring to read Eliot.

Start from the beginning. "The Lovesong of J. Alfred Prufrock."

Oh, it's all so familiar. Talking of Michelangelo. That is not it. That is not what I meant at all. So how should I presume? And so on. All the familiar lines, all the familiar images, the insights into what it meant, indeed what it means to live in this world that is still Eliot's world, the world my coffee-vendor's husband Bilal Khbeiz tells us remains—nearly a century after Eliot helped us understand this fact—dominated by the "manufacture of transient events."

But amid these familiar sounds—the roosters, soldiers chatting in their sentry box on the street corner, another Air France flight passing almost directly overhead—I read another familiar line and pause.

Shall I say, I have gone at dusk through narrow streets

And watched the smoke that rises from the pipes
Of lonely men in shirt sleeves, leaning out of windows?

I think of the narrow Beirut streets I walk, morning and evening. I think of the old men I pass, wizened old men, their eyes milky with cataracts, a grey stubble on their chins: the street vendor who sprinkled oregano in the round of kaak bread I bought on the way to Saturday's volleyball game, the vegetable seller just around the corner, the grandfather who sits in front of the mini-market run by his children and grandchildren, halfway up the hill from the Bain Militaire.

They are, I understand as I sit on the Sunday-morning balcony, not lonely.

"*Sabah al khair*," the middle-aged man in a sweat suit says to the *kaak*-seller.

"*Sabah innoor. Keefek?*" Good morning to you. How are you?

"*Hamdillah. Keefek enta?*" Fine. And you?

"*Hamdillah.*"

And then the conversation got too complicated for me, but I know the vendor told the other man to choose the bread he wanted, which he did, and then went on to ask the old man to dollop a bit more of the oregano mixture into the center of the bread. The old man told him that was the best way and spooned scoop after scoop into the hole he'd broken in the pocket of the bread, chattering on, while his customer chattered back.

Finally he handed him the bread.

"*Allah maak*," the old man said. God be with you.

"*Allah ya salmak*," the other replied, touching him on the shoulder as he walked away, eating his *kaak*. God give you peace.

No, I don't think there are many lonely men in shirtsleeves here. Crazy as this place is, its cardinal flaw is not the alienation of individual from individual.

I don't think there are many Lebanese who would tell us, as our South African neighbors did the other day, that when they go home to Johannesburg their siblings make no effort to bring the young cousins together. I don't think there are many Lebanese who would, like I did, have to explain that I didn't meet my grandmother until I was twenty-two and that I have cousins, nieces, and nephews whom I've never met.

There's a flipside to this, of course. Lebanon's problems can, to a great extent, be attributed to the fact that most people's identities are bound up tightly with small groups of people sharing a common religion and sense of common blood.

But, watching the *kaak* vendor chatter on with his customer and realizing that the customer was as engaged in the conversation as if he were talking with his own grandfather, I have to wonder about the trade-offs.

CHAPTER 6
Pilgrimages

Eid el Adha. The end of the Hajj, the pilgrimage.

I'd been here before. Sort of.

Buffy, Charis and I had arrived in Cairo almost a decade ago just in time for this same holiday. The image of men clustered around a frantic sheep on a narrow side street remains vividly etched in our minds. They held the panicked animal down, slit its throat, ecstatically dipped their hands in the spurting blood, and then touched things—cars, the walls of buildings, anything—leaving the blessing of red handprints everywhere, the fingers spread wide in supplication. In gratitude.

Adha means sacrifice, you see. *Eid el Adha* is the Feast of the Sacrifice. The time we thank god for having produced a ram from a nearby thicket, instead of asking poor, obedient Abraham to slit the throat of his puzzled son. Instead of asking Abraham to prove his love for his god at the expense of his love for his son.

Buffy, Charis, and I equally vividly remember the horrified reaction of the red-headed woman from Texas, who made her horror and disgust at the ritual very clear.

It turned out OK. Buffy made her disgust at the ignorant rudeness of the Texan's outburst equally clear, and her husband calmed her down.

But this is Beirut. There'll be a couple of sheep waiting outside butcher shops to be slaughtered for feasts, but no reveling in the act itself like we saw in Egypt. The signs of celebration are a bit more subdued here and a lot less anachronistic.

Last night, for example, as Buffy and I walked the three miles downtown to the Sofil Cinema to see "Late Bloomers," a Swiss entry to the European Film Festival that ran all last week, the traffic had ground to an absolute standstill.

"Everybody's out shopping," Buffy opined. "Three days of closed shops, so they're stocking up. Probably Christmas shopping too."

Good thing we'd decided to walk instead of paying somebody a few dollars so we could sit in an idling taxi watching people like us trundling along at a good clip, marveling at all the things one marvels at here.

Take the dance that crossing streets entails. The pedestrian must calculate whether the amount the driver would have to decelerate if the pedestrian stepped into the street at that very moment would be considered rude. Then, having determined the ratio to be an appropriate one, they must step confidently first in front of the oncoming car and then in front of the one in the next lane, who'll have to acknowledge that the pedestrian, having made it this far, has earned the benefit of the doubt, requiring that driver's deceleration. All the while, everybody knows that somehow it will work out, usually without anyone even shaking a fist at anyone else.

It is a dance indeed—to engage in it, you have to purge every preconception you have about how to cross any street in any city in the United States or in most European countries (Italy might be the exception). It's like speaking a different language, calling upon a different part of your brain, a different way of thinking about ordinary things.

You don't wait for an opening in the traffic. You decide what might be an appropriate place to create an opening.

Soon the dance—like responding "*Sabah innoor*" when someone greets you with "*Sabah el khair*"—becomes second nature.

Buffy and I walked on through the busy, noisy diversity of the city. The yellow banner draped below our apartment across Rue Baalbek wishes everyone a blessed *Eid el Adha*, courtesy of the mosque just down the street. Throughout the district, shopkeepers—Christian, Muslim, and Druze alike—have placed Christmas decorations in their windows, perhaps also hanging an artificial Christmas wreath on their doorway. No point in missing a sale, is there?

But as we leave mostly Sunni Hamra and Sanayeh and approach intensely Christian Ashrefieh, full-fledged Christmas decorations begin to proliferate, with neon images of trees, presents, sleighs, and the like lining the streets, Christmas tree lights blinking from apartment windows, "O Holy Night" pouring from some shop across the street.

The city never becomes all one thing or all the other, though. Hugging the narrow sidewalk of a long overpass, we look out on the huge new el Amine mosque, right next to which stands the tall, as-yet-unlit city Christmas tree. We assume those lights will come on when this Muslim celebration is finished on Wednesday. Beyond the mosque and the tree, the Christmas lights draping Virgin Megastore flickered on just as the call to prayer began from the four minarets scattered among the apartment buildings on the other side of the overpass.

We paused to watch, listen, and ponder for a few minutes and then went on to the theater, where we saw a movie set in a little Swiss village, its protagonist an eighty-year-old woman who decided to open a lingerie shop, much to the consternation of most of her long-time friends and neighbors. But—as you can imagine—it all worked out in this chick-flick for middle-aged women (and men, since we could use a kick in the pants too) that was set in a green, quiet, monocultural world so unlike the one we had walked through to get to the theater.

* * *

This morning—the first morning of the *Eid*—the call to prayer was different. Usually there's nothing after the dawn call until late morning. But this morning it was supplemented by a longer and more insistent one at 7:00 a.m. This one was less complex than most, simply "*Allah akbar*" again and again, interspersed with "*La allah illah allah*," Allah is the greatest; there is no god but god.

The chant went on for over half an hour.

The sermon was also broadcast from nearby minarets. The one a few blocks away was too distorted for me even to pick out an occasional word or phrase. But you knew it was a sermon—the voice dropping to signal that something very serious was about to come, a pause, and then the serious thing came, the voice rising, rising, then halting abruptly. A long pause as we all pondered the immensity of what had just been said. Then something lighter, something hopeful. And so on.

You didn't need a phrasebook.

* * *

Now the pilgrims return from Mecca, the pilgrimage having earned for them the honorific "Hajj" for a man and "Hajji" for a woman.

Several of the cable stations we get offer live video of what's going on at Mecca's grand mosque. The most interesting times of year, of course, are during the Hajj and during Ramadan, another time when many travel to Mecca to pay their respects to their god and their prophet.

Sometimes I watch. The Kaaba, the huge, tapestry-draped building in which a holy meteorite is housed, is the focal point of the worship. People walk around the thirty-foot-high edifice; others worship from the several vast floors of open space surrounding the wide plaza. Most wear white, symbolizing their purity—or their hope to acquire it, at least.

Interestingly, the Kaaba was holy before Mohammed declared it sacred to Islam in the early seventh century. The temple had contained 360 idols, and people from all around Arabia regularly visited to pay their respects to this or that of the gods represented there. The Jews and Christians in the region, of course, paid the idols no mind, but nobody much minded them either. When Mohammed came to the city with his new monotheistic message, some of the most violent opposition came from businessmen who were afraid that changing the nature of the holiness to be venerated in the city would hurt the tourist trade.

Once he returned to Mecca from Medina, however, he kept the shrine but tossed out the idols—there is, after all, no god but god.

During our unit on the rise and spread of Islam, most of my Muslim students were astounded to learn that the holiness of the Kaaba pre-dated the founding of their religion.

Standing at a microphone on one of the floors high above the Kaaba, an imam recites a verse from the Koran for the assembled masses—and it is truly masses who fill the several floors of this vast open-air building. "*Ameen*," he says when he finishes. "*Ameen*," the thousands reply. Then thousands of people kneel, forehead to the ground. "*Alla-a-a-ah Akbar*!" he calls. Thousands of people rise.

One evening I watched a call-in TV show on another channel. A glib young moderator fielded phone calls for a telegenic imam who responded to callers' questions about the hajj. I could pick up only bits and pieces, but his intent was clearly to make the callers feel comfortable, explaining the basics of what was involved.

There is something mesmerizing about the chanted recitation of verses from the Koran, the almost silent kneeling and bowing, the abrupt "*Alla-a-ah Akbar*!" that brings everyone to their feet.

And there certainly is something attractive about the religion: acknowledge the one god so great that he simply cannot be imagined, follow the simple rules he's laid out, be rewarded in paradise. Not really much more than that.

* * *

On Saturday, Buffy and I went on another sort of pilgrimage, I suppose you could call it. André Bechara, an ACS colleague, is the cofounder of an eco-tourism group called Lebanese Adventure. For this trip he had arranged a tour of several wineries in the Bekaa, just over the mountains.

Whenever I crest the six thousand-foot-high pass through the ridge of Mount Lebanon, I always recall that a friend of Buffy's who works in military intelligence calls the Bekaa "the most dangerous spot on the planet." Indeed, it is through this valley and across these mountains that Hizbollah's weapons are shipped. It is in various hidden camps that young men are trained to fight. It is here, from time to time, where some group unleashes the immense firepower it keeps hidden in its closets on some other group.

But what a beautiful site, the wide, green expanse of alluvial plain spread between two sets of mountains, the narrow Litani River meandering southward toward the gorge in the western range it has cut to flow to the sea near Sidon.

It was a wonderful day. Not much wine, but conversations with a UN economist about Lebanon's financial prospects, with a young journalist about an article she'd done on drama therapy in a Lebanese prison, with a public health intern about her frustrations working with the Ministry of Health, and with a group marketing professionals about their recent contract to create a set of ads denouncing drunk driving.

Then the sun began to set on the Anti-Lebanon Mountains on the eastern edge of the valley, turning them rose beneath the purple desert skies beyond. Damascus lies just over the ridge, and the Golan Heights lie just beyond snow-capped Mt. Hermon at the southern end of the mountains.

We drove up the mountain road from Chtaura and then wound our way through the twilight down to Beirut. Moussa, the taxi driver from over on Rue Sadat, was waiting for us at the pickup point.

"Have you been on the Hajj, Moussa?" I asked.

"I don't believe in the Hajj."

"Why?"

"Men go on the Hajj to be away from their wives, and when they come back they say they will divorce their wives because that is what they decided in Mecca. People go only so they can say they go. It is not good. It is for the wrong reasons."

He paused.

"I do not go to mosque either."

"But you pray," I replied.

"I pray. But I pray where I am. I do not need to go somewhere. I went before. I put my shoes in the place for shoes. I came back and my shoes were gone. There were old, broken shoes instead. I do not go to the mosque to trade my shoes."

* * *

CHAPTER 6

I paused as I stepped out the door of our apartment building a few days ago. Across the street several soldiers and a delivery boy from Petit Marché were chatting by the little sentry house. Two women passed, talking earnestly in low tones. An old man stood leaning on the balcony railing of his first-floor apartment, watching me watching him. In the street a woman leaned toward a taxi driver, negotiating the fare.

And I began to understand something about what attracts me to this place so much.

Beirut is intimate.

The moment I step into the street, it's as though I'm allowed into all the lives around me—only to watch, if I want, or to participate if I choose to take another step inside.

To wit. I've been exchanging greetings with one of the soldiers who regularly stands guard across the street for a couple of months now. He's a pleasant-looking young man with frameless glasses and a wide smile.

One day last week, as I approached from the side street carrying a couple of bags of groceries, he got up from his chair, crossed the street, and started walking toward me.

Uh-oh, I thought. We must've done something to worry the Hariri folks up the street, and he's coming to deliver the message.

"Good morning," he said.

"Good morning. *Keefek*. How are you?"

"Fine. You walked this morning?"

"Oh. Yeah. I went to Bou Khalil. Groceries," I said, lifting the bags to show how innocent they were.

"You are American?"

"Yes. *Ana min Ameerka*."

"My English is not good. You speak good Arabic."

"Your English is better than my Arabic. Where did you learn it? *Ween taalimt?*"

"In my school. But I do not practice. How do you learn Arabic?"

"*Ambudrous kil yoom.* I study every day. *Shway.* A little."

"I will speak English. You will speak Arabic. We will learn together."

I set one of the bags down and offered my hand.

"Sure. Together. *Maah bahd*. We'll learn together."

"Good-bye."

"*Maah salameh*."

Intimate. All you've got to do is show up. Maybe everything in life is pilgrimage if you only have sense enough to see it.

But I guess it's a good idea to keep an eye on your shoes.

* * *

All week I've tried to bring myself to write. That we're about to travel back to America for a few weeks seems such an auspicious time to reflect on why I'm here in Beirut, fraught with all kinds of symbolism and meaning. Maybe if I could plumb my feelings about the trip, some of my questions about what makes America and the nature of my relationship to my country would come into clearer focus.

But day after day I've sat staring at the computer screen; day after day I've not been able to write anything. And there's not much time to figure anything out; just a little before midnight tonight Moussa will take us to the airport, and we'll begin our long trip.

If being home entails being with loved ones in wonderful places, this certainly will be home. Our daughter and her partner, my brother and sister and their partners, my oldest and dearest friend and his wife. Wonderful, crazy Berkeley. A few days amid the thick, dark redwoods of Big Sur's jagged coast. What could be better?

But home? My home?

I don't think so.

I've actually been dreading the trip. Dreading first, of course, the ten-hour flight from Paris that I'll do my best to ignore as I try to bury myself in the several thick books that'll constitute my carry-on luggage.

But the dread lies deeper.

I tried to describe it to a colleague.

"Looking forward to your vacation?" he asked a couple of days ago.

"Yeah. To seeing family, drinking water from the tap, and stuff like that. But…" I hesitated.

"But what?"

"Bob, it's so hard for me in the US. I can't really say what makes me so mad when I'm there, but I it just does. I guess it's that we live in such a cocoon. When I'm in the US, I spend so much of my time biting my tongue. There's just this subtle, unspoken assumption that we're really special. It's like we assume that we should get all the those goodies. Like because we're American, we deserve the good stuff. I get angry at the sense of privilege we seem to feel." I paused. "I think I get even angrier that we don't know we feel the sense of privilege."

Bob smiled. A condescending smile. He clearly felt pity for me.

"Well, you'll need to get over that," he suggested. "Anger's not good for you."

Hmm. I decided this conversation wasn't headed anywhere.

"Yeah. Have a good holiday."

"You, too."

I still haven't learned much about what I feel about my relationship with my country. One thing, however, is gradually becoming clear to me.

America is no place for romantics.

Being a romantic is a complicated thing because being a romantic precludes the possibility of imagining any other way of being. This is simply because as a romantic, one assumes that everything and everyone is fraught with much more meaning than meets the eye, s, to the Romantic, even the most staid among us is merely suppressing the volcano that lies at the core of every human psyche.

Compare this with the way a hardheaded realist sees the world. To a realist, the world is simply what it is. Streets filled with traffic are streets filled with traffic; war's war, and inevitable; love's OK but not all it's cracked up to be; everybody's just another somebody. Some people do allow their volcanoes to spurt and spout, but it's all just sound and fury, and we all know what that signifies.

But to a romantic! Ah, the world is *not* what it is. The world is layers and layers of meaning, symbol, and possibility—not the possibility that alternative sources of energy might be found, but that energy itself might be something other than energy and that the very idea of finding might result in the discovery that what we thought we were searching for was so much different from what we finally came upon and…well, you get the picture.

So to the realist, romantics are just noisy dreamers, wishing for a world that is not, never has been, and cannot be. But to the romantic, realists simply lack the imagination to see what really is.

Realists think romantics are silly. Romantics think realists could be romantics if only they could see beneath the surface. Realists want romantics to quit imagining and feeling—to *get it* by understanding there's not so much to get. Romantics want realists to imagine, to feel, to invent the world.

Well, here's the deal. Americans are realists. It's American "knowhow" that has entranced the world for well over a century. We are, as a culture, good at doing things—at building roads, inoculating ourselves against yellow fever, running meetings, and figuring out how to dam the river and drain the swamp.

The rite of passage for American boys—until recently—was to rebuild the engine of a '49 Ford, the legacy of the man who essentially invented the assembly line and who went on to say, "History is bunk." What Henry Ford meant by this was that it is only today that matters, and what one can do with it, not the past, not an understanding of the things that got us to this point today. Not ideas, not study, not the life of the mind.

Practicality. Realism. Not romanticism.

Well, I never rebuilt a Ford, '49 or otherwise. The closest I came was watching Jim Clardy take apart and then put back together my 250 cc Maiko motorcycle back in 1965. I can still see him, hunched over that little engine, asking me to hand him this or that tool, astounded by this or that feature of the (as I recall) Czech motorcycle. I handed him this or that, being as excited as I could make myself about what he learned about the machine's innards.

But I didn't really care.

In retrospect, I can see that my twenty years in Vermont were, in part, an effort to Americanize myself. To get good at doing things with things. At being practical, a realist. So I built a pole barn—it never fell over, but the roof did leak. And I laid tongue-in-groove pine flooring throughout the second story addition to our house—try as hard as I might, I could never quite get rid of the little angled gap between the ends of the boards and the walls. Oh how carefully I measured where to cut holes for electrical outlets in the sheetrock and then watched as Steven Melanson and I hung the panels, only to find that I was usually off by an inch or two. I cleaned my chainsaw and sharpened its teeth; I made a rack in the garage for my tools and hung them neatly.

Oh how I admired and envied everyone who could do these things so well.

Oh how hard I tried to care.

But it didn't take.

In the end, I remained more interested in listening to the water burble in the brook on a pitch-black night or in watching the contours of the snow as it filled my boot track or in trying to figure out how Dan Jarvis connected himself in his mind with Weathersfield's hundred other Jarvises—and how they connected themselves with him in their minds—than in how straight I could hang a row of shingles.

So here I am now, living in a city where a quarter of the buildings—give or take—are unlivable. Some were abandoned during the civil war and have simply been left to deteriorate, vines overwhelming the balconies and reaching into the empty window sockets, doorways shattered, walls crumbling. Others have just gradually declined over the years, till fewer people lived there, then fewer, and now they stand dark and empty.

There is indeed some building life-cycle here that I cannot quite fathom. It is the kind of thing that no red-blooded American male would ever allow to happen. Either tear it down or fix it up, the realist's ethos insists—none of this shillyshallying.

But to the romantic, the tattered awnings and darkened windows of the upper floors of an abandoned building promise mysteries. Whose were the last lives to unfold in these apartments? What pushed each family over the brink, so they finally, one by one, gave up on the building? What Omani or Qatari entrepreneur is watching Beirut's real estate market, waiting to decide that this block of Rue Makdissi is just about ready for a shining new marble tower?

And all that mystery is enhanced by the darkened building's street-level realities, where diamond-encrusted gold bracelets glitter in the window of the jewelry store. Next door, the vegetable seller piles tomatoes into a pyramid beside another pyramid of pomegranates, while bunches of tiny bananas grown in greenhouses just up the coast hang on strings above the cucumbers. A closet-sized money-changer's stall is wedged between the vegetable seller and a lingerie shop, from which steps a woman clad in a black *tchador*, fully veiled, only her eyes darting right and left, making sure it's safe to cross the street, her parcel of new underwear clutched to her chest.

* * *

Buffy and I decided to have our last dinner before returning to the US at Le Petit Café, the Lebanese style restaurant overlooking Pigeon Rocks three-quarters of a mile from our apartment. We ate our hummus, grape leaves, and lamb kebabs at a leisurely pace, looking out on the floodlit columns of limestone that jut from the sea in the center of a wide cove, listening to the sad tones of the Arabic songs playing in the background, chatting, pausing to watch and listen, and then chatting again.

We made our way home along the crowded sidewalks, where clusters of people conversed in energetic Arabic.

"It's really interesting to live where you walk along and really have no idea what people are talking about, isn't it?" I said.

"It is. Of course, you know what it's about," she replied. "Children and friends and parents and how well their car's running and all that."

"Yeah. It's really sort of pathetic, how little we have to talk about, isn't it?"

"Oh, Nick. Don't you get it yet?" She smiled, meaning no harm.

I smiled. "I guess not."

She went on to remind me of what a professor friend of hers had told her years before: "Nobody wants to be a romantic. You just wake up one morning in your sixties and say, 'Shit! I'm a romantic.'"

* * *

Whose jets are those, the ones racing low over the city this morning? The local French-language radio station is running a program on pensions in France, not a blow-by-blow account of Israeli jets strafing southern Beirut. Naharnet and Yalibnan aren't posting minute-by-minute updates about illegal over-flights.

So maybe they're one of the two Lebanese Air Force jets, just out practicing (two, that is, until the twelve MIGs Russia has promised Lebanon—a gift the Bush administration, which is about to give the army a variety of small arms, has applauded—arrive sometime later this year.)

But I'm not comforted. Israel's invasion of the Gaza Strip has set too much in motion for my taste. How easy it would be for Hizbollah, taking advantage of the worldwide condemnation of Israel's actions, to launch a few sympathy rockets into northern Israel? Only yesterday, Hizbollah leader Hassan Nasrallah criticized UN Resolution 1701 for blaming Hizbollah for the 2006 war—the one Israel initiated in response to Hizbollah's capture of a couple of Israeli soldiers, the outcome of which turned Hizbollah into *the* major political force in Lebanon. Exactly what is Nasrallah telling us? What do his remarks signal for the future?

At the very least, they tell us that after two weeks spent basking in the ease of northern California and the welcoming warmth of family and friends, Buffy and I are back in Beirut.

After two weeks of noting front-page headlines warning of the loss of a quarter of a million United States businesses over the next few years and first-ever American plant closures by Toyota, I'm scanning the papers for news that somebody has set something in motion that'll cause Israel to carry out its promise to completely destroy this country if anybody here does anything that threatens a single Israeli.

We're back in a place where what's written and said between the lines seems to matter more than the lines themselves.

Back where, before I left for my pilgrimage to the US, I pulled Kafka's *Amerika* from a shelf in the school library's fiction collection. I'd read the novel decades ago and remembered being struck by how little about America Kafka—who'd never visited the US—had put into the book. How little, even, he'd seemed interested in putting into the book; the setting mattered much less than the setting in his more famous later works *The Trial* and *The Castle*.

I figured that it might be interesting to reread this work begun in 1912 and published posthumously in 1927 as I returned to America. It seemed somehow appropriate to revisit so inaccurate a look at my country just before revisiting the country I, myself, understood so poorly.

It doesn't take long to realize how little Kafka actually knows about America. Eight lines, as a matter of fact. Karl Rossman's ship is just pulling into New York's harbor. "A sudden burst of sunshine seemed to illumine the Statue of Liberty, so that he saw it in a new light, although he had sighted it long before. The arm with the sword rose up as if newly stretched aloft, and round the figure..."

Arm with the sword?

No wonder the author didn't give his protagonist much time to wander the city, other than a single brief foray through a crowd. He had no idea what that city looked like.

Further, what an irony that the day before we left Berkeley to return to Beirut Adam Kirsch published an essay in *The New York Times Book Review* entitled "America, 'Amerika,'" reviewing a new translation of this "least read, least written about" of Kafka's works.

By the time this review came out, I had made it almost halfway through the book. Karl had spent a few months living with his uncle Jacob, learning English and horseback riding. He then passed a disastrous evening with his uncle's friend Pollunder, finally setting off on the road, where he met up with two ne'er-do-wells before settling down for a bit.

Oh, I suppose Kafka captured—probably quite by accident—a bit of America here and there. I note the narrator's comment that "In this country sympathy was something you could not hope for; in that respect America resembled what Karl had read about; except that those who were fortunate seemed really to enjoy their good fortune here, sunning themselves among their care-free friends" (38). Or the depiction of driving through Manhattan: "the pavements and roadways were thronged with traffic changing its direction every minute, as if caught up in a whirlwind and roaring like some strange element quite unconnected with humanity" (53).

Of Americans' penchant for hard work, the "manageress" who offers Karl a job at the Hotel Occidental in Rameses, New York, explains to Karl, "America's a strange country. Take this boy, for instance; he came here only a year and a half ago with his parents; he's an Italian. At the moment it looks as if he simply wouldn't be able to stand the work, his face has fallen away to nothing and he goes to sleep on the job, although he's naturally a very willing lad—but let him go on working here or anywhere else in America for another six months and he'll be able to take it all in his stride, and in another five years he'll be a strong man" (136).

Well, that's as far as I'd gotten by the time we touched down at Rafik Hariri International Airport Monday night, picked up our luggage, and headed back to the Adel Building on Rue Commodore.

America, land of no sympathy, traffic jams, and hard work.

Maybe Kafka got some of it right, after all. At least under the outgoing Bush administration. But maybe, if my optimistic friends and relatives are right, there'll be a little more sympathy and a little less traffic under the Obama administration.

About the hard work, I've yet to see any American working as hard as the young men who showed up at construction sites in Nairobi at 7:00 a.m. and left for home at seven or eight in the evening or the old guy who totes his vegetables to the little hole-in-the-wall just off Rue Commodore at 5:00 a.m., usually staying open till 6:00 or 7:00 p.m. But, after all, Kakfa was writing about the industrial America of a century ago, not our information-age America.

Kafka really had no idea of what he was talking about. Knowing so little about the US that at one point he had Karl and his associates stop on an imagined hillside to look down upon Manhattan and Brooklyn, Kafka couldn't imagine the physical grandeur of the west coast of the United States, the part of the country that we had just visited.

Clearly he could never have imagined the inspiring beauty of the lights of the Livermore Valley twinkling in the dusk from our friends' house high on a nearby—very real—hilltop or of the waves rolling in along the coast at Point Reyes or Big Sur, or even of the sunbaked aroma of eucalyptus and redwood that pervades the UC Berkeley campus.

It is, indeed, an amazing land about which Kafka knew nothing.

And, if my friends and relatives are at all representative, it is a hopeful, optimistic land. It's a place where Steve wants to keep working at the lab where he's worked for almost thirty years to see if they can actually set off a controlled fusion reaction, laying foundations for an endless supply of clean and cheap energy. Meanwhile Phyllis puts the finishing touches on yet another iteration of her work blending paints with wax to create new ways of seeing the world. It's a world where Tommy Lee poured hours of love and energy into revising a movie script that's just been accepted by the producer, and Rob just finished putting the finishing touches on a grant proposal that will allow him to continue his work creating nanotechnological vehicles for the early diagnosis of some cancers. Charis has convinced yet another group of crusty academics that the insights she's gleaned from her year in Nepal merit journal-readers' attention; Sara continues to craft her stage character Alice, the funny little woman who has so much to tell us about America's prisons, about resilience, and about love.

Needless to say, these are the same people who share my hopes for America: that it can become, once again, a place of promise, not of fear, that it can become a place like the one that Thomas Friedman describes in the introduction to *Hot, Flat and Crowded*:

> Our air will be cleaner, our environment will be healthier, our young people will see their idealism mirrored in their own government, and our industries will have more tools to do good for themselves and the planet at the same time. This is also an America that will have its identity back, not to mention its self-confidence, because it will again be leading the world on the most important strategic mission and values issue of the day…the hour is late, the stakes couldn't be higher, the project couldn't be harder, the payoff couldn't be greater (24).

Meanwhile, although the mysterious jet over-flights have ceased, Naharnet reminds me it's still Lebanon. "Unknown assailants threw two hand grenades last night on an empty lot in Muhajereen Street in Tripoli's Bab al-Tabbaneh area. One of the grenades exploded while an army sapper worked on defusing the other."

Closer to home, tens of thousands of people are reported at this moment to be marching to a nearby stadium for a rally that Nasrallah has called "to renew your commitment to the resistance and to renew your animosity to Israel and the Great Satan which orders Israel…we have to act as though all possibilities are real and open with Israel and we must always be ready for any eventuality."

That's us, that "Great Satan."

So I guess that we too, whoever and whatever we may turn out to be, have to be ready for "any eventuality."

CHAPTER 7
Not in Kansas anymore; not at all

Decisions, decisions, decisions.

Well, at first it's not so hard as I wander Beirut's quiet Sunday-morning streets.

To the guy setting out bags of bread in front of the mini-market by Bou Hassan restaurant, it's "*Sabah al khair.*"

"*Sabah innoor*," he replies.

Same thing to the security guard sitting on the patio in front of the new Rotana Suites Raouche, that gleaming twenty-story granite enigma that was completed a year ago, but remains totally unoccupied; a casualty of the subprime crisis, or of some indigenous financial brouhaha?

"*Sabah al khair.*"

"*Sabah innoor.*"

The thirty-something woman skipping (literally) toward me along the Corniche, holding hands with her eight-year-old, also-skipping daughter is a no-brainer—you generally don't greet women you don't know.

Wrong.

"*Bonjour!*" she says, grinning as she passes.

"Oh! *Bonjour.*"

Here comes, I'm pretty sure, a "*Sabah al khair.*" An old guy wearing a slightly tattered sport coat, his muffler wrapped tightly around his neck to protect him from the sixty-degree winter weather.

Fooled again.

"Good morning. How are you?" he asks as we reach greeting distance.

"Fine, fine. And you?"

It had taken me a few days to remember Beirut's casual approach to language boundaries after returning from our couple of weeks in the US. For example, the proper reply to "*Bonjour*" is actually "*Bonjourain,*" adding the Arabic suffix for "two," taken from "*Marhaba*" (hello), the response to which is "*Marhabtain*" (two hellos).

By Saturday I had remembered.

I'd picked up Samir Kassir's *Histoire de Beyrouth* again—I'm not sure why I just couldn't focus on it sitting on Sister Sara's Seventh Street front stoop in Berkeley.

The book is really getting interesting now. It was in the nineteenth century that Beirut began to become the Beirut we recognize—complete with an 1860 bloodbath between the Maronites and the Druze in the nearby mountains. Still part of the Ottoman Empire, Lebanon was becoming part of the exotified Middle East that Edward Said railed against in his seminal 1978 work *Orientalism*.

The romanticization of Lebanon was well under way by mid-century, when Maxime de Camp, traveling from Alexandria to Beirut with Flaubert, wrote:

> The land around Beirut, the forests of umbrella pines, the roads lined with fig trees and myrtles, with pomegranates, where chameleons run everywhere; where the view of the Mediterranean and the sight of the wooded heights of Mount Lebanon rise against the sky with the purest of lines. This is a retreat perfect for contemplative people, for the disenchanted, for those who are wounded by existence; it seems to me that one could live happily here doing nothing but gazing at the mountains and the sea (135) [my translation].

As the century wore on, the city expanded further and further outside its Medieval walls. Along with "those wounded by existence" came missionaries—Protestant, Jesuit and Orthodox—to establish hospitals, high schools, and universities and teach in English, French, Greek, and Arabic.

Meanwhile, the Ottomans (possessors of that sprawling empire by then described by Europeans as "the sick man of Europe") had decided to try to catch up with the West. They upgraded their navy and modernized their army, of course. But they also replaced the turban with the fez or *tarboush* (which, ironically, Ataturk outlawed as a sign of Turkish backwardness in the 1920s), and encouraged Westerners to set up shop in its territories.

Gradually, western furniture began to appear in fashionable Beirut homes: dining, for example, was done with forks and knives from individual plates set at a table, the diners seated in chairs; no longer did diners sprawl around the mat that was laden with platters from which everyone scooped mouthfuls of whatever they wanted to scoop.

I wanted to read some of the authors who had visited this land when it was undergoing these momentous changes, and who had gone on to write the works that would set in motion the process about which Said would write:

> My contention is that Orientalism is fundamentally a political doctrine willed over the Orient because the Orient was weaker than the West, which elided the Orient's difference with its weakness…as a cultural apparatus Orientalism is all aggression, activity, judgment, will-to-truth, and knowledge (204).

Online I found Alphonse de Lamartine's *Souvenirs, Impressions, Pensées et Paysages Pendant un Voyage en Orient (1832-1833)*. After a long introduction acknowledging the wonderful works written about the East by the likes of Chateaubriand and Michaud, he explains:

> I burned, thus, from the age of eight, with the desire to visit the mountains from which God descended; the deserts where the angels came to show Hagar the spring from which to bring her poor child back to life; the rivers which ran from the earthly paradise; this sky where you could watch the ascent and descent of angels on Jacob's ladder. This desire was never extinguished in me; I always dreamed of a voyage to the Orient, like the grand act of my entire life (3) [my translation].

But I'm an old fart, so I wanted to hold the book in my hands. And now I wanted to read Chateaubriand, along with Renan and all the others I'd taken note of in Kassir's book.

Beirut has a marvelous collection of bookstores. Just down Rue Commodore is Friends, and a block away on Hamra is the Oriental Bookstore, which has a great collection. A few blocks east lies the best, Antoine's, so Buffy and I headed there on Saturday afternoon.

"I'm looking for the works of some nineteenth century French authors: Lamartine, Renan, Chateaubriand, Flaubert. Do you have them?" I asked a young woman shelving books.

"In English or in French?

"*N'importe*."

"*Allons voir dans l'ordinateur*."

So *nous avons cherché* these authors for some time, but found only *des poemes et des romans*, so I thanked her and gave up.

Off to the Esquire bookstore, the one my brother Richard had discovered on a TV documentary about Beirut from his home on Humboldt Street in Reno. Greetings all around. I passed along thanks from my brother for the book on Hizbollah I had picked up for him, then explained my plight.

No. No Renan or Chateaubriand or Lamartine. Perhaps Antoine's?

Been there.

"You might be interested in this book by Kassir," the owner said as we started to leave. "It's an excellent study of the civil war."

"After I finish *Histoire de Beyrouth*," I replied.

"You know he was killed, assassinated?"

"Yes." I remembered the blurb about the author on the back cover: born in Beirut, taught at St. Joseph University, author of several other books, writer for *Al Nahar*.

Then the single, final sentence, "*Samir Kassir a été assassiné à Beyrouth le 2 juin 2005*."

"Yes, they might have something." The bookstore owner paused. "Kassir was a respectable man. A very respectable man. Good luck."

We shook hands, and Buffy and I headed for the Cross Roads Bookstore on Rue Makdissi. A red banner that reads "Book Sale" has hung out front since at least 2000, when I first visited Beirut. Another banner boasts a collection of more than a million books.

This may be an understatement.

There are only tens of thousands upstairs, probably, from which Buffy decided that we needed a Shakespeare anthology to add to the three we have in storage: hers from college, her mother's and my mother's. Now we have the Beirut edition.

But downstairs, the shelves are packed, with books in at least six languages (I noted German, Spanish, and Russian in addition to English, French, and Arabic) stacked sideways, the visible stack often obscuring a second one behind it.

Leaning over several jammed shelves marked *classiques*, the saleswoman and I tried to narrow down our search.

"*Vous cherchez les romans, ou quoi?*" You're looking for novels, or what?

"*La. Biddi tarikh willa* essays of some sort." No. I'm looking for history or essays of some sort.

"*Emta?*" When?

"*Min abil mia wa khamseen sany.* They were French romantics *qui ont visité le liban et ont creé l'interesse publique dans les pays arabes.*" From 150 years ago. They were French romantics who visited Lebanon and created public interest in Arab countries.

We never found any of the books, but the young woman took our phone number and assured us she would call if she found anything.

Walking home, I reflected on this very Lebanese habit of shifting from language to language with no apparent reason for the shift.

Somehow, this intricately idiosyncratic practice reminded me of a conversation that had taken place in one of my history classes a few days before.

The students had just come back from vacation, so I'd wanted to make sure that anybody who had anything they wanted to share had a chance to do so. Nastassia, who'd been so excited about the prospect of spending the holiday in Paris, told of a few experiences. Toshi had gone to Oman, and Karen had gone to Syria. A couple of people went to Dubai. Camilla didn't have anything to say about her trip home to South Africa, and Evelyn was not back from Malaysia yet.

"I went to Iraq, Mr. Boke!" Donia said, beaming brightly.

"Iraq! What prompted that?"

"My mother's brother lives there. Not in Baghdad, but a few hours north."

Now what do you say to somebody who has just gone to Iraq for a holiday? Same thing you ask anybody, I guess.

"So did you have a good time?"

"Well, it was sort of fun figuring out when you were going to shower. See, nobody knows when the water will come on, so when it does everybody goes and cleans up fast. Then, of course, there's not much electricity."

"How about the checkpoints and stuff like that?"

"It made me nervous at first because there are so many places where you get stopped every few blocks, but I've got a Canadian passport as well as my Lebanese one, so they were pretty nice, and it was OK."

"Any bombs or anything go off near you?"

"Not very nearby, but there was something not too far. Nobody was hurt, though."

"How do your people feel about things, Donia?"

"Oh, they hate it. But what can they do? It was good to see my family, though."

So it turns out that I was searching for books by long-dead Frenchmen who were enchanted by this multifarious land while Donia visited her relatives in a country devastated by my government's foreign policy.

That same government where both the house and the senate just voted unwavering support for Israel's attack on Gaza, which has, by the latest count, taken over eight hundred civilian lives.

Meanwhile, every television station in this region regularly broadcasts film clips from the streets of Gaza: a young man runs toward the hospital carrying a bloodied friend in his arms, a blood-spattered child lies in the street, a woman wails, the carcass of an exploded ambulance smolders.

Meanwhile, at Friday's brief high school faculty meeting, Assistant Principal Laila explains that several students are trying to find out what kind of relief can be sent to Gaza. More information will be forthcoming.

Meanwhile, Lebanon's Maronite president and Sunni prime minister jointly insist that Lebanon will not become a second front in Israel's current conflict, about the same time the head of Hizbollah's parliamentary block told a rally of tens of thousands of Shia in southern Lebanon, "The Israeli aggression and invasion of Gaza will reaffirm once again the hatred the people of Arab and

Muslim regions have for the American administration that allowed the bloodshed and supported the Israeli enemy…we are ready to face any [Israeli] stupidity."

Meanwhile…

* * *

Sunday morning.

Beirut is asleep.

Not the overwhelming first sleep that comes at the end of an eventful day or later hours' dream-fraught sleep, but the restful sleep of early morning, when the sun has just crested the eastern mountain ridge, the night rain has washed the air clear, and only a few things stir. Like the awakening doves, who coo.

Rain is likely, so I'm out early.

I walk up past the heavily guarded Hariri palace, past the high-walled Lebanese American University campus. Then I turn east and walk up past the white marble Druze social services buildings to what I figure to be the top of one of Beirut's two 150-meter-plus-above-sea-level hills. Through streets I've never walked before. Narrow and winding.

These neighborhoods will not be highlighted on a tourist map. Not because they're dangerous, but because there's nothing here but apartment buildings, lined with balconies where ficus trees lean out over the street and laundry hangs to dry. At street level, a hair salon, then a notary public, a vegetable stand, a tailor, an Internet café. Walk on. Repeat the sequence, with minor variations.

This isn't the Beirut whose virtues *The New York Times* just extolled when it rated this city the number-one place (out of the forty-four it chose) you should visit in 2009. Number one! Here's what the *Times* had to say about Beirut on January 11:

> With a recent (though perhaps tenuous) détente keeping the violence in check, the capital of Lebanon is poised to reclaim its title as the Paris of the Middle East. Two hotels scheduled to open this year are raising the luxury quotient—the Four Seasons Hotel Beirut and Le Gray, the

> latter from the people behind One Aldwych in London—and a clutch of high-profile restaurants are transforming the city's culinary scene. Tradition Lebanese cooking finds its apotheosis at the cozy Al-Ajami restaurant, while the glitterati settles into Hussein Hadid's Kitchen, run by a nephew of the architect Zaha Hadid. But nothing symbolizes the city's gastro-intestinal awakening like Souk el-Tayeb, Beirut's first farmer's market. The market, founded in 2004, reconciles Lebanon's warring factions through their common love of their country's food.

As you can tell, those folks at the *Times* have a very different take on what matters in a city than I do. But, given the other cities they suggested visiting this year, that's no surprise: next on the list was Las Vegas, followed by the Persian Gulf shopping paradise Doha, Qatar. The list got a little livelier after that, with Bhutan, Monument Valley, Kazakhstan, Buffalo (really?), Madagascar, and Metz, France, coming next.

Anyway, it's nice to know that some people are beginning to erase the horrid images of Lebanon's civil war from their minds and to consider the possibility that this is a good place to visit, if not to live (the fact that the détente is tenuous should, however, be duly noted).

Of course, the horrors being wrought on Gaza less than two hundred miles to the south do make one uneasy. A friend expressed concern for our safety in a recent e-mail, the only appropriate response to which I could figure out was "When the headlines read, 'Beirut Strafed, Bombed by Israeli Aircraft' begin to worry."

I'm not truly so sanguine. One would be a fool to treat the volatility of this region lightly.

But I am learning how to deal with it.

Here's an example. I was shuffling papers while students sifted into the classroom for Creative Nonfiction.

"Did you hear, sir? Hizbollah shot some rockets into Israel," Mark said, a little catch to his voice.

If this were true, it would be really bad news. Israel has made it very clear that if Hizbollah fires rockets, the entire nation of Lebanon will be history. The great fear when a few rockets were lobbed into Israel from Lebanon a few days ago was that Hizbollah might have shot them. But the party issued denials, and Israel said they weren't the kind of rockets Hizbollah uses. Whew!

"Yeah. Why bother having class, sir, if we're all going to be blown away?" Firas asked. He was smiling, but everybody here has learned to smile through troubling circumstances.

So what should I, the teacher, do?

Ah. Got it. I was sitting at the computer anyway, so I opened Naharnet, the Lebanese news website I go to whenever something's going on. This site posts events minute by minute during such times, which is a wonderful feature during real crises, although it seems a bit much when it's just Michel Aoun lambasting Fuad Siniora in a speech again.

Anyway, I turned on the video doohickey that allows everyone in the classroom to see what's on my computer screen while I waited for Naharnet to download.

Indeed, there was the blue background above the other news stories that indicated they were following something closely.

Scroll down. Yup. There was the news about the firing of the rockets.

"Zalfa, would you read it aloud, please?"

It didn't sound good. After a few rockets were fired, there was an Israeli response to the area purported to be the launch site, both by air and from cannons just across the border. Zalfa read on, finally coming to the last entry, which was posted about fifteen minutes ago.

"Hizbollah insists that it is the government's responsibility to determine the source of such attacks."

"OK," I said. "What's that mean?"

Silence. Then, from Mark, "I get it. That means they're telling us they didn't do it, and they're using this as an opportunity to attack the government for doing something wrong."

"Right."

I looked around the room.

"Get it? So we don't get attacked by Israel today. Would you get your papers out please so we can get on with our work?"

You really have to think differently here.

There is no respite—in Beirut or in any other country in the Middle East—from the news when things heat up. All dials are tuned to events in Gaza. Turn on an Arabic TV news channel. There'll be a brief bit about the Ukrainian gas crisis and another about Obama's plan to follow Lincoln's train route to DC.

Then Gaza. A live broadcast of the speech by the President of the UN Security Council denouncing the Israeli attack; another of a speech by Mahmoud Abbas, the leader of Fatah. Clips of foreign minister Livni and secretary of state Rice holding a press conference together. Interviews with mourning grandmothers and academic experts.

Instead of a commercial break, there'll be silent footage of fathers carrying dead children and twisted bodies lying in pools of blood in the street. Rubble. Everywhere rubble.

Turn to a radio talk show: You won't know exactly what they're saying, but you'll hear "Gaza," and then "Israel," and then "Gaza" again. On and on and on.

I understand that Israel felt it simply could not tolerate Hamas—which denies Israel's right to exist, but which *was* duly elected to power by Gazans; put that in your pipe and smoke it, Neocons who simplistically insist that the vote and the free market provide the answer to all the world's problems—firing rockets into its territory every day.

I do understand that this couldn't go on.

But I also know that what they're doing now won't solve their problem.

Israeli defense minister Ehud Barak says they're pretty close to having achieved their goals.

By that I assume he means several things: that he believes a good portion of Hamas' munitions have been destroyed, a significant number of Hamas' leaders are dead, and the people of Gaza will insist that its leaders not allow rockets to be fired into Israel anymore.

That's not what I see, though.

I see simpler results. I see entire neighborhoods reduced to piles of concrete, rebar, broken children's toys, and scorched mattresses. I see young men—and children—whose lust for revenge is being whetted well beyond anything I can possibly imagine.

This desire for revenge by inhabitants of this region against Westerners insisting that the land was theirs by their god's grant is, of course, nothing new. Fulcher of Chartres describes the sack of Jerusalem by Crusaders in 1099 C.E.

> Count Raymond and his men...joyfully rushed into the city to pursue and kill the nefarious enemies, as their comrades were already doing. Some Saracens, Arabs, and Ethiopians took refuge in the tower of David, others fled to the temples of the Lord and of Solomon. A great fight took place in the court and porch of the temples, where they were unable to escape from our gladiators. Many fled to the roof of the temple of Solomon, and were shot with arrows, so that they fell to the ground dead. In this temple almost ten thousand were killed. Indeed, if you had been there you would have seen our feet colored to our ankles with the blood of the slain. But what more shall I relate? None of them were left alive; neither women nor children were spared.
>
> This may seem strange to you. Our squires and poorer footmen discovered a trick of the Saracens, for they learned that they could find [gold coins] in the stomachs and intestines of the dead Saracens, who had swallowed them. Thus, after several days they burned a great heap of dead bodies, that they might more easily get the precious metal from the ashes. Moreover, Tancred broke into the temple of the Lord and most wrongfully stole much gold and silver, also precious stones, but later, repenting of his action, after everything had been accounted for, be restored all to its former place of sanctity.
>
> The carnage over, the crusaders entered the houses and took whatever they found in them. However, this was all done in such a sensible manner that whoever entered a house first received no injury from anyone else, whether he was rich or poor. Even though the house was a palace, whatever he found there was his property. Thus many poor men became rich.
>
> Afterward, all, clergy and laymen, went to the Sepulcher of the Lord and His glorious temple, singing the ninth chant. With fitting humility,

> they repeated prayers and made their offering at the holy places that they had long desired to visit.
>
> *http://www.fordham.edu/halsall/source/fulcher-cde.html#capture*

Most people here—in Beirut, Gaza, Saudi Arabia, Iran, Tunisia, and all the rest—are not specifically conscious of this specific history. It is, however, part of the undergirding cultural fabric of the region.

It is just this deep-seated consciousness of the blighted relationship between this region and the West that caused such a furor when George W. Bush proclaimed a "crusade" against those who had crashed airplanes into American buildings a few years ago?

This round of the violence can't last. Someday soon Israel will stop bombing Gaza and, some day after that, pull its troops out, as it did a while ago.

Then what?

Then what will angry Gazans do?

And what about those "settlements" Israel has allowed to take over nearly one-fifth of the Palestinian lands on the West Bank? How will it deal with that kettle of fish?

Watching all this, how many people are remembering that it took almost two hundred years to drive the last crusader from the eastern Mediterranean? But they *were* driven out. Eventually.

Meanwhile, Naharnet has created a new platform for up-to-the-minute news flashes, the ones from Gaza. This morning it reports, in red type, that:

> Israeli PM Ehud Olmert said Israel's unilateral ceasefire in the Gaza Strip was fragile and was being reassessed on minute by minute basis.
>
> - AFP: Palestinian medics said they have so far pulled 25 bodies, including several children, from the rubble in the north of the Gaza Strip after Israel halted a war on Hamas.
> - Five rockets fired from Gaza landed in Israel in the first such attack since Israel began a unilateral ceasefire in its war on Hamas, the Israeli army said.
> - al-Arabiya: 10 Palestinian rockets fell in Sderot.

- Israel army: An Israeli tank unit fired at armed gunmen in Gaza City when troops came under fire just hours after a truce went into effect in the enclave.

Just below these items, in blue, we learn that at ten thirty this morning, "Lebanese security forces used tear gas to disperse anti-Israeli protesters trying to storm the US embassy" just outside Beirut.

So tomorrow at ACS a group of students will begin to raise money for a Gaza relief fund—you know, bake sales, talent shows, and the like.

Tuesday night Buffy and I will attend a dinner in honor of Obama's inauguration.

The e-mail invitation from Assistant Principal Laila Alamuddin read, "Democrats Abroad are holding a shindig on the 20th, and I have been asked to send the word out. Please see invite attached. RSVP is tomorrow. It is not actually a party per se because it does not seem appropriate, given Gaza."

Most of the thirty-five-dollar-per-person charge will go to Gaza relief.

CHAPTER 8
History: Made and in the Making

Imagine that!

There he was, more than half a century after I saw my first "colored only" sign above a water fountain and heard my South Carolina uncle strain to say "nigra" instead of "nigger" out of deference to my mother's liberalism. A young man of color ("colored," "negro," "African-American," and "black" having come and gone as terms of preference during the ensuing years) being sworn in as president of the United States of America.

And there we were, my wife and I amid a mildly frenzied crowd of ex-pats, Lebanese-Americans, and Lebanese at Bardo's restaurant, just across the street from Haigazian University, celebrating this inauguration and all it stood for.

Wine flowed and the room boomed with enthusiastic chatter as we waited for the inaugural show to begin on the wide screen at one end of the room. The CNN camera panned, capturing the crowd that stretched from the Capitol to the Lincoln Memorial to soon-to-be-ex-president Bush making his way toward the rostrum, then catching Dick Cheney looking grim in his wheelchair.

The ceremony was about to begin. A young woman came to the bar and tapped the microphone; the room quieted. She hurried through her remarks: Democrats Abroad in Lebanon welcomes you…the good work we've all done… the bright future.

Then three brief campaign anecdotes. I've forgotten the first two, but the last was about some canvassing she'd done in the US last summer. She'd been working a phone bank.

"So I made another call and got this guy in rural West Virginia, asking him who he was going to vote for, ready to give my Obama spiel. He said to me, 'Well, I'm gonna vote for Obama. That's because I'm a racist, but I don't want my son to grow up a racist.'"

Silence.

"Thanks for coming, and enjoy the evening."

Soon Diane Feinstein came on the screen reminding us that "the freedom to choose our leaders is the root of liberty."

I looked around the room. American colleagues from ACS, Jim and MJ, were there. And so was Renée Codsi, who came to Lebanon six years ago to recapture something of her past. "Codsi" is Arabic for "from Jerusalem." Her father was Palestinian. Samer Batlouni, one of my history students, was there with his mother, the director of the local branch of an international NGO. Her father was with her, visiting from the US. Ramsi, who graduated from ACS two years ago and was studying interior design at Lebanese American University, was there too.

Most of the people in the crowd were much closer to Ramsi's and Samer's ages than to mine. Too young to even imagine the reality of "colored only" in the land of the free. But also too young to imagine the violence of the civil war that unhinged Lebanon for fifteen years not so long ago.

My life is their history. Just as the gritty historical horror of the Great Depression and World War II comprised my parents' lives and the Gold Rush to California comprised my great grandparents'.

How could Ramsi and Samer—or Renée, for that matter—understand the historic significance of peacefully changing one's leaders, decade after decade? I am, myself, only slowly beginning to understand things like this.

I had thought about this layering of history and the even more complex layering of our ability to understand any of it as I had watched sixty tenth-graders taking notes on their school tour of Byblos a few days earlier.

"There have been seventeen civilizations here," the guide was explaining. "The Roman theatre we are sitting in now was actually built above the pre-Egyptian Obelisk Temple over there that we will visit soon."

The students leaned forward, writing, some glancing at others' notes to make sure they were getting it right.

"We will finish with the crusaders' castle, built after Byblos—or Jbeil—was conquered early in the twelfth century. Even there you will see constructions inside that are different, where the Mamluks and Ottomans who came afterward used different stonework techniques from the crusaders."

We walked past a row of Roman columns toward a three thousand-year-old Phoenician sarcophagus, where the guide explained that such heavy stone caskets were lowered into deep underground tombs by first filling the hole in the ground with sand, then placing the sarcophagus on top of the sand, then digging away the sand.

Then a brief halt by the vague foundations of a temple. Artifacts revealed, the guide explained, that worship had been conducted there by Babylonians in around 2,000 BCE, then by Egyptians in around 1,200, and finally by Persians in around 600 BCE—same spot, with new gods continuously enriching the pantheon.

I listened in awe. This was probably my sixth or seventh visit here, and I was always in awe.

I watched the kids, understanding that most of them could not feel awe. Oh, some of the boys would try to imagine the engineering feat involved in piling stone on stone to build the twenty-meter-high crusader castle. Some of the girls might consider this but would probably be more prone to try to imagine people, families even, treading the stone pathways ours were treading.

I tried to remember the first time I visited Byblos, probably in 1957 or '58. I recall coming only reluctantly and rather grumpily, probably one Saturday, with my mother and maybe a friend of hers. I vaguely remember being slightly intrigued by the interior of the castle. Of the rest, the foundations of Neolithic houses, the Phoenician ramparts, the Persian gate, or the Hittite temple? Nothing.

The older I have become, the more I have understood that even though I have no conscious recognition or recollection of much of what I saw here—or of the racism I saw in South Carolina while visiting my relatives, or of camping along the pristine shores of Lake Shasta with my father, or of so many of the many events that have made up my days....

The older I become, the more I begin—ever so slightly—to understand the vast complexity of the process of becoming human.

So I wonder if Amanda, who took copious notes and asked probing questions of the guide, will remember anything about this day. More important, will any of it make a difference in the kind of person she becomes, even if she doesn't remember anything about this day? And what about Ali, who spent most of the time hovering as far from the guide as he could with Danny, both of them moaning and complaining? Will he, years from now, conjure the image of seventy-five Genoese galleys laying siege to the city in 1104? Or did he, perhaps, find himself describing the dark, narrow underground passage to Ahiram's tomb to his family over dinner?

And Samer, who, in his mid-teenaged years, witnessed the inauguration of America's first non-white president and gazed from the rampart of a nine hundred-year-old fortress, looking out on the tiny natural harbor that made Byblos so strategic. What will he make of this?

What will Samer do with this much history?

What will he do with Obama's promise to the Muslim world that America will devise a foreign policy "based on mutual interest and mutual respect"? How will he blend what such remarks bring to mind with what he read about the sack of Jerusalem at the end of the tour on Friday, Fulcher of Chartres' first-hand account of mayhem, rape, pillage, hatred, and disdain?

How do we make all these things fit together? How do we make sense of our history? Of histories? Of history?

Further, what will they do, Samer and all the young people who stood in that elbow-to-elbow, smoke-filled room cheering Obama's insistence that "our patchwork heritage is our strength, not our weakness," while all around them the economic engine that has conceived, constructed, and transported this television screen to Ras Beirut, raised the salmon and grown the caper on his cracker, woven the fabrics, sewn the shoes, and made all the rest of the things that he and I and everyone else in this room, in this city, in this world have come to assume entails the world? What will we do as that world crumbles, layer by layer, segment by segment, product by product?

Byblos has housed seventeen civilizations over six thousand years. Ours will, more than likely, not be the last.

What will Samer do—what will we all do—with this unfolding history? On the same day that America celebrates the possibility of overcoming its own demons, Ban Ki Moon tours Gaza, shaking his head at the gratuitous damage America's most steadfast ally has wrought on Samer's and Ramsi's neighbors, on Renée's father's people.

All this goes on while Bangladeshi migrants, looking for work in Indonesia, are dumped on desert islands by Thai officials. While children die of cholera in Zimbabwe. While Tereza and Henrique, my friends in Recife, Brazil, explain that stopping for a red light can be hazardous if the ubiquitous street-corner thieves decide you and your car look ripe for robbery. While a friend here explains that rental cars in Lebanon—which are plainly marked as such by light-green license plates—are often targeted for theft, since their drivers will be less likely to put up a big fuss.

While Obama winds up his remarks. We are, he promises, about to enter "a new era of responsibility…[when we emphasize] our duties to ourselves, our nation, and our world."

We will "endure what storms may come."

And then, concluding, as dishes clink while the buffet is laid out in the adjacent room, "…and god bless you."

The applause begins, there in Washington and here in Beirut. And in many elsewheres. On this historic day. Part of history. Of histories.

"Well," the young man standing in front of me shouts above the din to his neighbor, "here we go."

* * *

I'm reminded that, in the long run, it's Samer's acts of touring Byblos and attending the inaugural event at Bardo's restaurant in the same week that tell us more about the true history of humanity than the castle he visited and the parades he watched on the widescreen.

Or that has more impact on the ways castles end up being constructed and inaugurations conducted. What really matters is what Tolstoy called, in the essay that introduces *War and Peace*, "the history of the life of the peoples and their impulses."

People like Mark Dorman.

Mark came to Beirut—well, actually, was brought to Beirut by his father, who took a semester-long teaching appointment at the Near East School of Theology—last August, knowing that in January he'd return to finish his senior year at his southern California high school.

So Mark came to ACS, where his father had studied thirty years ago while *his* father was the president of AUB. A homecoming for the elder Dorman, an uprooting for the wife and son.

Things at school were tough for Mark in the beginning. Lots of small strikes against him, many related to the importance of stylish cool among affluent young Lebanese, some related to the way the world works for teenagers anywhere.

Mark's a bit of an odd duck, not your typically style-conscious Lebanese teenager. So for quite some time he hovered on the outskirts of the society of his senior class, being, at best, tolerated, at worst, mildly harassed. He finally found a few friends to hang out with, but it still wasn't the best of all possible worlds for this very pleasant young man.

Then he got a part in the fall drama production, the bedroom farce *Lend Me a Tenor*. Not just a part. He got the lead. Long about mid-October word began to get around that he was really good.

Adults who'd been watching from the sidelines breathed a sigh of relief—doing a good job as the lead in the school play would get him a lot of high-fives, regular greetings from his peers in the hallway between classes, and maybe even an affectionate nickname.

Opening night.

He really was good, a very talented kid. His Italian accent cavorted appropriately up and down the tonal scale; he lifted that hefty body lightly around the stage; his lechery was exceptionally believable.

But then, right in the middle of a very busy scene where everybody was running hither and yon, Mark raced along the center of the stage toward stage right and slipped, then fell onto the floor right smack in front of the first row.

And then, without missing a beat, he hauled that bulk up from that floor, put his hands on the stage, hefted himself up, and continued stage-rightward, picking up his lines where he'd left off maybe two seconds before, when he lost his footing. It was all done with such aplomb that it took the audience a few moments to realize that his fall wasn't scripted.

Having goofed, very badly, and having redeemed himself, very excellently, Mark Dorman became a hero.

Every relationship Mark Dorman had with everyone in the school community changed from that moment.

Who could imagine—you heard in the halls—anyone having so much total cool as to fall off the stage, leap back up, and carry on, all without missing a beat?

Now I don't know if Mark visited Byblos during his stay here or what stories his father told him about the Beirut of his youth or what he now understands about the relationships between Israel and the inhabitants of the lands it occupies.

But I am sure that Mark's life was changed in those two seconds in the ACS auditorium.

Tolstoy continues, "So long as histories are written of separate individuals, whether Caesars, Alexanders, Luthers, or Voltaires, and not the histories of all, absolutely all those who take part in an event, it is quite impossible to describe the movement of humanity."

The history of all. The history of the small events that make all of us—each and every one—who we are, that teach us how to see the world, what strategies to apply to make the world work for us, when to stay and when to fold, and all the rest.

I contemplate this way of thinking about how history works as I read A. Roger Ekirch's piece from the recent *American Historical Review* that my friend Dick sent me, "Sleep We Have Lost: Pre-Industrial Slumber in the British Isles." Ekirch writes, "Until the close of the early modern era, Western Europeans on most evenings experienced two major intervals of sleep bridged by up to an hour or more of quiet wakefulness" (29), going on to discuss what people did during that wakeful hour or two in the middle of the night.

He cites an old English ballad that suggested, "At the wakening of your first sleepe/You she have a hott drinke made,/And at the wakening of your next sleepe/Your sorrows will have a slake" (34). Those not so fortunate as to have time for a toddy in the middle of the night might catch up on their laundry or, as a doctor from Bath advised, "Students that must of necessity watch and study by night, that they do it not till after their first sleep" (34).

I consider many things: Mark's fall from the stage and some Wessex clergyman sipping tea in the dark of the night as he thinks about his sermon. A I wander toward downtown early Saturday morning in search of buildings I've been reading about in *L'Histoire de Beyrouth*. Considering all these things, I wonder what difference little things like this ultimately make? What difference do such patterns make in the ways we unfold our own lives?

And what difference does the unfolding of each single life make in the unfolding of what we think of as history, of the grand narratives we conceive to make sense of the ways countries and cultures move through time?

Tolstoy tells us they make all the difference. History is the indivisible sum of all those parts. How I take my coffee, or how we take our coffees, might cause a war—or end one.

* * *

After several aborted efforts, I finally found Beirut's long-abandoned synagogue. I am told there are eight Jews left in the city now, nine if you count Saul, the ACS history teacher.

Having missed the building on several previous jaunts, I decided to walk along a road above the area where it was supposed to be. Indeed, I spotted the building below, its red-tile roof shredded by weather, the paint on its exterior walls almost entirely peeled away. I walked down the steps toward the street where the building stood, surrounded by new construction projects.

I peered through the wrought-iron gate. The front doors and windows were long gone, and the interior was overgrown with weeds and ailanthus and locust trees. Above the doorway, Hebrew lettering.

Once, Beirut's Jewish community thrived alongside the city's Armenians, Maronites, Druze, Orthodox, Sunni, Shia, and all the rest. Since the creation of Israel, it has dwindled to almost nothing.

I walked on, passing from the grander history of this city and that religion into a place where my personal history recently intersected with Beirut's. Coming to the Capuchin church, I remembered the day, almost a decade ago, that I chanced upon this church and, chatting with the guard, learned that the following day the church would be formally rededicated. It had been severely damaged during the civil war, and it had taken almost ten years to raise the money and rebuild the church, which is situated only a few blocks from the former green line that separated Christian Beirut from Muslim Beirut.

I arrived early enough to get a seat. Listening to the speeches and then the sermon in French, I felt myself part of something significant.

Taking a seat in the empty church this morning a decade later, I tried to recall that day, trying to imagine the role it had played in my ultimate decision to come back to Beirut.

Then I walked further into the reconstructed downtown, where French-Mandate-era buildings are coming back to life. Well, coming back to life again, having undergone several false starts since 2005, each of which was aborted by some violence—the Hariri assassination in 2005, the Israeli attacks of 2006, Hizbollah's street fighting last summer.

The beige sandstone of the late Ottoman and French Mandate periods predominates here: the solidity of the Parliament building that faces the Place de l'Etoile clock tower, the stockier municipal building a few blocks away, block after block of two-to-four story buildings housing street-level up-scale shops and restaurants. Scattered throughout the district are seventeenth– and eighteenth-century mosques, with the Maronite and Orthodox cathedrals flanking the recently excavated Roman ruins, all dwarfed by the blue dome and tall spires of the new Al Amine mosque.

Enough history. Time to go home and get some breakfast.

Passing westward through new high-end apartment and shopping complexes, I pause at the truck entrance of the "Beirut Square" apartment complex to investigate the project's progress. Architects' rough drafts and hand-scribbled notes make up a two-meter-high billboard posted on the walls adjacent to the entrance. In a brilliant touch of ad-copy design, the last paragraph of advertising copy in Italian is followed by an English translation, which reads, "We began to think about how the Lebanese people think of their houses…" but the words fade into a blur, then to black.

Turning from the promotional material, I step onto the building site itself. The roof of the synagogue is visible on the street beyond, and above that, the Grand Serail, the 150-year-old Ottoman military barracks that now houses the offices of Lebanon's prime minister. At the far end of the Beirut Square construction site, men are hard at work with bulldozers and backhoes preparing to lay a foundation.

Closer, I see clusters of men working with shovels, pushing wheelbarrows. Ah, more history! Every developer's nightmare: they've come upon the stacks of circular bricks that supported the floor of yet another, previously unknown, Roman bath a few millennia ago. These men are not building anything; they're conducting an archeological excavation. I wonder how the architects have integrated this probably unanticipated find into the original plans for the upscale ground-level shopping arcade.

Remembering that I'm hungry and am trying to get home for breakfast, I move on, past the soon-to-open Wadi Grand Residence (whose ad copy explains that living here will "Revitalize Mind, Body and Soul") and Noor Gardens ("Designed for Life Designed for Living"—check it out at www.noorgardens.com).

On past Baab Idriss into Hamra, which hopes it'll be able to hang onto its cache, even when all these new complexes come onto the market.

Hoping it'll be able to keep its toehold in the history of Beirut.

Shopkeeper by shopkeeper.

* * *

February 14. It's a big day. I'm checking Naharnet every few minutes to make sure that any blowback from today's massive commemoration of the fourth anniversary of Rafik Hariri's assassination remains minimal.

So far nothing to be concerned about. Some stones thrown at a group of pro-Hariri folks on their way home from Martyrs' Square. That was at three. It's after five now.

It's probably safe enough for us to take the number two bus down to the Monot Theater, where a traveling troupe is performing "The Grand Inquisitor." It's a bit of Dostoevsky's *Brothers Karamazov* that's often excerpted in anthologies on Existentialism, the one where the Grand Inquisitor explains patiently to a briefly-returned Jesus that people simply don't want what he had offered. They want "Miracle, Mystery and Authority," not freedom and truth.

That'll be an interesting series of juxtapositions, won't it? Watching a British troupe stage an excerpt from a Russian novel at a French-speaking university a few blocks from where some Lebanese have just commemorated a death that resulted in Syria's expulsion from the country, two days before other Lebanese will commemorate the assassination—probably by Israel—of one of their leaders in Damascus a year ago. Might as well cap it all off with dinner at the Chinese restaurant just down the street from the theater.

Lead stories on Al Jazeera and BBC both estimated "hundreds of thousands" of people packed into the broad Place de Martyrs facing Hariri's monument just south of the port.

CNN patched together a brief historical overview before the demonstration really got under way, suggesting that "thousands" would attend. Nothing since.

Nothing about the one o'clock moment of silence acknowledging the devastating bomb that dug a twenty-meter-wide crater in front of the St. Georges Hotel four years ago; nothing about how the echoes of Christian church bells blended symbolically with the call of Muslim muezzins through the afternoon sunlight.

Yesterday the United States embassy had sent out a more or less boilerplate "warden message":

> Saturday, the 14th of February will mark the fourth anniversary of the assassination of former Lebanese Prime Minister, Rafik Hariri. Thursday, February 12 will mark the one-year anniversary of the death of senior Hizballah official, Imad Fayez Mughniyah. There will be a remembrance ceremony for Rafik Hariri beginning at 10:00 a.m. on February 14th at Martyr's Square. Hizballah will commemorate the one-year anniversary

> of the death of Imad Mughniyah on February 16 at Al Raya Court in Sfeir area, Beirut, Southern Suburb. Americans are advised that they should avoid any areas where demonstrations, protests or other large gatherings are occurring.

But—I figured on Saturday morning—I could go early, before the young men have gotten all pumped up with adrenalin, before the crowds are too thick, the tempers frayed by too much standing cramped in a crowd in the noonday sun. No reason not to go downtown to watch the people pouring in from all over the country, scenes of which the Mustaqbal ("Future," pro-Hariri) TV station began airing as early as 8:00 a.m.

After all, I'd safely maneuvered situations like this before. And after all, these guys—the "March 14" guys—are the pro-Western ones, the ones who want a Lebanon where women can work and wear pretty much what they want, where religious affiliation is somewhat trumped by national allegiance, where most people don't believe in censoring films (unless they're pro-Israel) and videogames.

No reason not to venture out today, being careful, watching for groups of young men wearing green headbands, waving yellow flags—Hizbollah followers—who might be out looking for trouble.

Buffy just nodded and smiled, knowing I'd be careful, figuring that one way or another I'd make it back in time for lunch.

"Get us a Lebanese flag," she said as I left.

As she put it over dinner before the curtain went up on the play that evening, "Sometimes I get irritated with you, Nick, and lots of other things. But I've never been bored. Not once in our relationship have I been bored."

So I started walking toward Martyrs' Square several miles east of our apartment. As I came upon the main thoroughfare by Sanayeh park, the traffic picked up, almost all of the cars and buses plastered with Hariri posters, young men and women hanging out the windows waving flags: the Lebanese flag with its green cedar on a white background framed by two wide red stripes, light blue Mustaqbal flags, Lebanese Forces and Progressive Socialist Party flags, and others I didn't recognize.

Lots of chanting, lots of singing.

Lots of raucous and rowdy young people—you had to be careful not to get knocked on the head by an overzealous flag-waver. But older people as well, some women wearing traditional headscarves and dark, shapeless, ankle-length dresses and men in suits. Younger men and women dressed more casually. Lots of families. Grandma and Grandpa, Mom and Dad, a bunch of kids, all holding hands so as not to get separated in the crowds heading downtown.

I headed to the overpass just south of the gathering, figuring it would be a good place to get the full picture of what was going on.

Several soldiers stood leaning on the guardrail, watching people stream into the already jammed square.

Six young men strutted along the sidewalk below the overpass. One of them tried to take a blue Mustaqbal flag from an old man, who wrestled it away from him. Another taunted a young man carrying a PSP flag who was waiting off to the side for his friends.

But then their hormones trumped their politics, as three pretty young women passed, dressed to the nines in purple—headscarves, sweaters, pants and even high-heeled boots. The young men ogled, then catcalled. The young women looked at each other, giggled, and pointedly ignored the young men. The young men whistled and called more loudly, eventually, their efforts having come to naught, turning back toward the crowd to see what adventure might be next on their day's agenda.

I called Buffy to tell her all was OK and to let her listen to the deafening music being broadcast from the grandstand a quarter mile away.

Deciding to walk around the eastern edge of the crowd, then head home along the Corniche, I passed some of the new, expensive, several-story apartment buildings of Saifi Village, upscale dress shops and art galleries lining the twisting, narrow cobbled streets built to resemble the "real" Beirut. By the tony wine shop, by Café Paul, famous for its eggs benedict and the like, toward the harbor.

The crowds grew thicker. A young man stepped from the sidewalk and eagerly handed me a Lebanese flag on a sawed-off broom-handle. Another gave me a baseball cap that said *maak*, "with you." I unfurled the flag and put on the cap.

The music—mostly modern "I love Lebanon" types of songs by popular artists—was deafening. Scenes from Hariri's life flashed across widescreen television monitors set at intervals high above the crowds. At the top of the Alnahar building just ahead, a poster of Gebran Tueni, that newspaper's publisher who was assassinated—was that last year, or the year before? In the background, the huge el Amine mosque that Hariri had commissioned not long before his death, with the skyline of Beirut rising on the ridge beyond. Hawkers selling t-shirts, water, snacks, and flags did a steady business from the sidewalk.

I walked along Charles Helou Avenue, navigating the ambling throngs, then turning right into the several-acre patch of archeological excavations, Tell Beirut, that had been undertaken when the reconstruction of this part of the city had begun in the 1990s.

I stood looking at the site map. I'd been here a dozen times but had never really understood what was what or where. Today I took my time.

Oh, I see, on the right just down the path lies the Hellenistic road; just across the path from that is a wall from the Bronze Age. That would be what, one thousand years before the road? Yeah. And another wall, a Phoenician one—but who knows when that was—just beyond, next to a well from the Persian period, maybe 600 BCE. There's an arch from what remains of Beirut's small medieval castle. To its left, remnants of a building from the Ottoman period—that could have been built any time between 1500 and 1914.

A few other people wandered these erratic ruins, trying to make sense of them. But mostly, to my right, a steady stream of people continued—and would continue for the next two hours—to pour into Martyrs' Square.

Martyrs' Square. Originally named Place de la Liberté et de l'Union after the Ottoman Empire's Young Turk Revolution of 1908, then changed to Place des Martyrs in honor of the Lebanese nationalists hanged there by Jamal Pacha a few years later.

Two men sat sipping coffee beside several Roman columns that lay alongside the path leading toward the street, watching, as I was, the joyful people—families, high school classes, groups from churches and mosques—made their ways toward the ceremonies.

OK. Time to go. I don't much like crowds, and I wouldn't have understood much from the speeches, anyway. Turning toward the Corniche, I started home, negotiating against the tide of the tens of thousands of people who continued to swarm toward the Square.

I picked up my pace. I'd told Buff I'd be home by lunch.

CHAPTER 9
Day to Day

Saturday. It was almost seven fifteen before I rolled out of bed. No problem. I didn't have to be at school till around nine to meet the twenty seniors who'd be going to the Red Cross facility in Antelias to plant the olive trees donated by the ACS parents' group. Eighty-four trees. One for each senior.

A few years from now when the trees mature, the Red Cross will sell the olives under an ACS label, with the proceeds will go to the organization.

While my coffee heats up, I squeeze a large navel orange and a smaller blood orange, their eaves still dangling from the stems.

I sip my coffee while I read a poem before checking my e-mail and then eating my breakfast. I'm watching the time carefully. Almost eight o'clock. I close the book and head for the kitchen to get my breakfast just as Naharnet posts the day's first "live coverage" update:

7:50 a.m.: al Mustaqbl News: Two rockets launched from al Qulaiala and al-Mansouri, in the south close to Naquora toward Israel.

OK. Not big enough to keep us from planting the trees. Breakfast. I take it into the dining room and open *L'histoire de Beyrouth*. I'm reading about the 1920s.

> Whatever the obstacles may have been, however, the tendency was more and more clearly in favor of dropping the veil, which was understood as progress and defended as such, notably in a book published in 1928 by a young Muslim woman, Nazira Zeineddine, under the title *De-veiling and*

the Veil, with an explicitly evocative subtitle, "The liberation of women and social renewal in the Muslim world" (378).

Another Internet check.

8:15 a.m.: Press reports stated that one of the rockets blew up at a non-residential area inside Lebanese territory.

8:20 a.m.: UNIFIL did not monitor any rocket launching from south Lebanon, Israel responds with 3 shells.

OK. Ready to go. I have the cell phone. Buffy and I have agreed that the one who plans to venture farther from the beaten path will take the mobile phone we share. I put that and my little black notebook in my back pocket. Better take my residency permit. Rain hat and umbrella. Get a little money—you never know. Out the door.

As I walk toward ACS, the events continue to unfold.

8:30 a.m.: Al jazeera: Israel confirms one rocket strike at the western part of the Galilee in north Israel.

8:32 a.m.: Agence France Presse: One injured by rocket fired into Israel from Lebanon: radio.

8:35 a.m.: al-Arabiya: the rockets launched from south Lebanon toward Israel were Ketyoushas.

Maybe, I think as I turn the corner toward the newsstand, I'll pick up *L'Orient Le Jour* instead of the *Daily Star*. It has more complete theatre and art show listings.

I should be back by early afternoon. Eighty-four trees, twenty kids—how long can that take?

Damn, I forgot the camera. Plenty of time. Turn around at the vegetable seller and hustle back to the apartment.

Got it. Out again.

I'll get the newspaper on the way back.

No rain yet. Maybe we'll make it through the morning dry.

Down Rue Sadat, across Rue Bliss. Most of my colleagues take a "shortcut" through the International College campus to get from Bliss down to ACS. "Shortcut" is in quotation marks because it saves all of three—five if you're really slow—minutes. But it deprives you—or me, anyway, since nobody else seems to care—of a morning view of the wide panorama of the Mediterranean as I descend from the ridgeline of Ras Beirut toward sea level.

Each morning is different. Some days the sea's like glass. But usually the waves are rolling in, sometimes almost directly from the west, so they'll pass parallel to this shoreline, heading for the north-south coastline. Other days they'll come in from the northwest, and spatter or crash against the Corniche. If they're in from the southwest, all you see from this vantage point is the chop and swells farther out, while the waves burst against Pigeon Rocks and the Sporting Club on the southwestern tip the of the peninsula.

This morning the waves billow huge and break in wind-swept frenzies, storms bringing them from the northwest. The waves seem to echo the clouds that roll and roil directly overhead and the other clouds, thicker and darker, farther out to sea, heralding rain.

Only three kids have arrived when I get to school. But the bus is there, along with the car we'll follow to the site. All is well. I tell Karine—the young woman who organized this event—that I don't mind waiting a few minutes but that we need to get on our way by nine fifteen or so. She understands, but does not like the plan—these are her friends, and this is her project. And this is Lebanon; people are hardly ever on time in Lebanon.

On Naharnet, events continue.

9:00 a.m. AFP Three Israel rockets hit south Lebanon: Lebanese army.

9:02 a.m.: National News Agency: 6 Israeli shells landed between al-Huniyeh and al-Mansouri.

Karine's on the phone. Firas and Ryan say they're on the way. Sabine lives in that part of town, so she'll meet us at the Red Cross. Faisal is on his way. Kids show up. Karine keeps calling.

Everybody's here but Faisal. He's still on his way.

"Where is he?"

She calls again.

"He's at the McDonald's in Ain Mreisse. Can we pick him up?"

That's a mile and a half away, and he's walking. "Sure. Let's go."

9:10 a.m.: al-Arabiya: Hizbollah denied its knowledge of the Ketyousha rockets fired from the south toward Israel.

We stop for Faisal and then drive through town, over the cement-lined trough through which the Beirut River runs. The river is the formal boundary between the city and the suburbs. The suburbs look the same as the city: apartment buildings, offices, street-level shops, sidewalk kiosks, narrow streets twisting off into who knows where.

There's almost never more than a trickle in the Beirut River, but today it's red and rushing from all the rain that's fallen over the past few weeks. The rain turns to snow when it hits the tall mountain ridges—snow that'll melt gradually and furnish the country with its water for the subsequent eight months.

We turn northward along the coast, then up the steep hillside into Antelias, not far from the fortress-like American embassy. Halfway up the steep hillside we turn left off the main road and immediately right, pulling up in front of the three-story beige stone Red Cross building. Officials pile out the main door to welcome us.

Handshakes, kisses, greetings, arrangements. I'm introduced.

"*Enchanté*," the Red Cross director says.

"*En anglais pour lui*," Karine's mother says.

"*Non, je parle français assez bien*," I say. The director smiles and begins to explain, in French, the plan for this morning.

The plan, that is, unless the skies open up, as seems so likely.

The plan unfolds.

There's a little wooden sign to be set into the ground near one clump of olive trees: "American Community School at Beirut—Class of 2009." They'll put in a few trees, then the sign, then take lots of pictures. Fast, before the rains come.

The TV cameras begin to roll. Al Mustaqbl Television, Future Television, the station run by the Future Movement, Hariri's party, is here. They'll be filming and interviewing throughout the entire process, putting together a segment for a morning show on local culture.

A young woman hands a microphone to Joe, who's standing next to the newly planted trees, near the sign.

The little light on the TV camera blinks red. The interview begins. I lean forward, listening for words and phrases, astounded to find that I'm actually understanding a fair amount, both of what the interviewer is asking and of Joe's responses.

She wants to know what he's doing here, and how this fits into his work at ACS. Joe—the same Joe who seems to have recently decided to systematically skip many of his classes—articulately describes the school's community service requirements and then goes on to explain that these trees are being planted for the future of the community and even of Lebanon. He is poised and knowledgeable.

The microphone goes to Faisal, and the camera swings his way—the same Faisal whom I had chided for delaying our departure when we picked him up at McDonald's an hour earlier. Faisal is equally competent, equally poised, equally articulate.

And I am reminded of how precarious and unpredictable an enterprise education really is.

We want so badly to be able to say, "We did these specific, measurable things with these specific students, and they responded by being able to do these specific, measurable things. Our measurements, thus, demonstrate that we have succeeded."

Instead all we can truly say is, "Well, after years spent cloistered with these two kids, talking about everything from gerunds to quadratic equations, when they were asked to stand in the mud in front of a TV camera and talk about some of the things we'd mentioned off and on, they spoke articulately about why they were standing there in the mud."

That's really about all we can really say about education.

The irony is that if I hadn't been standing there in the mud with these two boys, having, valiantly and with great frustration, practiced my Arabic day after day, I'd not even have known that much.

The work party moved on to another planting area. There was Mihir, who still hasn't gotten his report card because he hasn't turned in the volleyball uniform he left at his host family's house in Cairo a few months ago. He's handing a sapling to Sabine, who takes it gingerly, not wanting to soil her white Northeastern University sweatshirt.

There's Khalil, who stayed home from school yesterday with a severe case of food poisoning—one of those kids who hides his kind heart behind a steady stream of mild sarcasm. And Gabby, who was uprooted from her cozy Catholic girls school in Manhattan for her last two years of high school and whose mother wonders why they didn't have sense enough to uproot the family years before. "This world is so much more real in some way I can't really define," she says. Mark too was dropped into the ACS maelstrom in the middle of his junior year, yanked away from Bethesda Chevy Chase High School, where he was a soccer star. He's applied to the University of Maryland, but maybe, he tells me, just maybe he'll stick around and attend AUB, down the road from ACS.

Elsewhere, other things are happening.

10:30 am: NBN TV: Security Forces find rocket platforms used in launching rockets at Israel at a field in al-Hiniyeh.

More holes dug in the red mud, more trees planted. The rain has held off.

I am interviewed. The reporter says she'll translate what I say into Arabic. But I give it a shot, anyway. It works, but not well enough for TV.

"Why does ACS do this?"

"This particular activity, or the broader 'this,' community service?"

"Both."

"We do this, like the young man told you before, and like the name of your television station, for the future, for *almustaqbl*." She smiles. "Specifically, these trees will bear fruit that will be sold to raise money for the Red Cross.

"More broadly, ACS believes that the purpose of school is not only to improve the mind," I tap my head, trying to remember the Arabic for "mind," or even "brain," "but because we believe that the purpose of education is to make better people, not just people who can pass tests.

"This is why our students work as tutors with our own middle school students, but also with Palestinian kids, and why they visit the elderly, and raise money for the 'sister schools' in southern Lebanon and Sri Lanka."

I wanted to add, "And so when kids stand holding microphones in front of TV cameras, they can explain how what they do blends with what the world needs." But I thought that was a bit over the top. Or at least hard to translate.

The trees are planted.

We go inside for snacks and coffee.

In the south:

10:50 a.m.: Fatah Secretary-general in Lebanon Sultan Abul Ainien said no Palestinian PLO faction is connected to the rocket launching to Israel early this morning.

11:00 a.m.: PFLP politburo member Ramez Mustapha to al-Jadeed TV: The Front has nothing to do with the rocket launching toward Israel

11:20 a.m.: Lebanese Military Command: An unknown and suspected source fired two rockets from the south (toward Israel) the investigation is ongoing.

11:30 a.m.: PM Saniora: The firing of rockets from south Lebanon and the Israeli response is a violation of UNSCR 1701. Such acts are rejected and denounced at a time when Israeli aggression toward Lebanon is repeated.

I ask an official to show the students how the blood bank works.

The students dutifully troop upstairs.

I'm chatting with Gabby when Ryan comes to tell me that he's going to donate blood. He's eighteen, hasn't had any of the proscribed diseases, doesn't have a tattoo, or any of the other things that would prevent him from doing this.

"Sure. We'll wait."

I remember when I first met Ryan two years ago. He was big then, but he's huge now—tall and wide and sturdy. He was new to ACS, having spent years at the German School. His spoken English was tolerable, but his written English was atrocious. I was his English teacher.

The problem was that he didn't want to work. No. Worse. He didn't know *how* to work.

He would write two sentences, call it a paragraph, and brag that he had actually done something. I gradually convinced—enabled?—him to write more, then to review it for correctness, and then to revise it for meaning.

Slowly, slowly, slowly.

Before I left for the US in June, 2007, he thanked me for what I had done.

"But I drove you crazy, Ryan, stopping you in the halls to tell you to do this or not to do that. You hated it."

"Yes, sir. I hated it. But I needed to hear it."

Ryan's blood flows through the tube. Fadool comes racing into the room.

"I want to give blood, but they won't let me!"

"Why not?"

"Because I've lived in Africa."

"Where, Fadool?"

"Libya."

"That's not the part of Africa they care about. Try again."

He left, then returned smiling, waving the form he had to fill out.

I looked it over with him.

"Uh-oh. I've had a tattoo."

"Go talk to the guy."

He raced back to the doctor. Then he raced back into the room. Fadool is a tall, lithe young man who could easily become a Valentino-type movie star. He races everywhere.

"Oh, sir, he really wants my blood. He said that the procedure was OK."

Back to the form.

"What's this?" He reads aloud an Arabic word we don't recognize.

"A tetanus shot," someone translates.

Back to the doctor.

Back again.

"Sir, he really wants my blood. He said the clinic where I got the shot was fine."

Fadool completes the form, takes off his shirt, and sits on the reclining chair.

Just a few weeks ago, Fadool had come to my classroom after school. He wanted to know why he hadn't received an A in my Creative Nonfiction class.

"Fadool, you have a real disadvantage."

He looked shocked. Fadool always looks *something*.

"What, sir?"

"Your charm. You are going to have to figure out how to learn not to rely on your charm so much."

He looked surprised. "What do you mean, sir?"

Now one of the fascinating things about working with young people is how interested they are, by and large, in talking about themselves, even when what you have to say isn't particularly positive.

You can imagine the conversation I had with Fadool—how important it is to have more than one trick in your bag, how easy it is to fall back on what comes naturally, how different it is once you get away from the safe, familiar little world of high school.

Did he listen? Will it make a difference?

Well, I had no idea whether Ryan was paying any attention when I regularly stopped him in the hall two years ago. And we still don't know if we can get Joe to make it to all his classes or Faisal to consider other people while he's standing in line to get his McDonald burger.

But I'm glad I didn't try to explain any of this to the interviewer from Mustaqbl.

Trees are planted, blood's been donated. We pile into the bus, still ahead of the rain. The sea still crashes against the rocks along the Corniche as we pull up to the school.

1:15 p.m.: Central Security Council convenes at ministry of Interior with Minister Baroud presiding, to discuss security situation in the country and the recent security incidents that took place.

2:45 p.m.: President Michel Suleiman: Firing the rockets from south Lebanon is a challenge against the Lebanese will, Israel's response is a violation of UNSCR 1701.

3:00 p.m.: Central Security Council: We shall continue strengthening the security and military deployment in all Lebanese regions particularly in Beirut and Mount Lebanon. Security forces are to deal with strictness with any violations

I walk home, picking up a *Daily Star* along the way.

* * *

Now I belong in Beirut.

Now I belong in the way I felt I belonged in the Fan District of Richmond, Virginia, the night I chased two burglars away from an open window in a dark alley. The way I felt I belonged in Weathersfield, Vermont, the day I came upon a fallen tree blocking Jarvis Road, parked my car, and walked home to get my chainsaw, then cut the tree into sections, which I dragged to the roadside, opening the way to traffic.

Thursday evening was beautiful. Buffy and MJ were having coffee at Younes Café just around the corner from our apartment, but I'd had enough of people. I decided to amble over to Raouché to watch waves crash against Pigeon Rocks and the pink and golden rays of sunset breaking through the storm clouds rolling in from the west.

It was a wonderful way to end the day.

Walking home, I thought about the way women are treated.

An older boy accused of harassing a young girl at school had brought this to mind, but questions of gender relationships are never far from the surface in this part of the world.

Of course, these questions lie just beneath the surface everywhere—when people complain about the status of women in the Middle East, I remind them that women were not allowed to vote in the United States until my mother was nine and that she'd have been fired from her job teaching school if she'd been seen consorting with a man.

I also remind them that—jumping ahead three-quarters of a century—just about the time many Americans thought we had put some of the worst of these sexist attitudes to rest, we hear our youngsters—boys and girls alike—singing about "hos" and "bitches" as though these were perfectly appropriate ways to speak about women.

But the issue is certainly more central to the politics and society of the Middle East than it is in the West today.

The bright, energetic young Lebanese elementary school teacher who's always stylishly dressed and mildly flirtatious told me she'd had a wonderful time visiting family in Riyadh, Saudi Arabia, over the Christmas holidays.

"Isn't it hard to adjust, covering your hair and wearing an abaya?" I asked.

"Oh, no. It's just the way things are. You don't even notice after a while."

"But you drive here, don't you? And can be seen with men other than family members?"

"Yes. But you adjust." She flashed a brilliant smile and returned to her photocopying.

Then there's Donia, a brilliant Iraqi-Lebanese tenth grader, who often pats me on the shoulder as she passes my desk, going to her seat in history class. "Hey, Boke. Good morning," she says, grinning broadly. Her Serbian friend Natalija puts her hand on my hand as I point out a problem with her paper. "No, wait, sir. I see what you're saying, but look here, at what I wrote in the next paragraph," as she moves my hand down so my finger points at the sentence she believes makes the point I'm saying she missed.

Touch is central to this culture. Walking around the classroom, briefly discussing the papers I've just returned, I might put my hand on each student's shoulder or forearm—male or female. It's almost required, though I don't touch girls or women who are covered.

In the public realm, there's Saudi Arabia's recent appointment of a woman—the first ever to hold any ministerial position—as Deputy Minister for Women's Education, a revolutionary event that made headlines throughout the region. And in Lebanon the controversy over whether a Lebanese woman married to a foreigner should be able to pass her citizenship to her children.

Questions of gender are never far from the surface here.

But the harassment issue at school nagged at me. I was considering the incident—and whether I had thawed the beans we were going to eat for dinner—as I turned off Rue Sadat onto Rue Commodore on my way home from

Raouché. Night had fallen; the wet streets glistened in the glow from still-open shops and streetlights.

Halfway down the block a young couple stood talking at the edge of the street. She wore a little black beret tilted to one side, high heeled boots, a dark jacket, and tight-fitting jeans—sort of the archetypical young Beiruti. He wore a heavy jacket and jeans. I smiled, remembering being a young man standing in the street talking intimately with a young woman.

But as I passed I noticed that all was not well with this couple. They were angry. When he took her by the arm, she pushed his hand away. She raised her voice. He raised his.

My smile turned wry, as I remembered the downside of being part of a young couple—the part that simply didn't have the slightest idea how to deal with the complexities of what we call love, for lack of a better term.

Crossing into the next block, though, I wondered just how serious this dispute was, so I stopped and turned back to watch.

She was, it seemed, trying to get past him, to continue walking in my direction. Each time she tried to pass him, though, he stepped in front of her. His voice got louder. Hers got shriller.

I stood watching. What are the limits here, I wondered? And what would happen to an *ajnabi*—a foreigner—who interfered before those limits were reached?

Standing on Rue Commodore, watching what looked like a situation that was escalating toward violence, I understood how little I understood.

Then I saw a man step between two cars and approach the couple.

I began walking hurriedly toward them. I watched him saying something to the them. The young man shouted at him. He walked away hurriedly.

The young man resumed his tirade at the young woman.

I touched the sleeve of the man who had spoken to the couple.

"Don't go," I said.

He turned toward me. He was in his thirties, shorter than I, balding. He had a narrow mustache. He wore a black windbreaker.

"But I don't want to face him alone."

"You're not alone," I said. "Come."

And I stepped between the cars, hoping he was following.

"Hey! Leave her alone!" I yelled. In English. As loudly as I could.

Other passersby stopped, turning toward the couple. The man was forcing her to move across the street, still yelling.

We all—I think there were six or seven of us by now—moved toward them.

The young man turned to look at us.

Then he turned back to the woman. He slapped her. Hard.

Then he slapped her again.

Then he started walking hurriedly back toward Rue Sadat, hunched over, his arms pumping.

The woman ran in the opposite direction, high heels clicking, her hand on her cheek.

We stood watching. First her, as she disappeared into the night. Then him, as he charged down the street and around the corner.

"Thank you," I said to the man who had stayed.

Then I turned and walked home, looking down the side streets for the young woman, whose cheek would be bruised.

* * *

Narrow streets and narrower alleyways, twisting left, then right, branching off here and there into a vague distance, all darkened by the shadows of buildings and lined with tiny shops.

I've visited two such places this weekend.

On Sunday, it was the souks of Tripoli, fifty miles north of Beirut. Downtown Tripoli was spared the ravages of the Civil War which turned Beirut's souks to rubble, so we got off the bus the school had hired for the outing not far from the central clock tower, then stepped into the souks and back in time.

Well, sort of. One of the great things about Tripoli's souks, unlike those of Sidon and Byblos, is that they remain vital, integrated into the community. So instead of being accosted by yet another shopkeeper desperate to sell at least one samovar or Palestinian headscarf to at least one tourist today, you are ignored. It's local residents who're perusing the wares—the shoes, blouses, sale-priced laundry detergents, and bushel bags of herbs and spices—that frequent these shops.

Oh, there are the samovars and headscarves (which have become a fashion statement for Lebanon's young, although I'm not sure how Yasser Arafat would've felt about the purple and mauve versions), the obligatory perfumed soap factory, and the under-employed tour guide who tries to talk me into a tour of the mosque, just at the end of the arcade.

Shoppers crowd the narrow walkway. How old are the buildings? I ask John Darcy, the ACS teacher who had arranged the outing.

"They're Ottoman," he explains.

"John, that doesn't tell me much. That could mean any time from 1519 to 1919."

He smiles and shrugs his shoulders.

John is Lebanese. The Darcy surname comes from his great grandfather, a d'Arcy who came to Lebanon from France in the mid-nineteenth century, when the allure of this part of the world began to attract entrepreneurs and cultural pilgrims. John is Roman Catholic and grew up in a strictly Christian district just northeast of the city.

"The first time I went to the Hamra district—I was a teenager—and heard the call to prayer, I was shocked. I had no idea what that was."

The Lebanese teachers who've come on the trip mostly wander and watch, as I do. At the end of our wandering, as we step out of the souk onto the main street, Arij takes her son Sammy into a shop that seems to have reasonably priced running shoes. I stand outside chatting with Najwa, her mother. But by and large, Katya, Nada, John, and the others haven't come to buy things. They've just come to be here.

The Americans, on the other hand, are perennial shoppers. They're in and out of stores—some tourist-oriented, others offering more mundane fare—each time coming out with yet another plastic bag full of more stuff.

What is it we've done to ourselves? When did the concept of "retail therapy" cease being a joke and become a way of life?

Of course, not only Americans see life as an opportunity to accumulate stuff you didn't know you wanted until you saw it.

I had stopped by Wassim's mosaic workshop yesterday, and he had raised just this point.

"What made us define ourselves by what we have? By what we purchase?" he asked. "How did American capitalism triumph so totally, even here, where we should be thinking about other things?"

I told him the story of my Southern Sudanese friend, Timothy, who had been astounded when I'd told him my wife and I had owned the same couch for several decades.

"But don't you get tired of what you own and need to buy a new one?" he had asked me.

"This young man," I'd explained to Wassim, "had grown up in a village in Southern Sudan, running naked from hut to hut. You'd think that he would understand that what matters is more than just owning things, after the war and devastation he'd lived through in south Sudan. Buffy says that's what happened to us is we go out into the world 'looking for something to want.'"

"That's it exactly," Wassim had replied.

And that was it exactly, there in those narrow, several-hundred-year-old narrow souks.

But it wasn't capitalism run amok that I had seen and understood as I'd wandered a different set of narrow alleyways the day before my Tripoli outing.

On Saturday I had gone with a half-dozen Americans to Bourj al Barajneh, the largest of Beirut's Palestinian refugee camps. We had gone to meet with some young Palestinian men and women who'd expressed interest in informal conversational English classes to the director of the camp's Women's Center, Miriam. She had in turn gotten in touch with David, an ACS colleague who's involved with some children's programs at the camp.

There's nothing romantic about the narrow alleyways of Bourj al Barajneh. We know that the several-story, ramshackle concrete-and-cement-block buildings that line them were built sometime after 1948, when hundreds of thousands of Palestinians fled the newly declared State of Israel.

We know that the half-meter-wide bundles of black wires that line the alleyways just above our heads carry pirated electricity to the camp's thirty thousand residents.

We know that the people we pass—old women who may remember a village in Palestine, young men who've never known anything but these alleys and the makeshift buildings that line them—are strictly limited in the jobs they can hold, the schools they can attend, and the rights they have once they step out of the camps and into "Lebanon," just beyond. The Lebanese government is very miserly in dispensing rights and possibilities to the Palestinians for two reasons: first, there aren't enough good jobs to go around for the Lebanese; second, if the Palestinians become too comfortable in Lebanon, they'll not want to go "home," when that longed-for day comes.

But we also know that this day will never come. Even if Israel eventually stops undermining the fragile peace process and actually halts the creation of new settlements on the West Bank (which it agreed to do long ago), it will never accept the Palestinian "right of return" for fear of an adjacent overcrowded Palestinian state populated by resentful former refugees. Further, for the vast majority of the residents of the camps, Palestine is just an old-folks' dream, a bunch of stories about olive groves and quiet evenings under the stars. Most of these refugees have lived their lives in this little island in bustling Beirut and have no desire to go back to a world that isn't what their grandparents tell them that it was anyway.

In Tripoli, even stopping to gawk and shop, it took less than half an hour to wander all the souk's zigzag streets and alleys. Walking at a good clip, it took us almost fifteen minutes to walk from one side of the Bourj al Barajneh to the other, and this was following only one route, ignoring the dozens of side alleys that would have led us into other parts of this warren-like maze of buildings that line the twisting and turning two-meter-wide walkways, most lined with a central gutter to carry off the rainwater, all of which lie in the perpetual shadow of the buildings, and all of which are festooned with bundles of electrical wires. No samovars and fancy soaps in these tiny shops—only cans of fava beans, toilet paper, t-shirts, and cheap shoes. Necessities.

Thirty thousand people are said to live here. Thirty thousand out of the four hundred thousand Palestinian refugees who live in Lebanon. Four hundred thousand out of a population of four million residents in Lebanon.

A television news clip last night showed an UNWRA (United Nations Relief and Works Agency—they've been helping Palestinian refugees since

1950, and they're the ones who first publicly reported on the unfathomable damage Israel recently wrought on Gaza) official celebrating the beginning of the reconstruction of the Nahr al Bared camp that was torn apart last year, first by internecine fighting, then by bombardments by the Lebanese army.

She was full of hope for a bright new future. A bright new future in a shinier, safer camp. A shinier, safer reservation-like arrangement in a country that simply wishes the problem, the people, would go away.

In the classroom at the Women's Center, our white plastic chairs scraped along the concrete floor as we pulled up to the table Miriam had reserved for us. I watched my colleagues set up their chairs at the far end of the table, noting that this would result in an us-them arrangement when the students joined us. Having learned years ago—working with "disadvantaged" parents in Vermont—how important it is to include the people you're working with as quickly as possible, I sat near the other end of the table so that I'd be sitting among the Palestinians when they came.

And it worked. Miriam explained—in Arabic and in English—why we were there and that we hoped to use this time to schedule some classes. Then the conversation began, going back and forth about days and times.

Once I saw that there was basic agreement and that the conversation had degenerated into minutiae about which Americans could and could not come at what times on which days, I turned to the students—eight young women and two young men—to begin to assess the English levels we'd be working with.

Two of the women who spoke fairly good English were sisters and told me they sometimes spoke to each other in English.

"You need to do that every day, you know," I said, explaining that I threw myself into as many situations as possible where I'd have no choice but to listen to Arabic and respond in Arabic. We joked about how hard it is to learn a new language—any new language.

Almost everyone had somebody they could practice with from time to time.

One young woman, however, spoke almost no English and told me in Arabic that she knew no one who spoke English.

"Say what I say. *Fhimti?* Do you understand?"

She nodded, smiling.

"I have…"

"I have..."

"no friends..."

"no friends..."

"who speak English."

"who speak English."

She tried to put it together into a complete sentence. I repeated. She tried. Others repeated. She tried. She got better. We were all laughing.

The other end of the table grew quiet. They had obviously finished arranging whatever needed arranging.

Everyone thanked everyone. Boxes of orange juice were passed around, the kind with the little straw you jab through the paper covering the hole.

The chairs scraped as we stood up to leave. A brief tour of the center's three other rooms—one with a sink and mirrors for hairdressing training and two other classrooms with stained whiteboards screwed to the wall, one lined by computers that had seen much better days.

Miriam asked us to please bring our own markers.

Then we left. I made a little map for myself, even though we went out the easy way: turn right, then right again, then left.

"You might want to note that landmark. It won't be going anywhere," David said as we made our last left-hand turn. He was right. The burned-out frame of a subcompact car stood just to the side of the entrance to the camp.

CHAPTER 10
Intersecting Cultures

I have a student teacher. Her name is Zeinab, and she's in her last semester at Haigazian University. She is covered, so I know only her smile, the soft curve of her nose, how her eyebrows wrinkle slightly and her eyes grow wide when what I say seems to puzzle her, and her hands, which are often folded in her lap. She usually wears a patterned hijab that rolls under at the rim, encircling her face. She seems to like browns and beiges.

She is very soft-spoken.

She didn't say much during the meeting with her and her supervisor from the university a few weeks ago. I was afraid that the depth of her traditionalism—her mode of dress revealing so much more about her worldview and attitudes, home life, family structure, ideas about maleness and femaleness and how these intersect than dress generally reveals in the West—would limit her ability to see what was taking place (or supposed to be taking place) in my classroom.

I was, in short, afraid that what I take to be the natural result of acknowledging the individual needs, demeanors, and interests of fairly typical teenagers would be perceived as anarchy, and I'd be of no use to Zeinab as a mentor.

My fears were heightened by the way she raced out of the first ninth grade English class she attended the moment I released the students.

"Uh-oh," I thought. "She's off to tell her supervisor that this just isn't going to work."

But she came back. I asked her to remain at the end of the class so we could debrief and I could get a feel for what she was seeing.

We'd been reading "Serpents in Paradise," an essay by Edward Abbey, the very explicit point of which was that human beings aren't so different from the other species that inhabit the planet, so we ought to be a bit kinder toward our kin, desert snakes included.

Zeinab and I sat across from each other at one of the long tables that form a U in my classroom.

"So tell me some of your impressions from the first couple of visits," I began.

A new Zeinab appeared, confident and articulate.

"I like the way they have to think about what they are reading, not only to say back what you tell them. They have their own opinions, but they have to justify the opinions from what they have read."

She went on in this vein for a while.

I must have misjudged her, I thought, breathing a silent sigh of relief. She must've gone to a more liberal school than I had imagined for her to see what was going on here so quickly.

When she finished, I asked her about her own experiences as a student.

"Oh, my classes were very rigid. We were never asked what we thought. It was the Lebanese curriculum. We only memorized what we read and what the teacher told us."

There have been many times in the almost half-decade I've spent working overseas when I've felt a bit like George W. Bush. Oh, not the Bush who insisted from an aircraft carrier deck that he'd solved Iraq's problems by destroying its infrastructure or who defiantly shook his fist at "a few dead-enders," challenging them to "Bring it on!"

I felt like the Bush who—if he was speaking the truth—seemed to believe that people really do think freedom is a good thing, however ignorant they may be of its complexities and internal contradictions and of the cultural convolutions that must take place for people to figure out what the hell to do with their new freedoms once they've got them and how to hang onto traditional values like respect for family and community while learning to love oneself as a self.

Here we have Zeinab—after 120 minutes of watching fourteen-year-olds mess around with ideas, asking questions about words like "writhe" and "evanescence," discussing why Abbey should (or should not) have added the mini-sermon at the end of his marvelously descriptive essay—a student even admitting unashamedly that he had gone ahead to finish the essay on his own the day before, being so fascinated by this prose.

Little understanding—or perhaps I'm giving Zeinab short shrift here—that once you've argued with a teacher about whether the author should have combined those three paragraphs into one, it's all over. Once you've done that, the next thing you know, you've ripped off your hijab and shaken your hair loose, rolled up your sleeves so any male non-relative you might pass in the street can see your forearms, and hemmed your skirt at, say, something daring like mid-calf.

I am, of course, overstating the case.

All the cases. For example, it's not as though what Zeinab saw in my classroom was totally new to her. She has most certainly taken classes at Haigazian—which was created just a few blocks to the southeast of the American University in the 1950s for Armenian students—where the kind of teaching and learning that goes on in my classroom has surely been propounded if not exemplified.

But this was certainly the first time this insightful young woman actually saw anyone doing with a bunch of high-school kids what she'd been reading and talking about.

Listening to Zeinab's observations, I was reminded of the radio scriptwriters I had worked with in Africa. Most of them had heard—and learned—all the jargon at some point in their university or post-university careers: "student-centered learning," "active learning," "authentic assessments," and all the rest. The irony, of course, is that all they had done was to memorize the terms so they could mark the correct box on a multiple-choice test.

Taban, one of the wisest and most articulate of my African colleagues, helped me understand the distance between the ideas and the realities we were dealing with only a few weeks after I arrived in Nairobi to work with the Southern Sudanese scriptwriting team.

It was our morning debriefing, an hour and a half into the work day. This was when I shared with the six scriptwriters things we needed to pay attention to and they shared with me their frustrations and satisfactions.

We had almost finished our meeting when Taban asked if he could raise another topic. Of course.

"Nick, we have been talking together about what we are doing here. The pedagogy we are discussing is familiar to us all," he said, pausing every few words to make sure he was capturing exactly what he wanted to say.

"We all know these terms. We have studied them in our classes and workshops and talked about them during our meetings at other places we have worked. But this is the first time we have ever actually used them,"

"Tell me more, Taban."

"Mmm. Well, you ask us what we think about things, and then you ask us to explain more what we mean. Then you respond with questions about what we have said. In the end, we all discuss the ideas together and make a decision about how to proceed. Then you write down our decision, and it becomes our protocol."

"You've never done that?" I looked at the Taban and then at the others seated around the table.

They all shook their heads.

They'd memorized the terms and passed the exams. But they'd never lived any of what they'd been learning.

It's sort of like adjusting to Beirut. When one first arrives here—or in any city where everything is unfamiliar—one is overwhelmed, unable to discriminate, seeing only the complex swirl of differences. The longer, however, one is here, the more one can distinguish thing from thing, sound from sound, smell from smell. The more one can begin to see what *is*.

My classroom is sort of Zeinab's Beirut—at first all new, all entirely different from anything she'd ever seen before; all fascinating.

After a week of classroom observations, Zeinab sat in the library while students dug around through books and then the Internet for information about a historical figure they'd selected to study from a list another teacher had developed and I'd modified.

The student who had read ahead in the "Serpents in Paradise" essay is looking into Edward Abbey. Two young women are intrigued by Virginia Woolf.

I asked Zeinab what she was seeing as she watched them at work in this less structured environment. She noted that in one class, the students might be chatting, but they did so while they took notes, remaining focused on their work. Good. She could see the positive aspects of the freedom, not the negative.

"In the other class, though, they stop working and just talk until you come around. Then they get to work."

Equally good. She was seeing the downsides. When you premise your teaching—your world view—on personal responsibility, you open the door to the possibility that Tatiana will take a quick glance at her Facebook page instead of googling Vita Sackville-West.

I contemplate such lapses and, momentarily, want to blame Western individualism for all the world's ills—for Bernard Madoff, for the credit crunch, for George W. Bush and global warming.

But then I remember that repressive worlds produce at least as many terrible people as liberal ones. At least, I think as I try to figure out how to wrap up these musings on Zeinab the proto-liberal, in more open worlds maybe the nice people have more of a chance to be nice.

* * *

When does a place become a home?

Is it when on a Saturday morning you open the door onto Rue Commodore and wonder which direction to walk in, knowing more or less what you'll find in either direction, pleased with all prospects?

Or is it when the policeman across the street, the rug merchant on the corner, the fruit vendor just a few doors down from him all greet you as you pass, maybe remarking on the weather, maybe not?

It's probably something more intangible. Probably something more akin to whatever made Buffy find herself thinking, "I live here now," one afternoon some months ago as she approached our apartment building at the end of the workday.

If Samir Kassir is right, this transformation happens especially readily in Beirut. Describing the city in the years leading up to the 1975 Civil War, he wrote:

> However effective the medical, hospitality and educational infrastructure may have been, however irresistible was the growth of the city's banks

> and commerce, however justifiable was the title "Switzerland of the Orient," all this mattered little in comparison with what—beyond all analogies—seemed a unique hallmark of Beirut: to provide a human environment that gave each visitor, however distant their home, the impression that the city was open to them. Open to the point of becoming their place, their home (442) [my translation].

Jayme Varco—a young woman who'd studied British Literature with me at Walsingham Academy last year and had, a few months ago, asked if I knew of any volunteer opportunities she might avail herself of while she took a semester off from college—experienced the eccentric welcome this city exudes during the three weeks she stayed with us, tutored in Palestinian refugee camps, had coffee along the Corniche, and wandered the city.

When Jayme stepped out the door onto Rue Commodore, she did not know what would be waiting in either direction. And the greetings she received were often unsolicited ones, from young men who assumed that the reputation young American women have for being more promiscuous than young Lebanese women meant that *all* young American women would readily sleep with any Lebanese man.

Jayme being here brought back memories of my first return to Beirut almost a decade ago.

Every day I had walked, trying to figure out what felt safe. Every day I widened the radius of my circle, until, in the end, I was covering miles instead of meters.

Like Jayme, I was amazed. Unlike Jayme, I had nothing familiar to go home to at night—Michel, the Mace Hotel night concierge who'd come to Beirut from Egypt decades before, talked with me about politics and tourism. But he was all I had.

But still. It was Beirut: the cacophony of languages and automobile horns, the stylish young women wearing hip-huggers and tank tops walking arm in arm with women in headscarves, the armored personnel carriers parked here and there, the occasional Syrian tank, the call to prayer echoing from mosque to mosque—all these things made me feel, as they made Jayme feel, alive, alert, present in, and part of the world in a way that very few places can make one feel.

Of course, Beirut doesn't make everyone feel that way. There's the neighbor whose spouse works for the UN—she hardly ever leaves her apartment. There's the young English teacher who insists that the reason Americans don't "need to wave their arms around when they speak" is because English is so much more expressive than Arabic. There are the many Westerners for whom the fact that nothing ever happens at the time it's supposed to happen makes them grumble about "Them," rather than, as I recommend, always bringing a book and being ready to wait.

Which Nick was I remembering as I thought about Jayme deciding whether to turn left or right on Rue Commodore? The eleven-year-old sent to Sifri's Market a few blocks away to bargain for a Christmas tree or the fifty-five-year-old trying to find a bus for Byblos, a half-hour to the north of Beirut? The thirteen-year-old catching a tram downtown to buy parts for his model airplanes or the sixty-year-old asking a Hizbollah underling to translate an anti-American billboard?

No matter. Jayme did exceedingly well. I knew things would go well for her when, at lunch mid-way through a long walk around the city her first day here, I suggested she order something familiar from the menu—you know, a hamburger or a tuna salad sandwich—and she very politely ignored my suggestion, asking what humus *lahme* was and *moutabal*. We ended up ordering plates of *mezza* to share. She loved it.

An auspicious beginning. In very short order, she had not only connected with people going off to tutor and teach in the refugee camps but had enlisted the help of a Qatari neighbor who'd been trying for months to find a way into such work; she'd not only begun tutoring at a nearby afterschool program but had taken over the classes several afternoons a week.

As much as Jayme was affecting the world, she was being affected. Her only foray out of the US prior to coming to Beirut had entailed spending a few days on a Caribbean beach.

Her father, with whom I spoke by Skype before she came, knew it would be a life-changing experience. Jayme knew it would be a life-changing experience.

But one can never really know what "life-changing" means until one lives the changes.

Changes such as finding out that all that French you memorized actually works if you're willing to risk looking foolish. Such as realizing that most of what you thought you knew about the Arab world—about the entire world beyond America's borders—is wrong.

Such as the unfathomable lessons that come from listening to an intelligent, well-educated young Palestinian woman explain that she cannot get a job in Lebanon because of the restrictions created by the Lebanese government and she can't travel to a country where she might get a job because of the near-impossibility of getting a visa with one of those brown, passport-like documents issued to "people of Palestinian origin living in Lebanon."

Such as the unfathomable lessons that come of trying to get a young American exchange student you've met on your trip to Beirut to recognize the narrow arrogance of his views, of watching a young orphan passionately lip synch a song about what it would be like to have parents at a Mother's Day celebration at an orphanage of the other side of the Bekaa.

The lessons born of ambling along the Corniche while the waves crash against the rocks below.

Of being someplace unlike any place you've ever been before.

I came to Beirut for the same reasons Jayme did—to be pushed to reconsider everything I thought I knew.

I came to be someplace where I might drop into M'Lord's clothing shop to chat with the owner on a lazy Saturday afternoon, only to have our conversation drift to politics—as conversations so often do here, where people remember that politics, messy and human affairs that they are, truly matter—and he asks me who put Ahmedinejad into power in Iran.

In Lebanon, the universal answer to most problematic questions is "Israel!" but I couldn't see how this was going to work, so I just said I didn't know.

"Bush! Look at him. Ahmedinejad is not one of the mullahs. He is not a Shia crazy man. Iraq is a mess, and religion is coming back to Afghanistan. What better man to have in Iran, a secular leader?"

Do I agree? Probably not.

But it's something to consider.

And that's all I wanted—that's all people like Jayme want—in coming to places like Beirut, in stepping away from the familiar. Not a new home; just new ways of looking at your old one, at yourself and your world.

CHAPTER 11
Identities

I'd been dreading this day ever since I'd cracked the spine of *L'histoire de Beyrouth* way back in November. I'd reached page 529, the beginning of chapter nineteen, the first chapter of section six, the concluding section of the book: "*La ville de tous les dangers*"—the city of all dangers. The chapter's entitled "*Sur le fil du rasoir*"—on the razor's edge.

It was perhaps doubly unfortunate that I had reached this point in this tale as the June seventh parliamentary elections loomed. The electoral lists had been posted, with 700-some candidates from dozens of parties and two competing blocks running for 128 seats.

More importantly, I'd reached this point in the history—perched on the verge of reading about the civil war that I know will unsettle my feelings about every street I walk down, every person I talk to, every unexpected sound I hear just at the time when everyone in Lebanon is wondering if the country will hold together.

Or will it disintegrate into bloodshed and hopelessness, as violent rhetoric devolves into violent action, augmenting explosive speech with the far-off "whump" of a car bomb, or the "tak-tak-tak" of automatic weapons fire?

Bright orange numbers on the top left-hand corner of every *Daily Star* remind us of the number of days till the election, just above a line drawing of a hand dropping a ballot into a box emblazoned with the red stripes and green cedar of the Lebanese flag. Today it's forty-three.

The campaign posters are up. Hizbollah's posters on the road to the airport are striking. The party's symbol—a green clenched fist brandishing an AK-47—washed out in the background. In red, in Arabic the phrases "My Lebanon," "Your Lebanon," "Their Lebanon" each crossed out, replaced by "Our Lebanon."

All the leaders of all the parties insist they want peace. Every editorialist prays for it. Everyone you speak with says there will be peace, *nshallah*.

But, then...

I had just finished reading "Composed on Westminster Bridge, September 3, 1803" to a ninth-grade class when, from the west, "Boom!"

I paused.

The students paused, their eyes darting left and right as they restrained themselves. They did not turn to the window behind them to look for a billow of smoke; they held their breath, listening.

Nothing.

Sarah nervously giggled very, very quietly, covering her mouth. Rami raised his hand to ask a question about the poem.

We're all wondering.

And I'm dreading reading what I'm about to read in Kassir's book, after months of two or three pages over breakfast every morning. Most recently I've reveled in the architectural achievements of the late '60s and early '70s, the spread of bookstores throughout the city, the building of the casino just to the north, and the development of seaside swimming spots like the Sporting Club, where I used to swim (unaware that it had been developed by a Palestinian entrepreneur and had become a favorite haunt of the city's intellectuals), and its slightly lower rent neighbor Long Beach, which, "with its three swimming pools and familial environment was perhaps the primary agent of the democratization of sea-bathing" (479).

Section six, chapter nineteen began, as one might have anticipated, simply: "The war did not take Beirut by surprise."

But after reading the preceding chapters, it had, in a sense, taken me by surprise. I'd relished the unfolding of this unique culture as I'd savored "The Switzerland of the Orient," "*Beyroutins et Beyroutines*," and, just before this section on the war, "Red Nights and Little White Beds."

The latter had concluded with a description of *albalad*, the downtown area where the city had laid its first foundations six thousand years before. Kassir remarks that this part of the city had escaped the confessional polarization that festered in the rest of the country:

> Nothing, in any case, could indicate that this downtown that seemed to resemble a country in itself would soon be one of the places to most rapidly catch fire, and that this fire would signify the coming of a suicide (526).

Reading on into the new chapter, I was reminded of exactly what "confessional polarization" meant here.

It was toward the end of my first teaching assignment at ACS, when I filled in for the spring semester after the Israeli invasion of 2006. Nabil had asked if I would serve as the advisor for his senior project. He wanted to write about Lebanon's Phoenician heritage.

Sure. Those intrepid adventurers had first caught my attention back in Miss Comer's fourth-grade classroom, the same year I'd played a Viking in the class play.

That was a long time before I'd learned—or paid any attention—that "Phoenician" was a Western name for the inhabitants of these shores, loosely referred to by its inhabitants as Canaanites, who thought of themselves as denizens of Acre, Tyre, Sidon, or Jbeil, not as any larger "-ician" or "-ite." You know, Phoenician like the Greek concept of the "Phoenix" because the sun seems to rise here if you're looking at it from the West. Just like *le Levant*, the land of the rising—another name the West has given the Middle East. East of what? Middle of what? And who says who gets to hand out names?

Oh, well. I hadn't read much Edward Said back in 1957. Or until the 1990s, for that matter.

Nor did I know then that some Lebanese, in their desire to clarify for themselves who they were, had picked up on this concept of "Phoenicia" and were claiming that the long-gone and misnamed people stood at the core of the true Lebanon—not the fervent Christians who spread their gospel up the coast a few thousand years ago nor the desert Arabs who brought Islam here in the seventh century and not the Maronites and Druze who, a few centuries later, split off from both these sects and took to the nearby mountains for safety.

People from the historic dawn of time, intrepid souls who'd sailed through the Straits of Gibraltar, all the way to Britain. The ones whose colonists in Carthage had almost toppled Rome before it had a chance to become the Rome that ruled this part of the world.

I didn't know anything about that quest for self-definition when I began working with Nabil.

I don't remember how the question of "confessional polarization" came up with Nabil or anything about the conversation, other than a few sentences.

"I'm Christian, Mr. Boke," he told me. "Well, I'm not Christian in the sense that I believe any of that, but I'm Christian in the sense that those are my people. My sect is Christian."

I remember trying to imagine if there was anything comparable to this statement in my life, in my sense of self.

"I'm American. Well, I'm not American in that I believe any of that..."

That doesn't work. The only way I really feel myself American is, in fact, in my beliefs about democracy, about equality, and all the rest.

And my religious affiliation—with Unitarian Universalism—is purely a matter of choice.

I certainly can't say, "I'm a Vermonter" or "I'm a Californian." I don't really have a state I can call home any more.

So Nabil's words were totally beyond my personal ken. There is nothing comparable in my life.

Kassir confirms Nabil's assertions about the relationship between his beliefs and his identity, writing, early in his chapter on the war, "In each community, the dogmas that formed the origin of the cult were little known...knowledge about them was not necessary in the sense that belonging to the community, acquired by birth, does not require a reflective engagement" (532).

He goes on, "Moreover, there is no way of pulling oneself out of the communal framework, even to those citizens who might want to" (534).

Reading this, I slowly begin to understand just how revolutionary the Minister of Justice's proposal to eliminate one's religious affiliation from the identity card actually is.

So Nabil's affiliation is not with a doctrine, even with the recognition that most people everywhere—Americans, Nepalis, Kenyans—actually know very little about what they "believe."

Nabil's Christian affiliation (I didn't think to ask if it was Greek Orthodox, Greek Catholic, Maronite, Roman Catholic, Evangelical, or Armenian) allows him legally to exist in Lebanon.

Curious, I opened the desk drawer and took my "Annual Residence Permit" issued by General Security from the back of my passport.

Let's see. There are all my names, my mother's and father's first names, my nationality and date of birth...

But, no, they don't care what sect I belong to. I'm a foreigner. We don't know any better.

* * *

Life goes on.

Two of my students at the Palestinian camp hadn't shown up for the last two lessons. Amani told me yesterday that they'd found work and didn't have the spare time anymore. Samer explained that Iyad had moved to a camp north of Tripoli because he found a job at a computer shop there. At ACS, the Palestinian reference librarian Moez got his visa for a summer trip to Canada. All good news.

And we'll go to Damascus next weekend, now that Lebanon and Syria have, for the first time since 1977, opened embassies and exchanged ambassadors and now that the Syrian regime doesn't seem as bent on punishing the Obama administration as it was on getting the Bush administration back for blowing up the alleged nuclear site it blew up in the north of that country a while ago.

Life not only goes on but remains, often, beautiful.

Last night we walked to a concert where two colleagues from school were to sing at the Greek Orthodox cathedral in *albalad*. When we arrived, we found the square filled with publisher's displays—I'd forgotten that UNESCO had declared Lebanon "Book Capital of the World, 2009," prompting Maronite President Suleiman to remark, at the gala ceremony, that Lebanon will remain "a center of radiance for civilization and humanity" while Sunni Prime Minister Fuad Siniora and Shia Speaker of the House Nabih Berri listened.

The concert—Gregorian chant-like pieces sung by the choir in Arabic—was glorious. The ornate altar and pulpit are glorious, as are the paintings that adorn the ceiling and the walls. Two reminders, however, have been left, two murals that were left untouched during the recent restoration. One shows Jesus facing Pilate, the other, Jesus in the Wilderness. Bullet gouges still pock the walls around each haloed figure.

After the concert we walked up the street for dinner. We ate at eight thirty, when the streets and café tables were just beginning to fill in this city that comes to life sometime between ten and eleven.

I remembered walking these streets alone two years ago. The waiters virtually pleaded with me to stop for a coffee at one of their empty tables. Clerks slept in the clothing shops and jewelry stores before just waiting to go out of business. The tent city Hizbollah had set up a quarter mile away, just outside the prime minister's offices, had driven everyone away.

Last night the streets were packed. Couples, families, groups of young people smoked their *nargilehs;* ate their pasta, steak, kebobs, and *mezza*; drank their wine, beer, arak, and Diet Pepsi; chatted; and people-watched.

Watching Beirut at its best, I wondered what chapter of this city's history we are in now. What's the title of the next chapter?

* * *

It's earlier this Sunday morning than I had planned to be up. Our day-trip to Damascus—or Balad aSham, as Syria was called under the Ottomans—had lasted longer than we had expected—quite a bit longer.

That was in part because many of those taking this particular road to Damascus did so because the city is a bargain-hunter's paradise, where everything from saffron to Oshkosh overalls (or knock-offs) is discounted significantly.

But that was also because crossing the border remains complicated, though it's not the three-hours-plus ordeal it was before Lebanon and Syria exchanged embassies.

Start with the fact that Lebanese who came with their ID cards are dealt with differently from Lebanese who brought their passports, to say nothing of the processes the half-dozen of us with German, British, American, and Indian passports must go through.

That's just to get out of Lebanon.

To get into Syria, which one does by driving through several miles of no man's land on the ridge of the Anti-Lebanon Mountains, we find the fixer we've hired at the border—charging seventy-five dollars per foreigner—to get us through immigration. Once again we divide into the three groups. We make our way to the front of whichever line we're in, hand over our documents, and wait for that final satisfying "whump!" of the bureaucrat's stamp that those who've traveled much have come to recognize as the "You're approved—get out of the way!" signal.

Then it's *Ahlan wa sahlan*. Welcome to Syria.

Sort of.

Damascus, lying at the foot of the mountains and on the edge of the desert, is a very different city from Beirut.

Maybe it's the omnipresent posters of Bashar al Assad, the president who noted, in a recent *Albalad* article, that "Syria is not a democracy. We are making changes, but we will go slowly" that add a note of ominousness to the place. Maybe it's somehow related to the fact that drivers obey traffic signals and pedestrians actually use the overpasses instead of dodging their way through traffic. Everything's pretty orderly and quiet.

And maybe all that is related to the fact that as you walk through the centuries-old Alhamidiya Souk—which is jam-packed with very serious shoppers—you're jostled and bumped in a way you're never quite jostled and bumped in Beirut.

But there are spices to be bought, Salahadin's statue and grave—as well as that of John the Baptist—to be seen at the Omayyad mosque, Corinthian columns in the plaza harking back to its Roman days, and mosaicked scenes of riverside palaces harking back to the structure's days as a Byzantine church.

And there are all those bargains to be had in the hundred-plus trendy stores at Cham City Center, six sparkling and glittering levels set next to the wide, tidy boulevard amid the neatly organized high rises at the northwest edge of the city.

And that wonderful three thirty lunch to be had at the Jdoudna restaurant, high on a ridge above the village of Bloudan. The bus wound its way into the hills for almost an hour, then pulled off onto a side street. The forty of us piled into rickety minivans that drove us the last mile or two up the hillside—a regular affair for this restaurant far at the end of a narrow, twisting and turning, barely two-lane roadway.

The usual—and wonderful—fare: humus, *fatouche* salad, kebabs and *kufta*, *kibbe*, fruit. And the usual conversation amid all the other conversations, the water pipes, the Turkish coffee, the wine and beer. Then back down to the main highway, and up, up, up to the Syrian border where we again split into groups and got back into the bus to drive across no-man's land, and—"whump!"—back into Lebanon.

We didn't get home till eleven thirty.

I had planned to sleep in the next morning.

But I was finished by six fifteen, so I made some coffee, picked up the *Norton Anthology of English Literature*, and settled down in the white plastic chair on the balcony overlooking Rue Commodore.

I skipped about in the first quarter of the book. A little Donne, a little Marvell, a little Dryden. I read the introduction to Aphra Behn's "Oroonoko," knowing nothing of this mid-seventeenth-century playwright, poet, and proto-novelist who flaunted her womanhood rather than hiding it. Back to Ben Jonson.

His poem "On My First Son" begins "Farewell, thou child of my right hand, and joy."

I read the footnote. "1. A literal translation of the Hebrew name 'Benjamin,' which implies the meaning of 'dextrous' or 'fortunate.' The boy was born in 1596 and died on his birthday in 1603."

Of course. Benjamin.

Ibn yameen. Son of the right.

Like I tell the taxi driver. "*Ala yameen, minfadlak, abil al hoteel commodore.*" It's on the right before the Hotel Commodore, please.

And Ibn becomes Ben.

As Ben, the grandson of our friends Chris and Sally, becomes Benzo.

Like Beverly was "beaver lea" or meadow. Which became Buffy. Like Charis was "grace," the name given to an aunt who died seventeen years before I was born, to honor her mother, Grace. Like Nicholas is "founder of cities" or "destroyer of cities" or something like that, and here becomes "N'qula," identifying the bearer of the name as Greek Orthodox.

How all these names that once meant something melt into their origins, becoming little more than the consonants and vowels that we find—or once found—pleasing or displeasing.

And so Damascus is Sham. Or Dimashq. Egypt is Misr. Greece—Hellas, to a Greek—is Yunaan.

Saul becomes Paul. Joshua is Jesus, which you can name a child if you're Roman Catholic but not if you belong to most Protestant sects.

How we name things.

And what that name comes to mean. As, when I stepped out of passport control into the cool mountain air of Lebanon—part of Balad Sham until the French took over in 1919—last night I felt safer than I had felt in Syria, where President Bashar al Assad, looking out on us from a huge billboard just outside the souk, reminded us that he loves Syria.

Bashar means "Bringer of glad tidings."

Last May the Lebanese parliament finally got around to electing a president after the country toyed with civil war for a week or so. His name is Michel Sleiman.

Solomon.

But names, like all words, Wittgenstein explained, barely meaning what we think they mean even at the most superficial level. Names certainly carry with them no power other than that which we may—on a Sunday morning when the city is finally beginning to wake up—grant them.

Well, I think I'll step out onto Rue Commodore for an amble. The street is named after the hotel in the next block. This is not actually the first Hotel Commodore, where my high school friends and I used to buy day-passes to go swimming, but its replacement. The first served as command central for foreign journalists covering the civil war and was destroyed in the 1980s.

But the street is also called Rue Baalbek. To be fair, we should probably call it Sharia Baalbek, using the Arabic rather than the French word for street to go along with its older name.

Which is not actually an Arabic name. The street is named for the city in the Bekaa Valley known for its Roman ruins, having been designated a UNESCO World Heritage Site in 1984. The *baal* part comes from the Canaanite word for god. Alexander the Great—a late-comer to the region—built a temple to Zeus here and renamed the place Heliopolis, or city of the sun. Then the Romans came and built the monumental temple to Jupiter, keeping the city's Greek name. When the Muslims took over during the seventh century, it was renamed *alcalat*, or fortress.

But Baalbek stuck.

Anyway, I'll go out for a wander, starting from here in the Hamra district.

You know, "hamra" like the exquisite building some of you have visited, the one built by the Muslim rulers of Granada in southern Spain in the fourteenth century, "Calat Alhambra," the red fortress.

* * *

"Acts of Violence grip Lebanon ahead of polls," reads the *Daily Star* headline.

What have I been missing? I skim the article.

A break-in at a political office. A couple of politicians' cars set ablaze. Shots fired near a restaurant in Jbeil, twenty-five miles north, while a candidate was speaking.

Oh, that's all. I knew that.

No car bombs. No assassinations. No automatic-weapons exchanges in the streets.

That's not real violence. No wonder they put it on page three.

Have I been here too long? My assumptions about how the world works seem to have shifted.

Or is it something bigger that's shifted, something more organic, as I've taken on some new identities, become a different me?

Identity. That's what I came here to try to understand.

So I've listened to lots of stories.

Like when Rima came back from taking a bunch of Model United Nations students to Istanbul. She—whose grandmother was Spanish, but whose father's family is Shia, from the south of Lebanon; her mother and father met and married in Côte d'Ivoire—and her students were astounded by the gradations of Islamness she and her students encountered.

Most noticeable were the boys from Saudi Arabia—only boys because in "The Kingdom" boys and girls are not allowed to mix—and the way they left the proceedings en masse to pray five times a day. They did not, of course, even consider coming to the dance. This is all complicated, of course, by the fact that at least some of those very students' parents had probably just returned from a weekend in Paris or London, where they had shed their conservative dress and gone to a trendy new night club for cocktails, or more.

Then there were the girls from Kuwait, all of whom were covered. Well, not so much the girls themselves, as the Istanbulis' reactions to them. Wherever the girls went, they generated whispers and hostile glances—this in a city rich with mosques, in a country governed by a moderate, Islamist-learning party.

Meanwhile, in Beirut, more women are deciding to wear the hijab, the headscarf. A high school teacher came back from her Easter break hajj to Mecca wearing the scarf. Last year it was an elementary school teacher.

All this reminds me of Shahinas, our tour guide in Egypt some years ago. She too was covered. She too had made a conscious decision to dress conservatively. As we drove from Memphis to Sakkara, she explained, "My husband and I were looking at some photos of us at the beach when we were younger. I couldn't believe it—that I would wear a bikini, showing so much of myself. How could I do that?"

I recently sat sipping coffee with Khalil at Younes Café, just around the corner from our apartment. We were talking about Amin Maalouf's *On Identity,* which Khalil had loaned me a few weeks before.

Maalouf begins, "How many times since I left Lebanon to live in France in 1976 have people asked me, with the best intentions in the world, whether I felt 'more French' or 'more Lebanese'? And I always give the same answer: 'Both!' I say that not in the interest of fairness or balance, but because any other answer would be a lie" (3).

So there's Khalil, history department chair at the American Community School at Beirut, his MA from Syracuse University, raised a Maronite Christian in Zgarta, far to the north of Beirut, prone to help me with my Arabic verbs and to send me articles from *Foreign Affairs*.

We're discussing the part of the book where Maalouf hypothesizes a citizen of Sarajevo, explaining that in 1980 he'd have referred to himself as a Yugoslav from Bosnia-Herzegovina who happened to be Muslim, while twelve years later when the war was at its height he might've responded, "I'm a Muslim," adding that he was from Bosnia.

> If he was stopped and questioned now [in 1998] he would say first of all that he was a Bosnian, then that he was a Muslim. He'd tell you he was just on his way to the mosque, but he'd also want you to know that his country is part of Europe and that he hopes it will one day be a member of the Union.
>
> How will this same person want to define himself if we meet him in the same place 20 years from now? Which of his affiliations will he put first? The European? The Islamic? The Bosnian? Something else again? The Balkan connection, perhaps? (11)

Our conversation shifted. What about our students? Who is Yussef, with both his Polish passport and a Lebanese one, who has to study the Lebanese curriculum because he hasn't been out of the country for three years in a row? Who is Rudy, with his French mother? And Camilla, whose South African parents have taken her to live in Uganda, then Lebanon? Natalja, the young Serbian woman? Zeina, whose family just brought her home to Lebanon after years in New York, where she studied in French schools? Ali, most of whose male relatives live in West Africa? Maher, returned from Amazonas years ago, with whom I chat in Portuguese from time to time?

"And who are you, Khalil, with all the facets of your background?"

He chuckled. "It's complicated."

"Who am I?" I continued.

It's complicated.

Maalouf tells us we have two identities. The "vertical" one is passed on from our ancestors and heritage. The "horizontal" one comes from our contemporaries and the world we live in.

"It seems to me," Maalouf goes on, "that the [horizontal identity] is the more influential of the two, and that it becomes more so every day. Yet this fact is not reflected in our perception of ourselves, and the inheritance we invoke most frequently is the 'vertical' one" (86).

I'm reminded of a feature on one of the cable news networks recently, probably Al Jazeera, about vigilante border patrolmen in the American southwest, clinging desperately to a culture that cannot survive intact for long—by definition, of course, since no culture survives intact for long.

I think about those vigilantes as I read about right-wing Dutchmen raising the alarm against the changes being wrought on that country by its steadily increasing Muslim population.

About China's insistence that it is allowing Tibetans to retain the most important aspects of their identity, even as they try to fully integrate their territory into China.

All this while my tenth-grade history students—including Yussef, Zeina, and Ali—study the desperate attempt by England's Puritans to turn that country into a theocracy in the 1650s. How did Jameel, the bright young Saudi, feel about my remarks about the narrowness of theocracies and the specific references I made to Saudi Arabia and Iran?

Did he feel the way Zalfa said she had felt—in another discussion in another class—to the response she had occasionally gotten when she'd explained on a recent trip to the US that she was Lebanese? "Watch out! Don't get her angry. She's Arab." It was, Zalfa explained, probably intended as a joke.

But they're right. Don't get Zalfa angry about things like the unjust ways some domestic workers brought to Lebanon from Bangladesh and Thailand are treated. Don't get her started. She'll quickly become furious and start quoting the Declaration of Independence and Bill of Rights.

* * *

I recently passed some of these musings along to a Lebanese friend. She e-mailed back:

> Thank you for sharing this with me. It's so nice to know the depth of a non-Lebanese's thoughts about "Our Lebanon." I especially enjoyed reading about the identity part and different sects...for me being raised in the States but with the majority of my upbringing being Lebanese traditions; I feel this complicated my childhood and continues to affect my life here in Lebanon as an adult. But, that's another story.

> I replied:

> But your comment about the complications of your childhood affecting your life here, I don't think it is "another story"—I think it is the story of Lebanon, all Lebanon and all Lebanese. This is barely a country, more a collection of traditions and value-systems all intricately woven together into a fiber that holds together sometimes, falls apart at others.

> To me, the fascinating aspect of this country is exactly this complexity, the difficulty in answering, 'Who are we, anyway?"

> The US has so homogenized cultures that there's not really much room for real diversity--oh, sure, there are Italian street festivals, and St. Patrick's Day, but all that is fluff, meaningless.
>
> I came back here, and immediately felt at home, I think in part because nothing is simple and homogenized here, with everything bumping up against everything else, trying to remain true to itself, while trying to leave room for others' ways. Until it doesn't work anymore and people take to the streets with AK-47s.

Meanwhile, the Pope, while visiting Nazareth, sang a song he'd written, chorusing in Arabic and Hebrew, "Shalom, Salam, Lord grant us peace," bringing to mind visions of church-school campfires and "Kumbaya."

Meanwhile, twenty-two days before Lebanon's parliamentary elections, Hassan Nasrallah, the Iran– and Syria-backed leader of the Shi'ite movement Hizbollah, intertwines Lebanese politics with the fate of Israel. The *Daily Star* tells us:

> Nasrallah criticized those "who doubt [our movement's] ability to run the country" saying, "The Resistance that defeated Israel can govern a country that is 100 times larger than Lebanon."
>
> In a live television speech during a graduation ceremony in Beirut's southern suburbs, Nasrallah lashed out at the Lebanese judiciary and declared May 7, 2008, which saw deadly clashes in Beirut [between his followers and supporters of the current, Western-oriented majority], a "glorious day" for the Resistance.

This is not a good sign, I think as I unsuccessfully test Maalouf's strategy, wondering how Nasrallah might identify himself a few decades from now.

* * *

Sunday morning. Time to head down to the Manara Palace for a breakfast of scrambled eggs and *manakish*—the thyme-and-sesame-seed mix called *zatar* spread with olive oil on thin mountain bread—while the surf begins to pick up just the other side of the retaining wall, and customers set themselves up for the morning with water pipes and Turkish coffee.

My coffee comes just as I reach the climax of the first chapter of Rowse's *Bosworth Field and the War of the Roses*. Richard II is about to endure the Revolution of 1399, after the few years of peace that followed the beheadings, betrayals and banishments of the 1380s.

"For himself," the chapter ends, "Richard now felt strong enough to carry out his long-nursed, secretly cherished designs of revenge upon his enemies" (47).

That's just what we're afraid of here.

And it's not unlike the warnings Dick Cheney's unleashing about the vulnerable position the Obama administration is putting the US in. Not unlike the calls to try members of the Bush administration for various breaches of justice.

I look around at the people sitting at the seaside tables, chatting, trying to be as oblivious as they can of what our future—this country's future—may hold, just as my friends back in the US do their best to ignore the worst of what their own politics has to offer.

The world's not a very nice place most of the time, is it? More often than not, all of us—those running the show as well as the rest of us—fall into the trap King Richard found himself in:

"He demanded to be regarded as more than a man, but in his conduct he fell below the average standards expected of a man. The result was to be seen in the deep-seated sense of insecurity within himself, and the insecurity he spread all around him" (48).

Familiar, isn't it? What strange comfort, to be reminded that our flaws are so universal, so timeless.

* * *

Fourteen days till the elections.

Fourteen days till we find out how Lebanon wants to define itself at this point in its history.

Tarek, the math teacher who's taught at ACS for decades, and Hassan, the energetic young Arabic teacher who only this year joined the staff, think things will work out.

Tarek keeps the kind of distance a lot of Lebanese maintain from things political, working hard to prevent skepticism from turning to cynicism. Hassan, though, recently got connected with the Mustaqbal, the "Future" movement made up of Sunni Hariri supporters. He went to a weekend downtown rally a month or so ago. "I'm just going to learn. I'm not going to get involved, I don't think," he told me on Friday. On Monday he was an enthusiastic convert.

So now he not only believes things won't fall apart, but he thinks—again, contrary to most of what I'm reading and hearing—that the electoral results will favor the Western-leaning March 14 forces of which his movement is the leader.

This is so different from what Hassan Nasrallah—not the imam in charge of Hizbollah but an acquaintance who works as an accountant with the Ministry of Agriculture—who is a fervent supporter of the March 8 "opposition" coalition believes.

"We have to get rid of corruption. All the old employees at the Ministry, the old guard, just accept it, but there are a number of us who came to work in the last few years who're trying to eliminate it."

"And," I replied, "you think that the March 8 people really mean it about getting rid of corruption? You don't think that the other Hassan Nasrallah's interested in establishing an Islamic Republic, led by Hizbollah?"

"Yes, they mean to get rid of it. And no, he's not. They understand what Lebanon is and needs, which is not an Islamic republic."

"What about what Nasrallah said a few days ago, about all that fighting in the streets between the Sunni and the Shia last year being good for Lebanon, a 'glorious day,' and how it saved Lebanon from a civil war."

"It did," he replied intensely. "They had to do that because March 14 was bringing thousands of uneducated, unemployed, armed Sunni men to Beirut.

The fighting was to show that the Shia would protect Lebanon and not let it be taken over by force."

"Hassan," I replied hesitantly, "I paid a lot of attention, but I never read about that anywhere. It doesn't ring a bell at all."

"It was in all the news. CNN ran it, and so did Aljazeera. It happened. It was the cause of the fighting. If the 'majority' had not done that and threatened Lebanon's stability, Nasrallah would never have sent Hizbollah's forces into the streets of Beirut."

What do you do with a statement like that? Well, first you decide to look up what you can about it when you get home. Then you try to figure out how what this man wants to believe has to do with who he is. Next you realize you can't sort this out over canapés and Almaza beer at the party where you're having this conversations. So you let it go, change the subject.

Just a few hours earlier that day, hearing voices at the end of the second floor hallway, I had dropped into the math department office.

An American colleague was talking with Rima Halabi about the Ministry of Education's last-minute decision to declare a nationwide school holiday in recognition of Israel's pulling the last of its troops out of the south of Lebanon in 2000. It's a day that Hizbollah claims as a victory for the "Resistance," of which it is the self-proclaimed leader.

Rima spoke not as a Druze or as a Beiruti. She spoke as a Lebanese.

"It's just shameful," she was saying, "that they could not have made this decision earlier. Every year we get closer and closer to days like this, and we all know that they will be declared holidays, but the Ministry waits till the last minute. I am embarrassed for my country."

My American colleague laughed.

"But it's why we love working here. All these little unexpected political holidays. We love getting days off like this. We love it!"

I waited till he had left the room and then asked, "Why does it embarrass you, Rima?"

"It makes my country seem so undeveloped, so primitive. It's so inefficient, and it's all because of all this political squabbling. It makes us look foolish. They could have made this decision weeks ago, and we all could have prepared for it.

"Next we all expect that the day after the elections will be a holiday. But we will have to wait till June fourth or fifth to find out. All because we're not really a modern nation yet and just can't operate efficiently."

"Rima," I said, "did you know southerners in the US would not vote for Republicans for a hundred years after the Civil War because the leader of the opposition to their secession, Abraham Lincoln, had been a Republican? And you do know that our civil war was fought, in part, over whether or not one human being could treat another human being as an animal?

"Today we've got people who fight tooth and nail over what language should be used in schools, whether people should go to jail for burning a flag, just a red-white-and-blue piece of cloth.

"And what about in France, where schoolgirls can wear crosses around their necks but not headscarves?

"How 'advanced' or 'developed' are those things?"

She smiled.

"People are all a bunch of idiots, Rima," I said. "It's just amazing we get along as well as we do. Oops, time to go."

I had to hurry home to catch a nap, then go grocery shopping in the cool of the evening. While I was out, Jim called, inviting us to the party, the one where I was to have the talk with Hassan Nasrallah.

CHAPTER 12
The End of the Year

"East Coker," the second of Eliot's *Four Quartets*, begins:

> In my beginning is my end. In succession
> Houses rise and fall, crumble, are extended
> Are removed, destroyed, or in their place
> Is an open field, or a factory, or a by-pass.

"In order to arrive at what you are not/You must," he goes on, tellling us midway through the poem, "go through the way which you are not."

And finally, what comes of all this? "In my end," he concludes, "is my beginning."

This year is drawing to a close, this personal year, this professional year, this political year, this year I've spent trying to sort out what my being here instead of being in all the other there's I've been to reveals about here, about there, and about what it means to be someone in any of these places.

My wife and I have been invited to the prom. She's spent more hours than either of us would care to count trying to figure out what to wear to a dress-up affair in a country that treats sequins, eyeliner, cleavage, accessories, and bronzed skin very, very seriously. The dance will begin a few hours from now at the Intercontinental Phoenicia Hotel, just down the street from where Hariri was assassinated four years ago. It's the new Phoenicia—the one that had to be totally rebuilt after the Battle of the Hotels that raged during one point in the civil war.

Fireworks just down the street remind us that Lebanon's parliamentary elections are only eight days away, Sunday June seventh. The bars will close at nine o'clock next Saturday, and not reopen till Monday evening. Road construction will be halted, and no trucks will be allowed on Lebanon's roads during that same time period. Monday the eighth is a holiday.

It's all pretty obvious: close the bars to keep down the fights and keep the roads open in case the army or the police need to get from here to there fast. Trucks: 1) block traffic, and 2) can explode. People will need Monday to drive back from their villages, where they voted—and it's better to have at least the government employees off the street and buildings empty in case there's trouble.

At school, exam schedules have been posted—they'll begin on the twelfth

Buffy and I have train and hotel reservations for our mid-July swing through part of Eastern Europe and offers of places to stay for our early-August trip to the US.

So many endings.

Endings amid beginnings.

I've begun spending early Saturday morning at the Manara Palace Café. It's the one set a meter or so above high tide at the western-most end of the promontory that is Ras Beirut. Sometimes I grade papers or, like this morning, bring something to read.

And watch. The young couple who've roused themselves for an early seaside coffee, leaning intently toward each other. The aging American businessman expounding on Lebanese commerce to several young men. Another old man, like me, sipping his coffee and reading his newspaper. All of us pause from time to time to glance at the waves lapping against the rocks a few meters away; the sun, risen above the mountain ridge, glistens its light on the swells; the fishermen stand on the rocks with their long poles, waiting.

The *Daily Star* tells us the fallout continues from the *Der Spiegel* article alleging that the Special Tribunal has found a direct connection between the Hariri assassination and Hizbollah. Then there's the irony of Vice President Biden—on a recent stopover in Beirut—insisting that there should be no foreign (code for Syrian and Iranian) interference in Lebanon's elections, then going on to explain that if Hizbollah and its allies were victorious, the US would have to re-examine its policies toward Lebanon, thereby attempting to involve itself in Lebanon's elections. This results in Hizbollah leader Nasrallah's response that Lebanon can buy the weapons it needs to defend itself against Israel from Iran and Syria, anyway, so it doesn't need the US.

What are these? Beginnings? Endings?

I don't suppose you can really tell which is which until enough time has passed to see what's come of whatever you were wondering about.

Eliot has something to say about that, too:

> There is, it seems to us,
> At best, only a limited value
> In the knowledge derived from experience.
> The knowledge imposes a pattern, and falsifies,
> For the pattern is new in every moment
> And every moment is a new and shocking
> Valuation of what we had been....
> The only wisdom we can hope to acquire
> Is the wisdom of humility: humility is endless.

* * *

The weather's warmed up. Beirut has begun to go swimming.

Beirut offers several options for people who like to swim.

Just around the bend from Pigeon Rocks are the Sporting Club—where I often swam as a boy—and Long Beach—where I didn't. For an entry fee of fourteen dollars for the day, you have access to the open sea, to a protected inlet, or to one of two saltwater pools. No sand; you dive into the water from the natural rocks that form this promontory or from the concrete decks covering most of the rocks. Changing rooms. Chaise lounges under umbrellas. Guys who'll take your order for a beer, a coffee, or a sandwich.

A mile-plus away, north and eastward along the Corniche, is "AUB Beach." Same sort of set-up, minus the guys who'll bring drinks and sandwiches, and the changing rooms. And minus the pools. Just open sea. It's two dollars with an ACS ID.

But anywhere in between Sporting and AUB Beach you can just slip through the railing, climb down any of the several makeshift ladders to the rocks—or, in the spot between the Riviera Hotel's seafront and a little clubhouse for local fishermen, walk through an opening in the fence, then down a gentle slope to the sea—and swim.

The most visible difference between Sporting/AUB and this several-mile option is that no women ever swim at the ad-hoc beaches, though the others glisten with well-oiled, nearly naked young women (and occasional more matronly types) who sometimes even—Truly! I have seen this with my own eyes!—go into the water.

While families often take the path to the seaside beach—the covered mothers and older daughters organizing little picnics beneath beach umbrellas they've brought, while the men and children swim and play on the seaweed-green rocks—most of those who swim at the free areas are between fourteen and twenty-eight and quite vociferously male. They spend as much time smoking their water pipes, calling loudly to each other, and eating snacks bought from vendors along the Corniche as they do swimming, but they have a good time. Noisy, but innocent.

I like the cost of the open rocks. I like the blend of people at AUB and Sporting. I like the access to sandwiches at Sporting, and, recently having been given a reduced-fee pass by a graduating senior, Buffy and I will probably swim there till the pass runs out. Then we'll review our options.

* * *

I stood on a submerged rock, knee-deep in the chop at AUB beach. Just beyond, the heads of two swimmers rose, then disappeared from sight behind a swell. Beyond them, two container ships passed, heading toward the port a few miles east. A motor boat whizzed by, bouncing and splashing through the waves.

Far to my right the long ridge of Jebel Lubnan, Mount Lebanon, rose knife-blade-like.

These mountains had been Druze until, a hundred-plus years ago, the Maronites moved in from the north, pushing the Druze into the Chouf, farther south.

The outcome of the elections are said to hinge on the Christian vote, on the region I'm looking at. The Sunni and Shia votes are accounted for, and most Druze will vote with the March 14, pro-West, faction. But Christian former general and former president Michel Aoun has aligned himself with the March 8 opposition, with Hizbollah and its allies, promising to clean out the corruption that plagues Lebanon.

Apparently he's being heard, thereby dividing the Christians. No one knows just how they'll split their vote, though all assume the final outcome will be close.

It's in the foothills of Jebel Lubnan, then, where the election will be decided, an area called the Metn. Here, Aoun's candidates are running neck and neck with the March 14 candidates.

Nobody really pretends to understand the politics. There seems to be no end or beginning to these, just a continuous more-of-the-same.

Lebanon just hasn't quite turned itself into a country yet. Samir Kassir, writing about the days before the civil war, explained:

> Independent of the sects as of all specific anthropological substrata, the real demarcation between the communities depended—and still depends—on the fact that an individual is obliged to belong to a group. Determined thus by his ancestry, he finds himself *ipso facto* distanced from those who belong to another group (533).

But it does change, I thought, as the swells rolled against me. The civil war pitted Christian against Muslim. A hundred years before that, Christians and Druze had slaughtered one another.

Today, it's Hizbollah's Shia who're calling the shots against the more moderate—and more prosperous—Sunni. Christians and Druze seem virtual bystanders.

Or is this different? After all, it's still the group you belong to that determines whom you'll get along with. The only thing that changes is your friends and your enemies, based on which have been classified as your group's friends and which as its enemies. You are still, in the end, who you were.

* * *

Lebanon votes today.

Well, it's not exactly "Lebanon" that votes. And this, it has finally dawned on me, is yet another piece to the puzzle of this tiny country's immense complexity.

"Will you go back to your village to vote, Hassan?" I asked the young Arabic teacher.

"No, I'm a Beiruti."

"So where will you vote?"

"At a school in Sin el Fil."

"Oh, you live that far from ACS? That's a long way to come every morning."

"No, I live in Hamra. But that is where I am from, Sin el Fil."

That is where I am from. So if I'm "from" Nabatiyeh, forty-five miles to the south, I'll drive there and vote. If I'm "from" Bechare, ninety miles north, or Baalbek, fifty miles northeast, or wherever, I'll go there.

Moreover, if I'm a married woman, no matter where I'm "from" I'll drive however many miles to my husband's polling place. He's the one whose origins matter.

Every label we give ourselves is, of course, a construct. I call myself "American," but I can donate blood to Kenyans or Kosovars as well as to Vermonters and Virginians.

But constructs are complicated and take a while to incarnate themselves. We've seen in recent years how hard it is for Kenyans and Kosovars to arrive at satisfactory constructs, at clarity for themselves and for the world exactly where they're "from," who they are. Kenyans still tend to think of themselves as Luo or Kikuyo before they think "Kenyan." Kosovars have struggled violently to establish themselves as Kosovars, not as second-class appendages of Serbia.

The strikes against the construct "Lebanon" seem endless. But it's much more than the question of whether Lebanon is a truly "Arab" country or whether it should be reunited with the Syria that France and England decided to separate it from more than half a century ago.

The voters, I have come to understand, are not Lebanese. They are Beirutis or Nabatiyans or Baalbekis. No matter where they may live in their country, they must go to their true home to cast their ballot—they must go to where their people are.

Another impediment to the creation of Lebanon, the country.

* * *

The "warden message" we received from the embassy last week was milder than most, reading, in part:

> Lebanese Parliamentary elections will be held on June 7, 2009. The U.S. Embassy in Beirut expects greater than normal traffic congestion, and large crowds at or near polling stations that day. The Embassy expects that the elections will be conducted in a peaceful and orderly fashion, but reminds American citizens in Lebanon that even peaceful gatherings and demonstrations can turn violent unexpectedly.
>
> American citizens in Lebanon during the election period are reminded to exercise caution and take appropriate measures to ensure their safety and security.

The message the headmaster sent out a few days later was, from a purely practical standpoint, a bit more disconcerting:

> On Sunday the Lebanese people will vote for their parliament. As a precaution, the government has closed all offices and banks on Saturday and Monday. In addition on Saturday evening all restaurants and

> entertainment places are to close at 9:00 PM and will remain closed until Tuesday. Please check with your local grocer to determine if they will be open on either Sunday or Monday.
>
> On Monday, we believe around noon, the results of the election will be announced. The likelihood of celebrations, fireworks, cars speeding around and other manifestations of victory will be evident. We caution all members of the community to plan to be at home on Monday and not to join in any street celebrations.
>
> School will continue on Tuesday unless you receive a direct message to the contrary.

Well, we hadn't really planned on joining any street demonstrations, but the bit about "restaurants and entertainment places" was unsettling. So I set out to conduct a random survey: Costa Coffee and Younes Café would be closed. Bread Republic and Starbucks would be open—"Well, unless..." and the barista's voice trailed off as she smiled faintly. Roi des Frites—or Malek al Batata; take your pick—with its two-table sidewalk set-up would be open.

I guess that's how you deal with things you don't want to deal with. You avoid imagining what it would be like to huddle in the corridors of your apartment building as the shooting starts. Instead, you wonder where you can go for an espresso.

I try to imagine what it would be like to be one of the seniors who sat in their hot robes and awkward mortarboards across from the faculty in the AUB Assembly Hall last Friday night. They'd taken exams only three out of their four high-school years because "political turmoil" had forced the cancellation of one set; they'd entirely lost two summers—2006 when Israel attacked and 2008 when Hizbollah launched its attack on Beirut.

So Saturday morning I stopped in here and there on my tramp around the city to see if I'd be able to get a coffee or a pastry. I do that instead of acknowledging my fear that sometime late Sunday—or Monday, or mid-July, or late September— I won't be able to stop in anywhere to ask about anything.

I go about my business. I meet Ramesh, the Indian UN police consultant who's married to a colleague of mine, for coffee, intending to let him talk about his mother's recent death, but instead spending an hour comparing India's and America's judicial systems.

In the afternoon I go to Bourj al Barajneh, where the faithful three young Palestinian women—Hiba, Amani, and Miriam—show up for our conversational English lesson. There we discuss concepts like "stroke" and "blood vessel," spinning the lesson off from Hiba's nutrition class and resorting, finally, to comparing the English with the Arabic words for the ingredients on Amani's bag of potato chips.

Amani is disappointed that I won't be in Lebanon on August 1, when she'll hold her wedding party in Ouzai. I am too.

* * *

There's almost no traffic on the way to Bourj. Everyone who's going to leave town has left. Rima went to Sidon: "I've never voted before," she told us. "But I'm going to vote this time." Rima is in her mid-thirties.

Wafa has gone to her village in the Chouf, which is mostly Druze. She will vote, but her artist brother Wassim won't. "Politics is all bullshit," he says, though he went to the village for a little peace and quiet.

Ariij will go to her village, which is mostly Shia, but not to vote. She is one of those who says she will never vote for a party led by someone who made her hide from their bullets in the hallway of her apartment building. Unfortunately, this applies to the current leaders of all Lebanon's parties.

Rada, who is Sunni, will drive her mother to Tripoli, where they will vote today, then return in the afternoon.

Hassan Nasrallah, the Environmental Ministry official who has offered such convincing arguments for Hizbollah and its March 8 allies, tells us he will not vote. He does not elaborate.

Math teacher Samer will not vote either. I am surprised, since he seems so interested in politics.

"I can't. I'm Australian. Well, I'm really Jordanian, since my father was granted citizenship by Jordan when he left Palestine in the 1950s, but then I went to Australia and got citizenship there." Samer's wife hasn't decided whether she will vote or not.

Ramesh and I talk about the elections on the way home from the coffee shop. I had hoped he might offer some credible predictions about the possibilities for violence, given his job as an advisor on security issues.

"Well, let me tell you an opinion, instead," he says. "I hope Hizbollah will win because then it will have to moderate itself. It will have to find ways to get along with the West other than simply condemning Obama for trying to sweet-talk Muslims.

"If it stays in power for a few years, it will see that it's not so easy to govern, and it will have to cooperate with the other side. I saw this happen with the radical Hindu party in India."

"So you don't think it wants to establish an Islamic republic?" I asked.

"Well, it may. But now it can acquire power only by allying with Aoun and his Christian supporters. If Aoun stays with them, he will be another factor moderating their plans."

"And if he doesn't?"

"That's another story, isn't it?"

* * *

The streets were quiet Sunday morning, so quiet that I could actually hear the surf as I walked by the long sandy beach south of Pigeon Rocks. I realized I'd never heard the crash of surf there before, only the roar of traffic.

On my five-mile walk I passed three polling stations. The street in front of each one was blocked off, and nearby parking lots did a brisk business selling everything from parking spaces to bags of potato chips and bottles of water. A few blocks from each, young men and women wearing blue or yellow or white hats, the color depending on the party, passed out fliers. At each station, lines of men and women—dressed a bit formally, as though for a graduation or a wedding—threaded their ways toward the entrance to the school where they would vote.

All was calm.

Knowing, however, that it would take only one angry, armed young man to destroy this calm, a line of olive-green trucks and armored personnel carriers stood at the ready along the Corniche just this side of the sandy beach.

Dozens of soldiers chatted, sipping coffee, waiting.

* * *

Blasts and bursts dragged me from my sleep.

Gunfire?

No, it's just fireworks.

From over at the Hariri palace a couple of blocks away.

Mmm. Too early for the results to be in. Must be they've all come home from their villages, jubilant and hopeful.

Hope the noise doesn't go on too long.

Wonder what time it is.

Back to sleep.

* * *

Dawn. I tried to fall back asleep but gave up at six fifteen.

Squeezed a couple of oranges, took Said's *Humanism and the Democratic Prospect* to the balcony, and picked up where I'd left off in the chapter about Eric Auerbach's *Mimesis*.

Ironic. It was Said's citation in *Orientalism* from Hugo of St. Victor in Auerbach that I'd chosen as my e-mail signature two years ago: "The man who finds his homeland sweet is still a tender beginner; he to whom every soil is as his native one is already strong; but he is perfect to whom the entire world is as a foreign land."

Auerbach's reflections on what it takes to understand how history unfolds itself offer some insight as we wait for the results of this complicated and virtually incomprehensible election:

> When [people] begin to appreciate the vital unity of individual epochs, so that each epoch appears as a whole...when, finally they accept the conviction that the meaning of events cannot be grasped in abstract and general forms...[and] must not be sought exclusively in the upper strata of society...but in also in art, economy, material and intellectual climate, in the depths of the workaday world and its men and women, because it is only there that one can grasp what is unique, what is animated by inner forces (111).

Of men and women driving along Lebanon's twisting roads lined by political posters, going "home" to vote for their representatives. Or, in twenty-five countries northwest of here, of men and women going to their own polling places to vote for representatives to their fledgling experiment in internationalism, the European Parliament. Or, in a few days, men and women doing the same thing in Iran.

Or, a few months ago, American men and women who showed Republican strategists that their plan to create a Democrat-proof electoral system just couldn't hold up against the popular will.

All these people passing judgment—limited judgment, to be sure, since those they vote for have been selected by people with their own sets of interests and those they vote for have often been severely tainted by their own pasts—doing what they can to ignore the public promises their leaders have made and broken, the secret deals they've arranged, the money they've pocketed.

But, to paraphrase Winston Churchill, it seems to be the best we've got.

Checking the time, I interrupt my musings in recognition of the fact that if I'm going to take a walk I should go before the results are in. It'll probably be safe till noon or so. There's no point in anybody getting really angry with anybody else till they know whether it's in their best interest to be generous or self-righteous, and pundits predict that we'll have the results by early afternoon.

Ah, might as well check the *Daily Star* online first. Might've been some skirmishes in the streets last night, and I'd want to avoid those areas.

Gmail opens. My homepage opens. The *Daily Star*, loaded with images and gimgaws, opens. Very, very slowly.

The headline: "March 14 coalition retains majority after parliamentary elections. Opposition source concedes defeat, accepts 'will of people,'" by Mirella Hodeib.

Now there's a surprise. So parliament will not, in the immediate future, at least, serve as a springboard for the creation of an Islamic republic; nor for a systematic intensification of hostilities against Israel.

Lebanon, in its own fragmented and convoluted way, voted for Lebanon, not for Iran or Syria or Islam or against Israel.

And, the article reveals, the results from the Metn, the Christian district just northeast of Beirut I was watching from the beach a few days earlier, aren't even in yet.

> BEIRUT: Lebanon's opposition conceded defeat against the March 14 coalition in pivotal polls Sunday after weeks of fierce campaigning. "We've lost the election," a senior opposition source, who declined to be identified, told Reuters. "We accept the result as the will of the people."
>
> "We'll go back to the way we were," the source added.
>
> The opposition source said the March 14 coalition is expected to ensure between 69 and 70 seats in the 128 parliament. The number matches figures predicted by the March 14 Forces.
>
> Progressive Socialist Party leader MP Walid Jumblatt on Sunday warned the March 14 Forces against "isolating the other party."
>
> Now there's a surprise.

No wonder all those fireworks at March 14 headquarters just around the corner last night.

If I'm going to take that walk, I'd better do it now

* * *

The mid-morning city was quiet. Beirutis seemed to be believing that things might work out. All the snack shops were open, and at Taj al Malook, the fancy-pants Lebanese patisserie on Rue Bliss, a few matronly types sipped coffee and nibbled honey-drenched sweets.

The several-mile walk downtown was uneventful. At the Place de l'Etoile, the several sidewalk cafés facing the parliament building hadn't opened yet, but staff was inside, reading newspapers and chatting before they opened their doors. No more soldiers than usual standing in the square.

In fact, no more soldiers than usual anywhere.

On the Corniche, only the usual mix: groups of amblers talking together intensely and solitary walkers seriously working up an early morning sweat.

"There's peace in the streets today," I said to the old man sitting in the shade of MB café's single umbrella while I waited for my coffee. I am learning to keep my Arabic efforts simple.

"What do you think will happen tomorrow and after tomorrow?" I continued.

"I don't know," he replied.

"Who knows?"

"Allah knows."

My coffee arrived. I crossed the street. A group of deeply tanned middle-aged men were swimming. I sipped my coffee and listened to the high-tide wavelets lapping against the rocks, then continued my roamings.

The Manara Palace Café, down the road from this little beach, was filling.

Just as I began to wonder where all the soldiers had gone, four armored personnel carriers came racing around the corner, treads clattering loudly on the pavement.

"Uh-oh," I thought. "Trouble must've broken out somewhere."

Then I watched as they turned into a vacant lot, ground their way up the steep hill, and parked. They'd apparently been called off duty, sent back to the barracks. Somebody must've decided that all would, for the nonce, be well—or well enough.

Indeed, the tourist shops on Hamra were just rolling up their corrugated shutters, and around the corner, Younes—the trendy café that had been closed the day before—was beginning to fill.

Approaching our building, I came upon Khaled, the concierge, heading for the market.

"Hizbollah has been shamed," he said. "Now they will not cause problems."

As I opened the door, building owner Nabil stepped out.

"They haven't decided what to do," he said. "There's nothing on the Hizbollah radio station but classical music. This is not a good sign."

A few minutes later, Naharnet quoted Hizbollah parliamentary spokesperson Mohamed Raad: "The majority must commit not to question our role as a resistance party, the legitimacy of our weapons arsenal, and the fact that Israel is an enemy state."

Oh, right. I keep forgetting about Hizbollah's twenty thousand rockets. Or is it forty thousand?

* * *

Sporting Club was packed.

Everybody was smiling. I guess not many March 8 true-believers hang out on Sporting's rocky outcrop where the beer and the whiskey flow pretty freely.

A light breeze blows. The swells rise and fall.

The final result turns out to be quite an upset—the March 14 coalition took seventy-one seats, compared to the opposition's fifty-seven. An almost 60 percent turnout. One really exciting aspect of the elections is that they were conducted on a single day, rather than staggered, week by week, region by region as they had always been before.

US Secretary of Transportation Ray Lahoud, who'd been sent to Beirut as an observer (along with Jimmy Carter's electoral watchdog group, which deemed the elections fair), was interviewed by the March 14 TV station anchor. Of Lebanese extraction, Lahoud, like so many here, could not conceal his pleasure at the results.

But it's more than the numbers. It's the fact that this place didn't blow apart.

It's the fact that Buffy and I are just going to watch the international news in a few minutes, then I'll pack my lunch for the next day, we'll make dinner, read for a while, and go to bed.

Tomorrow we'll just go to work.

We just might make it through an entire school year without a single "Political Turmoil Day." Not one.

Nshallah.

EPILOGUE

Looking Back

It's 2011. Indeed, we did make it through that year without a political turmoil day. And through the next. And through the first seven months of this school year.

I've been in Beirut for nearly three years now, closer to four if you add the semester I worked here after the 2006 Israeli attacks—more than double that total if you count those teenaged years I spent here.

How things have changed. I don't mean since 1961—that's a given. I'm noticing the changes that have taken place since 2007, when I began to reflect seriously on what it means to be back here, back in Beirut. And how that meaning is connected to what it meant to have lived here all those years ago.

It's February fourteenth, the sixth anniversary of the Hariri assassination. Schools are closed. This year's commemoration will be held indoors at the large International Exposition Center, not, as has been the case in the past, outdoors in the wide expanse of Martyrs' Square.

Lebanon's in the thick of another political stalemate, with Hizbollah having won this round by clever political maneuvering. I have a feeling that Hizbollah will be winning most of the rounds in the foreseeable future.

Schools will also close tomorrow in celebration of the Prophet's birthday.

Will schools have to close a few weeks from now when the Special Tribunal for Lebanon formally indicts Hariri's suspected assassins? Or a few weeks after that when Israel, threatened by the unexpected upheaval in Egypt, decides to create a diversion in Lebanon? Or a few weeks from then, when...?

How long will it take Najib Miqati to put together a cabinet? Will March 14 participate? Will America follow through on its threats to reevaluate its relationship with Lebanon now that Hizbollah's running the show?

Will Dan and Rickey Poor come to visit from New Hampshire, given Beirut's ongoing instability and given the demonstrations in Amman, where they'd planned to go after spending a week with us?

Everything's up in the air again.

Sipping Turkish coffee at the Bread Republic café, just around the corner from our apartment, I contemplate Lebanon's recurrent instability, wondering—again—exactly what this little country is, who its people are, how its people conceive themselves.

I recall a trip I'd taken to Hasroun on a Saturday not long after the 2008 parliamentary elections. A bit of serendipity had brought some questions about Lebanon's identity into high relief that Saturday, if only briefly.

Buffy and I had decided we needed a break from the city. Huda Chatah had recommended a tidy, inexpensive hotel in Hasroun, not far from the Cedars. I called. They had a room. I made a reservation.

The weekend before our holiday, I decided to scout the route we'd take to Hasroun. I took the bus from Beirut to Chekka, just south of Tripoli, where I disembarked, having been told I could pick up a bus into the mountains from there.

A taxi approached. The driver told me I'd have to go five miles inland to Koura to catch the bus to Hasroun.

OK.

He let me off at the intersection with the road from Tripoli. An old man stood waiting at the corner.

Is this where I catch the bus to Hasroun? Yes. *Ahlan wa Sahlan*.

We chatted.

A battered yellow Toyota sedan pulled up in front of us. The driver beckoned to my companion, who went to talk to him, then turned and beckoned to me.

"Come on. We've got a ride," he said.

My companion got into the backseat. I got into the front seat, greeted the driver, and we headed east, into the mountains.

It turned out that the driver was just looking for company for his twenty-five-mile drive to Bechare, just across the valley from Hasroun. He was a wizened old man who seemed to have a bit of trouble keeping to his side of the road as his car—as old in car-years as its driver was in human—sputtered and lurched its way into the mountains. We spoke, sometimes in Arabic, sometimes in French, occasionally in bits and pieces of English, as we made our way up the winding road. Soon it was just the driver who spoke.

He was very Christian. Everything, he explained enthusiastically, came in threes, just like the father, son, and holy spirit: father, mother, child; air, water, earth; sun, moon, stars. Wasn't this—he insisted, again and again—proof of the existence of god, specifically of the Christian god and of the truths of the New Testament?

Sure. Why not?

He offered more threesomes as we chugged along.

He let me out by a mini-market in Hasroun. I stepped across the narrow street to an overlook where I stood gazing into the deep chasm of the Kadisha Valley and at the steep mountain ridge beyond.

Looking out over the silence of the valley, I contemplated the fears and religious fervors that had sent my driver's Maronite ancestors into these protective reaches a thousand years ago.

Then I thought about the driver.

He remains picturesque fodder for a foreigner's reflections about a morning in north Lebanon as long as all he's doing is chattering away about his faith to a couple of accidental passengers on a drive into the mountains.

But was he always so innocent?

After all, it was his people who had violently driven the Druze further to the south a few generations before. It may have been he himself who, only a few decades ago, had enthusiastically pulled the trigger of his AK-47 when it was Christians and Muslims who were killing each other, each believing that Lebanon had no room for the other. It may have been he who, for that matter, in the midst of that same violence, had massacred Palestinians in Beirut's refugee camps, and even fellow Christians in Zgarta, not far from this village.

This old man is Lebanese. But which Lebanese is he? The proud descendent of nineteenth-century conquerors, insisting his ancestry dates back to the

Canaanites who lived here three thousand years ago, not to the Arabs who overran this land a millennium and a half ago? The warrior who murdered his neighbors and kinsmen at the end of the last century? Or just the quaint, cheerful proselytizer, looking for company on a Saturday afternoon?

To complicate the matter of his identity, those bullets he may have fired and the weapon that fired them may have been provided, at least indirectly, by my government, as such guns and bullets have been in so many places around the planet over the past half-century. Each time it has provided such weapons, my government has believed—or at least has convinced itself—that America was helping people who were defending values we agreed with. People who were, in a way, like us; people we could identify with.

Back in the 1980s, the American government had assumed it knew this man, so it gave him the gun that shot the bullets that killed the mutual enemy.

But how America fools itself. How unconvincingly we convince ourselves that the world is what we'd like it to be, not what it really is. How wrong we so often are about the identities of those we help—and of those we harm.

Consider Lebanon's recent elections. No analysis that I've read in the local English– or French-language news media made any reference to Obama's recent Cairo speech, in which he'd expressed his respect for Islam and his openness to the Arab world in general. Not once.

Western analyses of Lebanon's elections, however, often led with references to the speech. Consider this from salon.com by Juan Cole, a professor of Middle East Studies at the University of Michigan:

> June 10, 2009 | President Barack Obama's speech in Cairo last Thursday may already have borne fruit. His call for political moderates in the Muslim world to fight extremism may have helped tip the weekend's parliamentary elections in Lebanon to the anti-Syrian March 14 Alliance. Obama did not explicitly call for the defeat of Hizbollah in the elections, but the Lebanese already knew where the administration's sympathies lay.

I have no doubt that many of Lebanon's voters knew America's position on Hizbollah. But just in case, several American politicians and diplomats, including

Vice President Biden, had recently dropped by Beirut and had made it very clear that United States aid to Lebanon—especially military aid—would be seriously jeopardized if the March 8 coalition won the elections.

But no one who understands anything about Lebanese politics would have even remotely considered the possibility that my driver and my fellow passenger might have sat huddled over coffee at a café in Koura after Biden's visit, one of them saying something like, "You know, if we don't vote for the pro-Western March 14 coalition, we won't get those helicopters the US has promised us."

Sorry. Almost every vote cast in Lebanon was virtually foreordained. You were going to vote for the leader of the group or sub-group you had always voted for—you were going to vote for your people. The only unknowns were a few tens of thousands of Christians. Nobody could gauge exactly how angry some Christian voters might be at Michel Aoun for not speaking out against his Hizbollah colleagues when they started a mini-civil war in Beirut in May, 2008.

It turns out enough of these were angry to sway the vote toward March 14: 335,705 to 275,078 in predominantly Christian districts.

But that had nothing to do with Obama or with helicopters or with Biden's visit.

Reading articles in the American news media about the Lebanese elections—from CNN International online to central New Hampshire's *Valley News*—I was unsettlingly reminded of how Americans had viewed the politics of Vietnam forty-five years ago, when we thought that those nice South Vietnamese Roman Catholics must be just like us, so we should, indeed, send them more helicopters. And more. And then send them people to fly the helicopters and finally people to shoot at other Vietnamese from the helicopters.

After all, they're not communists.

After all, they're really a lot like us.

* * *

Layer upon layer of misconception. Maybe that's the most important lesson I've learned from my time in Beirut.

The oh-so-obvious lesson that everything I think and everything I think I think is conditioned by assumptions I've been lugging around since I first watched my mother reading the newspaper over her morning cup of coffee in Sacramento, swam in the American River with my father, overheard my parents and their friends rail against 1950s liberals' archenemy Joe McCarthy, and listened to the Lone Ranger on the radio.

And years later, as I watched my mother and Dallas Ostergaard play bridge with Fuad and Fadool while Jackie served canapés and freshened their drinks.

But how difficult it is to unravel all these influences, to imagine how they—and the zillion other things that I've experienced—wove themselves into the person sitting here at this keyboard, trying to unravel the unravelable, thinking that there was some value in such a project.

If it's this difficult to figure out how I became the person I became, how much more difficult would it be to understand the nature of any individual's identity, or the essence of any culture?

Georges Corm, in *L'Europe et le mythe de l'occident: la construction d'une histoire*, complicates the matter further, as he forces me to understand that even what I thought I understood about some of my culture's intellectual underpinnings—about the "West" as a belief system—is just the product of other unravellers' conceptualizing, of their fantasizing.

Sure, we know that the grand narratives—whether these entail the assumption that the United States was, indeed, fated to run from "sea to shining sea," that China had no choice but to join up with the unstoppable momentum of global capitalism, that Phoenician mercantile acumen would turn Beirut into the financial center of the Middle East—are hindsight interpretations that are better thought of as after-the-fact rationalizations than as explanations.

We forget this truth, though, because we also understand that remembering it leaves us with so little to go on.

Our intense need—I had written "desire" but then realized that this word was not nearly strong enough—to make sense of the world forces us to misconstrue so much.

For example, I want to think that my values are part of an organic evolution of what America did with what Europe had created—by combining various Germanic subcultures with Judeo-Christianity and topping it all off with reconceived myths about Greece and Rome—and then passed across the Atlantic on leaky wooden ships a few hundred years ago. But Corm reminds us that there is no "Europe." It, like Lebanon, like America, like Nick Boke, is a construct that can be understood in any of many ways, each of which essentially contradicts the others. He enumerates some specifics:

> We would say that the essence of Europe is Christian, or is the success of secular liberty; the land of reason or of intuition; the cradle of nationalism or the force that reduced and limited nationalism...she is socialist, or liberal, or Catholic, or imperialist (57).

By these clearer, though still murky, lights, one responds to America's initial acceptance of slavery, saying, "Oh, sure. That was the way things worked," not "Omigod! How could they have done that?" We no longer wonder that America continuously sticks its nose into other people's business. We say, "Of course it does. Superpowers always do." We are not surprised that American businessmen can be greedy, short-sighted sons of bitches. That's how big business operates, we say, American or otherwise. And how it has always operated, we elaborate.

We understand that those who argue that a Hizbollah-led Islamic Republic of Lebanon would be anathema are wrong—it would simply be a different Lebanon, emphasizing different aspects of this not-yet-a-country's identity.

As there is no single Europe, no single America, there is no single Lebanon—other than in people's imaginations.

We begin to understand, in short, that history's not going anywhere specific. It's just moving along, as it always has, taking the people who live in history along with it, suggesting to them that they find a way to define themselves, that they call themselves something. And for as long as this perplexing little species inhabits the planet, it will continue to do so.

We begin to understand that terrible things will take place, no matter how the committer of the sins conceives himself or herself, no matter how he or she explains those things.

The search for identity, then, might seem a red herring, an intriguing but distracting enterprise one engages in when one might well be doing something more important.

* * *

That little boy flying over the Mediterranean on that dark night fifty-some years ago, listening to the engines throb, was wondering where he was going, what he was coming to.

He certainly wasn't wondering who he would become.

How could any of us ever, truly, wonder that, beyond imagining ourselves doctors, mothers, or basketball stars?

How could any of us ever truly imagine the person we would spend a lifetime making, as we absorb and meld the sights we've seen and the sounds we've heard, the recollections these become, so often misremembered, so much more often forgotten.

How could we ever imagine that we are constructing an identity? How could we ever understand just what that identity is? How could we ever see what we have become?

How could we ever, in short, have the slightest idea of who we are or how we got that way?

Or of what's next?

Made in the USA
San Bernardino, CA
21 May 2013